TALK OF THE NATION

Talk of the Nation

Language and Conflict in Romania and Slovakia

Zsuzsa Csergo

Cornell University Press
Ithaca and London

First published 2007 by Cornell University Press

Printed in the United States of America

Library of Congress Cataloging-in-Publication Data

Csergo, Zsuzsa.
 Talk of the nation : language and conflict in Romania and Slovakia / Zsuzsa Csergo.
  p. cm.
 Includes bibliographical references and index.
 ISBN 978-0-8014-4537-8 (cloth : alk. paper)
 1. Linguistic minorities—Romania. 2. Linguistic minorities—Slovakia. 3. Anthropological linguistics—Romania. 4. Anthropological linguistics—Slovakia. 5. Post-communism—Social aspects—Romania. 6. Post-communism—Social aspects—a Slovakia.
7. Romania—Languages—Political aspects. 8. Slovakia—Languages—Political aspects. I. Title.
 P119.32.R6C74 2007
  306.4'49498—dc22

                          2006102925

Cornell University Press strives to use environmentally responsible suppliers and materials to the fullest extent possible in the publishing of its books. Such materials include vegetable-based, low-VOC inks and acid-free papers that are recycled, totally chlorine-free, or partly composed of nonwood fibers. For further information, visit our website at www.cornellpress.cornell.edu.

Cloth printing   10 9 8 7 6 5 4 3 2 1

Contents

Tables and Figure

Figure

Acknowledgments

This book developed from my long-standing interest in the politics of language use. As a student of post-Communist societies, the question underlying my research was why the issue of language use became a touchstone of majority-minority conflict in virtually all democratizing states that incorporated relatively sizable language minorities. What explains the continuing divisiveness of "national languages," and is democratic integration possible across language divides? I wished to get to the bottom of these questions and better understand the motivations of those who shaped the terms of the language debate through a study of both majority and minority perspectives. I wanted to investigate the positions of both those who deepened the majority-minority division over language and those who worked for reconciliation. My own position as an American-trained social scientist who grew up as a bilingual speaker in Central Europe offered important resources for research in that region. None of those resources, however, would have been sufficient in making this book possible without the contributions of a great number of individuals, too numerous to name, who placed their trust in me, and advised and assisted in essential ways.

The project has traveled a great distance from early drafts to a printed book, and in the course of this journey it benefited from support and advice by generous members of the academic community. Above all, Sharon Wolchik and Lee Sigelman have been fabulous advisers, mentors, and friends, as well as unfailing critics over the years. It is difficult to express the value of their contributions to this book. Special thanks are due to Valerie Bunce, whose support for the project helped maintain my faith in its merits and whose insights shaped the book in significant ways. I am grateful to Elizabeth Franker for years of invaluable research assistance, and to Ilona Teleki for similar help during the last months of the project. Mark Beissinger, Ingrid Creppell, James Goldgeier, Jon Harris, Zoltán Kántor, Rasma Karklins, Charles King, Ronald Linden, Alan Patten, Christina Paulston, Cristina and Dragoş Petrescu, Peter Reddaway, and Vladimir Tismaneanu offered critical readings of earlier drafts or parts of the manuscript, and several anonymous reviewers provided suggestions that helped improve the final text. I express my sincerest thanks to them all. I cannot overstate the importance of the help I have received from Elek Horvath in clarifying and improving my drafts. Thanks are due to László Sebők and Tamás Szémann for their help in creating the art. I am also grateful to Roger Haydon for his expertise in guiding the process from manuscript to book.

The research on which the book is based would not have been possible without financial support from a number of organizations, including the Institute for World Politics, the American Council of Learned Societies, the Social Science Research Council, the George Washington University, the George Hoffman Foundation, and the Woodrow Wilson International Center for Scholars. I thank the Open Society Institute in Bratislava and Cluj, the Political Science Institute of the Hungarian Academy of Sciences, the Teleki Foundation in Budapest, and the Public Opinion Research Institute in Bratislava for providing research material and office space. For their generosity in lending me social capital and expert advice during the various stages of my field work, I am grateful to Zora Bútorová, Péter Eckstein-Kovács, Iván Gyurcsik, Gábor Hajdu, Zoltán Kántor, Darina Malová, Silvia Michaliková, and Ildikó Szabó. Beyond sharing valuable resources and memorable experiences of field work in Slovakia, I thank Kevin Deegan-Krause for presenting a high standard in comparative empirical research.

"Talk" became more than just the subject matter of this study: it formed an integral part of the research process. A great number of politicians and civil servants gave their valuable time to talk with me during my repeated research trips, and their contributions were essential even if I cannot list their names. I am also indebted to friends and colleagues for inspiring conversations in living rooms and cafés of Bratislava, Bucharest, Budapest, and Cluj.

Fundamentally, however, it was the continuous support I received from my extended family that enabled me to complete the book. Above all, I am grateful to my mother and to Olga for loving my children and caring for them during my absences. Finally, my children Eszter and Daniel and my husband Gábor enabled me to find a long and difficult process enjoyable, meaningful, and worthwhile. It is to them that I dedicate this book.

List of Abbreviations

Slovakia

AD   Alliance of Democrats (HZDS splinter, formed in March 1993; merged with APR to form DÚ in 1995)

ANO   Alliance of the New Citizen (formed in 2001)

APR   Alternative for Political Realism (HZDS splinter, formed in March 1994; merged with AD to form DÚ in Summer 1994)

Coexistence   The Coexistence Political Movement (formed in February 1990; merged with MKDM and MPP to form MKP in 1998)

DS   Democratic Party (formed in October 1944; changed name to Party of Slovak Revival in 1948; returned to name DS in 1989; ODÚ merged with DS in 1993; in 1998, joined SDK)

DÚ   Democratic Union (formed in Summer 1994 by the HZDS splinter parties AD and APR; in 1995, the SNS splinter NDS-NA merged with DÚ; in 1998, joined SDK; became part of SDKU in 2000; a splinter resumed independent operation after 2000)

FMK   The Independent Hungarian Initiative (formed in 1989, became part VPN; split from VPN in 1991; changed name to MPP in January 1992)

HP   Movement of Agriculturalists (formed in Spring 1990)

HZDS   Movement for a Democratic Slovakia (VPN splinter, formed in April 1991)

KDH   Christian Democratic Movement (formed in November 1989; joined SDK in 1998; resumed independent operation after 2000)

KSS   Communist Party of Slovakia (separated from the Communist Party of Czechoslovakia in March 1990; the main body of the party changed its name to SDĽ in February 1991; a small group within the party rejected the change, eventually reclaiming the name KSS)

KSU   Christian Social Union (changed name from SKDH in 1993)

MK   Hungarian Coalition (electoral coalition in 1990, included Coexistence and MKDM; in 1994 also included MPP; became Party of the Hungarian Coalition in 1998)

MKDM   Hungarian Christian Democratic Movement (formed in March 1990; merged with MKDM and MPP to form MKP in 1998)

MKP   Party of the Hungarian Coalition (established in 1998 from the electoral Hungarian Coalition)

MNP   Hungarian People's Party (formed in December 1991)

MPP   Hungarian Civic Party (changed name from FMK in January 1992; merged with Coexistence and MKDM to form MKP in 1998)

NDS-NA   National Democratic Party-New Alternative (SNS splinter, formed in December 1993; merged with DÚ in 1995)

ODÚ   Civic Democratic Union (changed name from VPN in October 1991; merged with DS in 1993)

RSS   Peasants' Party of Slovakia (founded in October 1990)

SD   Social Democracy (electoral coalition in 1990, included SDĽ and SDSS)

SDK   Slovak Democratic Coalition (electoral coalition formed in 1997, including KDH, DÚ, DS, SDSS, and SZS; became the Party of the Slovak Democratic Coalition in 1998; stopped in 2001)

SDKÚ   Slovak Democratic and Christian Union (formed in 2000 by leaders of SDK, integrating DÚ, the Union of Businessmen and Tradesmen).

SDĽ   Party of Democratic Left (changed name from KSS in February 1991)

SDSS   Social Democratic Party of Slovakia (formed in January 1990; merged with SDK in 1998)

SKDH   Slovak Christian Democratic Movement (KDH splinter, formed in March 1992; changed its name to KSU in 1993)

Smer	"Direction" (formed in 1999)
SNS	Slovak National party (founded in December 1989)
SOP	Party of Civic Understanding (founded in 1998)
SV	Common Choice (electoral coalition in 1994, included SDĽ, SZS, HP, and SDSS)
SZS	Party of Greens in Slovakia (separated from Czech Party of Greens in 1991; merged with SDK in 1998)
VPN-FMK	Public Against Violence—Independent Hungarian Initiative (founded in November 1989; split into VPN and HZDS in April 1991; VPN became ODÚ in October 1991; FMK became MPP in 1992)
ZRS	Association of Workers in Slovakia (SDĽ splinter, formed in 1994)

Romania

AC	Civic Alliance (formed in November 1990; in 1991, its founders also created the Civic Alliance Party; AC continued as a liberal organization)
CD	Democratic Convention (formed in November 1991 by 13 parties and political organizations, including PNTCD, PAC, PNL, PSDR, RMDSZ, and others; later changed name to CDR)
CDR	Romanian Democratic Convention (changed name from Democratic Convention; in 1992; its composition changed over time; after the withdrawal of PNL in 2000, reconstituted as "CDR 2000")
FDSN	Democratic National Salvation Front (FSN splinter formed in March 1992; changed name to PDSR in June 1993)
FSN	National Salvation Front (founded in December 1989; split into FSN and FDSN in March 1992; the FSN splinter changed name to PD-FSN in May 1993)
PAC	Civic Alliance Party (formed by founders of Civic Alliance, registered as PAC in July 1991; joined CD—later CDR—in 1991)
PD	Democratic Party (successor of PD-FSN; its composition changed over time after absorbing other parties; formed the Justice and Truth Alliance with PNL in 2003)
PD-FSN	Democratic Party—National Salvation Front (party of original FSN; changed name from FSN in May 1993; joined USD in 1996; changed to PD in 2000)

PDSR	The Romanian Social Democratic Party (changed name from FDSN in June 1993; changed to PSD in June 2001, incorporating also the former PSDR)
PNL	National Liberal Party (founded in January 1990, as heir to interwar party by the same name; joined CD in 1991, left before the 1992 elections; rejoined CDR before the 1996 elections, left again in 2000; formed the Justice and Truth Alliance with PD in 2003)
PNȚCD	National Christian-Democratic Peasant Party (founded in January 1990, as heir to interwar party by the same name; joined CD—later CDR—in 1991)
PRM	Greater Romania Party (organization founded in January 1990; registered as a party in May 1991)
PSD	Party of Social Democracy (registered in June 2001, after a fusion between PDSR and PSDR; heir to the FSN-splinter FDSN, which underwent several changes of name and composition since 1990)
PSDR	Romanian Social Democratic Party (founded in January 1990, as heir to interwar party by the same name; joined CD—later CDR—in 1991; in June 2001, PSDR merged with PDSR to form PSD)
PSM	Socialist Labor Party (formed in 1991)
PUNR	Party of Romanian National Unity (changed name from AUR; founded in January 1990)
RMDSZ	Democratic Alliance of Hungarians in Romania (founded in December 1989; joined CD—later CDR—in 1991; left CDR in 1995; since then, "umbrella" Hungarian minority party incorporating liberal and conservative factions)
USD	Social Democratic Union (formed in 1996, included PD-FSN and PSDR)

TALK OF THE NATION

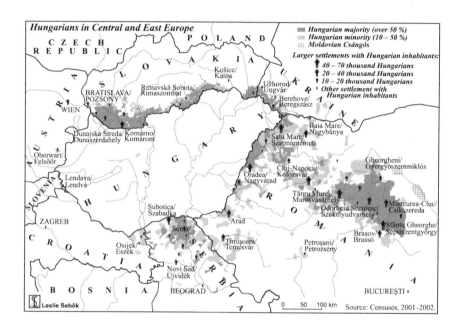

Hungarians in Central and East Europe

Hungarian majority (over 50 %)
Hungarian minority (10 – 50 %)
Moldovian Csángós

Larger settlements with Hungarian inhabitants:
40 – 70 thousand Hungarians
20 – 40 thousand Hungarians
10 – 20 thousand Hungarians
Other settlement with Hungarian inhabitants

Source: Censuses, 2001–2002.

Leslie Sebök

0   50   100 km

Chapter 1

Linguistic Territoriality

In less than fifteen years, the societies of Central and Eastern Europe experienced one of the most dramatic institutional and social changes in modern European history. As regimes collapsed and states disintegrated, new states and regimes took shape throughout the region. These changes created unprecedented opportunities for political debate and provided newly elected political elites and emerging political parties with opportunities to design new social contracts. Political leaders reasserted sovereignty after decades of Soviet dominance while simultaneously promising to take their societies "back" to a more prosperous and democratic European Union. Many Western theorists and policymakers expected that the desire for democratization and European integration would help weaken the traditional appeal of nationalism that had historically been associated with violent ethnic competition over state institutions and territorial boundaries.[1] Yet the interest in democratizing and "returning to Europe" remained bound up with a similarly powerful desire among ethnically conceived national majority and minority groups to assert *national* sovereignty over the territories they considered their "homelands" and to assume ownership over institutions they considered key to the reproduction of national cultures.

Against this backdrop, post-Communist societies offer invaluable lessons about one of the most important questions of our time: how can

---

[1] John Van Oudenaren, *Uniting Europe*, 2d ed. (Lanham, MD: Rowman and Littlefield Publishers, 2005), 339.

democratization resolve conflicts over cultural difference in places that are marked by legacies of nationalist competition? This book explores that question through a comparative study of more than a decade's worth of contestations over language use in the heart of post-Communist Eastern Europe, a territory encompassing Romania, Slovakia, and Hungary.

Based on extensive field research in these countries, conducted over a decade, the book speaks to the power of domestic majority and minority actors in making democracy work under conditions of continued nationalist competition. Recent scholarship on post-Communist democratization pays a great deal of attention to the role of Western (especially European) institutions, norms, and actors in compelling governments and minority groups to reach agreement on divisive issues. By focusing on domestic majority and minority political elites and parties as the key agents of change, this book contributes to a more balanced understanding of the way international and domestic actors work together to move multiethnic societies beyond cultural division.

A better understanding of the coexistence of democratization and nation-building in contemporary Europe—within the European Union, that many expected to become the first postmodern, post-Westphalian institution—requires a better understanding of the factors of both continuity and change. Two main arguments emerge from the analysis that follows. First, debates over language use demonstrate the continued significance of nationalism (both majority and minority) and territoriality in the heart of Europe, despite the overwhelming ambitions to integrate into a common European space. Second, although the issue of language use has remained politically significant, the domestic process of negotiation has enabled majority and minority actors to reach consensus on key issues and change important aspects of the social contract. When the major political elites and parties committed themselves to the democratic process, this process compelled them to engage each other in a debate in which they articulated and contested their positions peacefully. International influence was always filtered through domestic lenses. Changing international norms about minority protection and the membership opportunities promised by the European Union reinforced commitments to democracy, but it was primarily the domestic process resulting from that commitment that helped these actors resolve divisive issues.

A widely shared assumption among Western scholars and policymakers has been that conflicts over so-called ethnic issues such as language use often turn violent, endangering the stability of an entire region.[2] A similarly

---

[2] For a critique of this assumption, see Charles King, "The Myth of Ethnic Warfare," in *Foreign Affairs*, 80, no. 1 (November/December 2001): 165–70.

prevalent expectation has been that the more integrated with Western institutions societies become, the less salient and divisive issues of ethnicity and nationalism become for them. From this perspective, language conflicts, just like other manifestations of ethnic competition, are "transitional" phenomena that should disappear in societies that integrate and democratize.[3]

The story of post-Communist European state-building and democratization belies these expectations. Although the traditional face of nationalism—the drive to ensure that "the political and the national unit should be congruent"—made an impressive appearance after the collapse of Communism, in the majority of cases the overwhelming interest in state- and nation-building did not become violent.[4] Yet the significance of nation-building and language rights did not decrease as countries lined up to join the European Union. In the three Baltic states as well as Bulgaria, Romania, and Slovakia—where international integration was a prominent goal—nation-building and language rights have remained key political issues.[5] (The Baltics and Slovakia became EU members in 2004, Bulgaria and Romania joined in 2007.) Neither did strengthening the democratic modes of competition decrease the importance of language rights. To the contrary, this process has demonstrated the continuing relevance of language for the social contract. Where questions of linguistic diversity have not been resolved to the satisfaction of language minorities, such as in Latvia, they remain sources of conflict. Where language use no longer features prominently in political debates, language regulation has become an integral part of the social contract in a manner acceptable to important majority and minority national groups in society.

This book does not aim to downplay the role of international influence on interethnic relations. Rather, it seeks to highlight the combination of domestic agency and international influence so underemphasized in current scholarship. Clearly, any nuanced discussion of the factors that shape the dynamics of ethnic competition must take international factors into account. No region has made this necessity more evident than post-Communist Europe, where the European Union has profoundly influenced nationalist strategies

[3] E. J. Hobsbawm, *Nations and Nationalism since 1780* (New York: Cambridge University Press, 1990); Jack Snyder, *From Voting to Violence* (New York: Norton, 2000); and Mark Beissinger, "How Nationalisms Spread," *Social Research* 63, no. 1 (Spring 1996): 97–146.

[4] Ernest Gellner, *Nations and Nationalism* (Ithaca: Cornell University Press, 1983), 1. This meaning of nationalism is adopted also in John Breuilly, *Nationalism and the State* (Manchester, UK: Manchester University Press, 1982) and Hobsbawm, *Nations and Nationalism since 1780.*

[5] Nida M. Gezalis, "The European Union and the Statelessness Problem in the Baltic States," *European Journal of Migration and Law* 6 (2004): 225–42.

in the post–Cold War period.[6] The scholarly agenda that focuses on the ways in which Western institutions contributed to democratization (and interethnic peace) in post-Communist Europe has made lasting contributions to our understanding of social change. The works that resulted from this agenda are both theoretically interesting and analytically rich. Straddling the boundary between international and comparative politics, they move beyond the question of whether international organizations matter to ask which international actors matter, how, and under what conditions. Scholars have extensively explored the norms that international institutions have advanced, the strategies they have employed, and the impact they have had.[7] This literature has demonstrated that Western institutions made concerted and large-scale efforts to "socialize" post-Communist countries into "Western" norms of interaction and that the European Union assumed the central role in this activity.[8] Comparative analyses have shown that the European Union has contributed to the emergence of power-sharing arrangements in multiethnic polities such as Romania and Slovakia and to the adoption of more inclusive citizenship and minority policies in the Baltics.[9]

Much of this scholarship accords primary agency to international actors, celebrates the successes of Western influence, and points to domestic factors as constraints to the positive changes that international actors have worked to bring about.[10] Most studies acknowledge the limitations of international efforts, comment on the difficulties of measuring their impact on policy change, and take domestic actors into consideration. Yet few present domestic participants as anything more than recipients of international influence who either succeed or fail in complying with the goals of international actors.[11]

[6] Michael Keating and John McGarry, "Introduction" in *Minority Nationalism and the Changing International Order*, ed. Keating and McGarry (Oxford: Oxford University Press, 2001), 9; Zsuzsa Csergo and James M. Goldgeier, "Nationalist Strategies and European Integration," *Perspectives on Politics* 2, no. 1 (March 2004): 21–37.
[7] Ronald H. Linden, ed., *Norms and Nannies* (Lanham, MD: Rowman and Littlefield, 2002); Judith G. Kelley, *Ethnic Politics in Europe* (Princeton, NJ: Princeton University Press, 2004); Milada Anna Vachudova, *Europe Undivided* (Oxford: Oxford University Press, 2005); Patrice McMahon, "Managing Ethnicity in Eastern Europe," paper presented at the annual meeting of the International Studies Association, Montreal, Canada, March 17–20, 2004.
[8] Linden, ed., *Norms and Nannies*; Vachudova, *Europe Undivided*, 3.
[9] Martin Brusis, "The European Union and Interethnic Power-Sharing Arrangements in Accession Countries," *JEMIE: Journal on Ethnopolitics and Minority Issues in Europe* 1 (2003); Helen M. Morris, "EU Enlargement and Latvian Citizenship Policy," *JEMIE: Journal on Ethnopolitics and Minority Issues in Europe* 1 (2003); Kelley, *Ethnic Politics in Europe*.
[10] Vachudova, *Europe Undivided*; Ronald H. Linden, "Security and Identity in Southeast Europe" in *Norms and Nannies*, 179–201; Kelley, *Ethnic Politics in Europe*; James Hughes and Gwendolyn Sasse, "Monitoring the Monitors," *JEMIE: Journal on Ethnopolitics and Minority Issues in Europe* 1 (2003); David J. Smith, "Minority Rights, Multiculturalism and EU Enlargement," *JEMIE: Journal on Ethnopolitics and Minority Issues in Europe* 1 (2003).
[11] For emphasis on domestic actors, see Peter Vermeersch, "EU Enlargement and Minority Rights Policies in Central Europe," *JEMIE: Journal on Ethnopolitics and Minority Issues in Europe* 1 (2003).

This book shows that domestic actors are key agents of cooperation and change in their own right, and it highlights the continuing power of an international norm in constraining interethnic reconciliation. Before turning to the analysis of the way majority and minority actors used democratic debate to reach consensus on divisive issues, the pages that follow discuss the constraining effects of a fundamental international norm—territorial sovereignty.

Language and the Territorial State: A Continuing Relationship

In Europe, national languages have become the most important means of national cultural reproduction—an ongoing process that perpetuates the connections linking individuals, "nations," and "national homelands." National languages provide this link primarily through historiography, geography, and national literature. Although often overlooked, territoriality is a key underlying logic that made language use fundamental to political organization in states that followed the Westphalian nation-state model that emerged in Europe, and this principle also remains powerfully influential in the contemporary world, even in an enlarging Europe that many have expected to become the first postmodern, post-Westphalian institution.

Leading scholars of European political development agree that a key characteristic of the qualitatively different kind of political entity that grew out of the transformed empires, city-states, and feudal structures of early modern Europe was—in the words of Ertman—"the exceptionally penetrative sovereign, territorial state."[12] This type of state relied on language standardization and homogenization to perform such functions as the maintenance of a national army, administrative control, and compulsory education. Prominent modernization theorists, such as Karl Deutsch and Ernest Gellner, argued that language standardization was a developmental necessity for the state in the age of industrialization. Gellner explained that this state demanded an education in the universal high culture of mass literacy in the official language, thus creating the "cultural infrastructure" without which a modern industrial economy could not function.[13] Placing it in the framework of Max Weber's theory of state rationalization, David Laitin calls this process

---

[12] Thomas Ertman, *Birth of the Leviathan* (Cambridge: Cambridge University Press, 1997), 3; See also Ernst Hartwig Kantorowicz, *The King's Two Bodies* (Princeton, NJ: Princeton University Press, 1957); and Charles Tilly, *The Formation of National States in Western Europe* (Princeton, NJ: Princeton University Press, 1975).

[13] Karl Deutsch, *Nationalism and Social Communication* (Cambridge: MIT Press, 1953); Ernest Gellner, *Thought and Change* (London: Weidenfeld and Nicolson, 1964); and *Nations and Nationalism*.

"language rationalization," defined broadly as "the emergence of a single, dominant language in each state, which becomes the official one for education, administration, and cultural life."[14]

It is a matter of scholarly perspective whether one considers the state's bureaucratic efficiency or the nation's cultural homogeneity to be the primary driving force of language standardization and homogenization in the modern European nation-state.[15] As an outcome of this process, however, European nationalism contributed to the emergence of the powerful concept of *linguistic territoriality*. Central to this concept was the expectation that the national space would be mapped by a national language: To establish itself as an exclusive authority in a territory, the state marked its ownership in its *own* language both in physical spaces (place names and public signs) and within the public institutions that assured state sovereignty (such as public administration, legislation, the judiciary, and the military). To assure the continuity of ownership, the national language also linked people to the national space through socialization by an educational system where education took place in the spirit of national ideology. Major tools for perpetuating a national culture were the national literature, national historiography and geography, and national holidays, which also used the national language to pay homage to the history of the nation. Thus, language became more than an ethnic marker in the territorial state, gaining special significance as a *national* marker—in other words, the means by which individuals became socialized into the idea of belonging to the nation and being connected to the state.

Today, there is debate in the literature on nationalism about whether the politicization of language allegiance follows the design of political elites or evolves in response—as Anthony Smith puts it—to "the call of ethnic origin and culture."[16] What is less debatable, however, is that linguistic territoriality has become a lasting feature of state-society relations in the European state. In contemporary Europe, such territories are conceived not necessarily as states but in some cases as substate units on which national groups aim

[14] David Laitin, *Language Repertoires and State Construction in Africa* (New York: Cambridge University Press, 1992), ix.
[15] Political scientists influenced by Max Weber's theory of state rationalization (such as David Laitin) tend to place more emphasis on bureaucratic efficiency and less on nation-building than scholars of nationalism (including those in the modernization school, such as Gellner, Hobsbawm, and Benedict Anderson).
[16] Smith criticizes "instrumentalist" perspectives for downplaying the intensity of such mass responses in "Culture, Community and Territory," *International Affairs* 72, no. 3 (1996), 446. For his discussion of the debate among modernists, primordialists, and perennialists, see Anthony D. Smith, *Nationalism and Modernism* (London: Routledge, 2001). For a study that makes an excellent case for the elite-driven perspective, see Robert Greenberg, *Language and Identity in the Balkans* (New York: Oxford University Press, 2004).

to perpetuate their culture.[17] (The Catalans in Spain, for instance, consider a substate autonomous region to be their national homeland.) *Homeland community* is a useful concept for describing groups that claim a lengthy history on a particular territory and that usually have a historiography, geography, and literature that tell the link between the community and the territory.[18] Not all ethnicities are homeland communities. Immigrant groups, for instance, usually do not claim historic homeland rights in their country of residence. Roma populations, even though they have resided in Europe for centuries, do not typically define themselves as historic homeland communities.[19] Moreover, not all homeland communities aspire to self-governing institutions. The desire for self-governing institutions is what distinguishes nations from other ethnic groups. Smith articulates this distinction particularly well:

> Despite some overlap in that both belong to the same family of phenomena (collective cultural identities), the ethnic community usually has no political referent, and in many cases lacks a public culture and even a territorial dimension, since it is not necessary for an ethnic community to be in physical possession of its historic territory. A nation, on the other hand, must occupy a homeland of its own, at least for a long period of time, in order to constitute itself as a nation; and to aspire to nationhood and be recognized as a nation, it also needs to evolve a public culture and desire some degree of self-determination. On the other hand, it is not necessary . . . for a nation to possess a sovereign state of its own, but only to have an aspiration for a measure of autonomy coupled with the physical occupation of its homeland.[20]

The overwhelming success of languages in perpetuating popular conceptions about cultural ownership of the homeland has also contributed to many of the current problems confronting post-Communist European states with sizeable language minorities. This region has experienced dramatic shifts in territorial borders and reversals of dominance and subordination. As André Liebich summarizes,

> West European political and linguistic boundary changes over the centuries have been moderate compared to those in East Central Europe. . . . Minorities in

---

[17] Csergo and Goldgeier, "Nationalist Strategies and European Integration."
[18] Milton J. Esman, *Ethnic Politics* (Ithaca: Cornell University Press, 1994), 6.
[19] For a distinction between immigrant and historic communities, see Will Kymlicka, "Introduction," in *Can Liberal Pluralism Be Exported?* ed. Will Kymlicka and Magda Opalski (London: Oxford University Press, 2001), 23–24.
[20] Smith, *Nationalism* (Malden, MA: Blackwell, 2001), 12.

East Central Europe are living testimony to the meanders of the past, and perhaps also to the uncertainties of the future. . . . Moreover, the history they recount is one of past domination. It is the negation of piously cultivated narratives of continuity and of identity between a land, a state and a majority people. Minorities are a disturbing reminder that, in political terms, Slovakia was not always Slovak, the Czech Republic was not always Czech, Bulgaria was not always Bulgarian, and so on. At the very least, they recall that even recently parts of today's Poland were not Polish as parts of Romania were not Romanian. Inasmuch as the legitimacy of state units in East Central Europe is founded, to an even greater extent than in Western Europe, upon myths of national continuity, nay, of perennity, minorities are an unwelcome presence.[21]

Against the backdrop of this history, well-established loyalties to the language have been so effectively reproduced in the cultures of various groups within states that language loyalties can no longer be easily switched in favor of the majority language and the majority cultural landmarks.[22] Moreover, the minority political elites that demand the inclusion of their language in public institutions base such demands on the claim that their community is a "national" entity and therefore is *entitled* to institutional guarantees for reproducing its culture.[23] They confirm Borneman's argument that territoriality, which was initially a top-down strategic solution that the state employed, became a bottom-up principle of national and international order supported by a host of interested actors.[24]

It is due to the paradoxical success of nationalism that significant members of both majority and minority "national" communities share linguistic territoriality and thus assume an important connection between language rights and sovereignty—but they draw opposite conclusions for the ordering of languages. National majorities that define themselves as "titular" nations aim at establishing their language as the official ("national") language

---

[21] André Liebich, "Ethnic Minorities and Long-term Implications of EU Enlargement," in *Europe Unbound,* ed. Jan Zielonka (New York: Routledge, 2002), 120.

[22] The literature on language maintenance and language shift suggests that language loyalties *do* change under certain conditions, but only given incentives that are valuable to speakers in a particular context. See, for example, Susan Gal, *Language Shift* (New York: Academic Press, 1979); John Gumperz, *Language in Social Groups* (Stanford, CA: Stanford University Press, 1971); Kathryn A. Woolard, *Double Talk* (Stanford, CA: Stanford University Press, 1989).

[23] Alan Patten and Will Kymlicka, "Language Rights and Political Theory," in *Language Rights and Political Theory,* ed. Will Kymlicka and Alan Patten (Oxford: Oxford University Press, 2003), 5.

[24] John Borneman, "Towards a Theory of Ethnic Cleansing," in John Borneman, *Subversions of International Order* (Albany: State University of New York Press, 1997), 273–319.

in the state.[25] Language minorities that also define themselves in national terms reject the national hierarchy and demand the inclusion of their language in self-government. These structurally opposite conclusions do not simply reflect an ethnolinguistic cleavage in society. Rather, they follow the logic of the national definition of culture within the territorial state embodied in the modern secular "nation-state" model.

The global reach of this state model as well as its continuing relevance in the contemporary world are also subjects of ongoing scholarly dispute. Nineteenth- and twentieth-century political history provides abundant evidence that language became a major source of political power (and therefore of conflict) in multilingual societies organized in states modeled after the European territorial state. The overwhelming military and economic success of this state model fostered the view among political elites outside of Europe that state consolidation depended on a unified national language. As Laitin remarks, "The idea that real states have unique national languages became the conventional wisdom by the turn of the twentieth century for people as diverse as Lenin and Woodrow Wilson."[26] Language indeed served as a primary tool in efforts to forge national community in nineteenth-century Japan, early twentieth-century Israel, and a number of states that emerged from European colonization in late twentieth-century Africa.[27] Leading scholars have also claimed that the link connecting language, state, and nation is losing its significance in the contemporary world. Laitin, for instance, predicted that this pattern will no longer have much relevance for the future European state. Rather, language outcomes will likely follow individual rationality conditioned ultimately by market forces.[28] In a similar vein, Michael Billig envisioned a "free market of identities" in the integrating European Union.[29]

---

[25] "Titular nation" was the term used for the nation from which the name of each Soviet republic was derived. I adopted the term in this study because it reflects the concept of majority nationals that they have "ownership" rights in the state. For a similar adoption of the term, see Rogers Brubaker, *Nationalism Reframed* (Cambridge: Cambridge University Press, 1996) and David Laitin, *Identity in Formation* (Ithaca: Cornell University Press, 1998).

[26] David Laitin, "The Cultural Identities of a European State," *Politics and Society* 25, no. 3 (September 1997): 282.

[27] Laitin, *Language Repertoires*; Eliezer Ben-Rafael, *Language, Identity, and Social Division* (Oxford: Clarendon Press, 1994); Christina Bratt Paulston, "Linguistic Minorities and Language Policies," in *Sociolinguistics,* ed. Christina Bratt Paulston and G. Richard Tucker (Malden, MA: Blackwell, 2003), 398.

[28] Laitin, *Language Repertoires* and "Cultural Identities." Laitin later acknowledged the continued relevance of language rationalization in Europe in *Identity in Formation.*

[29] Billig, *Banal Nationalism* (London: Sage Publications, 1995), 133.

Such influential arguments notwithstanding, national languages maintain their power in Europe and continue to be linked to notions of territoriality. The last decade of the twentieth century saw a host of governments in the successor states of the dismembered federations in post-Communist Europe (the former Soviet Union, Yugoslavia, and Czechoslovakia) adopt language rationalization strategies.[30] Many of these governments simultaneously pursued membership in the EU. Strategies of language rationalization also accompanied the collapse of Communist regimes within previously existing state borders, such as in Bulgaria and Romania.

Linguistic territoriality is not limited to the post-Communist part of the continent. The evolving policies of language use within the European Union similarly belie the expectation that national languages would lose their relevance as a result of increased transnational integration.[31] In the societies that form the European Union, languages have played a key role in institutionalizing a strong link between individuals, national communities, and "homelands." Once established, the link between language and national cultural reproduction appears to remain strong even under the conditions of transnational integration. Although Europeans are currently experiencing a weakening of state sovereignty along with the creation of supranational institutions, the member states of the EU have been more willing to give up their sovereignty over economic policies than to surrender control over minority policy and policies of cultural reproduction (especially education and language policies). The mental map that links the concepts of state, nation, and language remains profoundly influential, and its influence is in some cases increasing. Although English is increasingly becoming the "lingua franca" in the institutions of the EU, governments and substate groups continue to pursue strategies to maintain and reproduce particular "national" cultures by strengthening, and in some cases even reviving, national languages.[32]

The same logic of linguistic territoriality also is a significant limit on efforts to create "complete multilingualism" within the EU boundaries.[33]

---

[30] Vesselin Vatchkov, "Divided by a Mutual Tongue," *Transitions* 4, no. 4 (September 1997): 76–81; Gordana Igric, "Education is the Key in Serb-Kosovar Negotiations," *Transitions* 3, no. 4 (March 7, 1997): 19–23; Rasma Karklins, *Ethnopolitics and Transition to Democracy* (Washington, D.C., and Baltimore: The Woodrow Wilson Center Press and the Johns Hopkins University Press, 1994); and Greenberg, *Language and Identity in the Balkans.*
[31] Gabrielle Hogan-Brun and Stefan Wolff, eds., *Minority Languages in Europe* (New York: Palgrave Macmillan, 2003).
[32] Abram de Swaan, *The Language Constellation of the European Union* (Amsterdam: Amsterdam School of Social Science, 1995).
[33] Suzanne Romaine, "Language Contact in Relation to Multilingualism, Norms, States, and Standardization," in *Language Contact and Language Conflict*, ed. Unn Royneland (Volda, Norway: Ivar Aasen Institute, Volda College, 1997), 9–18.

Although the European Community granted official status to each of the member states' "national languages" from the beginning of its formation, this policy in reality continued to favor "titular" majority languages of member states. The resulting hierarchy is reflected in the terms used for the classification of languages spoken within the EU: state languages are recognized as "national languages," while the languages of *historic* national minorities are considered "regional languages," "minority languages," or "lesser used languages." The most significant document that lays down the rules of language policy in Europe, the 1992 European Charter for Regional and Minority Languages, explicitly excludes the languages of immigrants.[34] Among recognized nonstate languages, the status of the Catalan language captures the inherent territorial biases of classification: Catalan has considerably more speakers in the EU than Danish or Maltese, yet the latter are recognized as an official "national" languages, while Catalan is a considered a "minority" language.[35]

As long as the territorial principle remains influential within an integrated Europe, the potential for language choice based on individual rationality will continue to be bound by the logic of the state. This logic drives the institutionalization of language rights in ways that serve the stability of states and the continued cultural ownership of their territory.

Democracy and the Constraints of Linguistic Territoriality

The same "exceptionally penetrative sovereign, territorial state" that emerged in Europe during the process that we now associate with modernity also gave rise to the institutions of democracy that Western institutions pressured post-Communist Europeans to adopt.[36] Yet this process has failed to engender universally applicable institutional tools for resolving issues of cultural difference. Although the idea of the social contract was rooted in universalist concepts of individual rationality and freedom, the universalist logic of liberalism was bound by the territorial logic of the state. Popular sovereignty was territorially defined, so the stability of the state as a spatial entity remained a central concern for democratic government.[37] Language became

---

[34] Gabrielle Hogan-Brun and Stefan Wolff, "Minority Languages in Europe," in *Minority Languages in Europe,* ed. Gabrielle Hogan-Brun and Stefan Wolff (New York: Palgrave Macmillan, 2003), 4.

[35] Catalan is an official language in Andorra, but Andorra is not a member of the European Union. Romaine, "Language Contact," 12.

[36] Ertman, *Birth of the Leviathan*, 3.

[37] An influential articulation of liberal ideology is in John Rawls, *A Theory of Justice* (Cambridge, MA: Harvard University Press, 1971).

an element of the social contract, because it helped fulfill important necessities of the democratic state. State stability demanded loyal citizens, and the stability of democracy required a political community of citizens with shared civic values. A common language facilitated equal access to the state's resources and helped socialize the population into the values of citizenship. The institution best suited to serve these needs was the national educational system, a system that also perpetuated a common national culture. It was through this process that two of the most powerful mass political ideologies, nationalism and democracy, emerged together in Europe.

The centuries that followed the birth of democratic nationalism, however, saw fierce competition in the name of this ideology among multiple political units in a relatively small space. After a series of wars that reinforced and challenged competing national loyalties, shifted territorial boundaries, and altered demographic patterns on the continent, the original relationship between democracy and nationalism changed substantially and substantively. Exclusive ideas of "nation" replaced the originally inclusive idea of "sovereign people." In Liah Greenfeld's words: "As nationalism spread in different conditions and the emphasis in the idea of the nation moved from the sovereign character to the uniqueness of the people, the original equivalence between it and democratic principles was lost. . . . As it did so, the nature of sovereignty was inevitably reinterpreted."[38]

It is a lasting legacy of this political process that elevating the language of one particular group to the status of a common national language is not an unequivocal source of inclusion but also a potential source of dominance and exclusion. Consequently, the way linguistic relations are established has become a fundamental issue of the social contract in multilingual democracies. In a comparative study of language and hierarchy in Britain and France, Grillo convincingly argues that language is also an important element of social differentiation in advanced industrial societies, even those not commonly associated with cultural pluralism: "Every European society is, and has always been, 'multilingual.' . . . It is also the case that in every European society languages and their speakers are usually of unequal status, power and authority, and there is commonly a hierarchical ordering of languages, dialects and ways of speaking."[39] These cases remind us that democratic governance is best viewed as a "work in progress" in all democracies—no

---

[38] Liah Greenfeld, *Nationalism* (Cambridge, MA: Harvard University Press, 1992), 10. On the historical tension between state sovereignty and national sovereignty, see Samuel J. Barkin and Bruce Cronin, "The State and the Nation," *International Organization* 48, no. 1 (Winter 1994): 107–30.

[39] Grillo, *Dominant Languages,* 1.

matter how old they are. The social contract is continuously redefined and renegotiated within territorial boundaries, and in multilingual societies this process inevitably involves questions about language use in important social, economic, and political institutions. Languages manifest the culture and status of their speakers; therefore the way languages are ordered reflects and reproduces social relations of hierarchy or equality.[40]

Multilingualism continues to raise questions about two of the most widely debated principles of democratic government: equality and inclusion. These questions concern whether language should be viewed as a matter of individual right, collective right, or civic duty, and, consequently, whether language minorities should be viewed as legitimate actors in the democratic process or as dangers to democratic stability. The answers that democratic political theory and practice give to these questions reveal the inherent tension between the universalist individualism at the core of liberal democratic ideology and the continued relevance of territorially defined collective identities in democratic states.

Although a number of contemporary democracies have no official language policy, as Romaine remarks, "It is quite naive to delude oneself that laissez-faire represents absence of a policy."[41] As already mentioned, it follows from the logic of the territorial democratic state to pursue a form of collective identity—a specific political community—to assure the continuity of both the democratic regime as a form of government and the state as a spatial entity. In the secular democratic state, language continues to serve as the primary means by which such a collective identity can be created and perpetuated through the institutions of cultural reproduction. In the absence of explicit language legislation, educational policies usually serve as the main vehicles of language planning.[42] Beyond competence in a common public language, schools and other institutions in all democratic states cultivate language loyalty and attachment to particular national literatures, historiographies, and geographies.

The universalist logic of liberalism could take us ultimately in the direction of a global free market of languages, where individual rationality and

---

[40] Pierre Bourdieu, *Language and Symbolic Power* (Cambridge, MA: Harvard University Press, 1991).

[41] Romaine, "Language Contact," 22. In broader terms, language policy involves—borrowing Weinstein's definition—"deliberate and conscious choices of language form and/or language function made by important institutions believed to be capable of long-term implementation over a significant area and among a significant population." Weinstein, *Language Policy,* 5.

[42] For the importance of education in language planning, see, for example, Robert B. Kaplan and Richard B. Baldauf Jr., *Language Planning from Practice to Theory* (Clevedon, UK: Multilingual Matters, 1997). The term "language planning" was coined by Einar Haugen in a 1959 article. See Romaine, "Language Contact," 9.

informal social norms rather than language legislation determine language choices.[43] In matters of language use, however, few theorists take a consistently liberal position. Even a passionate advocate of liberalism like Brian Barry claims that "a state cannot adopt a neutral stance" on language use.[44] On the one hand, Barry is emphatic on the necessity in a democratic state of "privatizing" cultural difference, claiming that "cultures are simply not the kind of entity to which rights can properly be ascribed" and that cultural diversity "has nothing to do with public policy."[45] On the other hand, he finds it appropriate for the democratic state to pursue a public policy objective to assimilate immigrants into its culture and makes the case for language uniformity or at least for the requirement that all individuals learn the "national" language.[46] In his conception of liberal democracy, the question of which language should be used in various domains of life ceases to be an issue of political contestation: "Any language will do as a medium of communication in a society as long as everybody speaks it."[47]

From the liberal perspective, a common language is primarily a question of equal access. Individuals need a common language to communicate, move around, and make choices about their lives within the boundaries of their citizenship. A shared language is also necessary for achieving social and economic integration and, ultimately, equal membership in a political community. The individualistic concept of identity does allow for language preferences and attachments to specific languages, but from this perspective the cultivation of group loyalty to a particular language and to the culture it carries is an illiberal process. Accordingly, a language minority acts in an illiberal way when it rejects its state's integrative language policies and struggles to preserve its own language.

The liberal perspective reaffirms the relevance of the Enlightenment tradition of universal rationality and the ethos of the autonomous individual, and it encourages us to assume that most speakers (that is, the majority) in democratic societies hold individualistic and rational ideas about language use. Majority-language speakers are indeed less likely to manifest their language loyalties collectively, as they usually face fewer constraints on the use of their language. Yet there is no reason to assume either that majorities are

[43] Universalism is such an important principle for this paradigm that liberal theory did not develop a distinctive theory of boundaries. See Brian Barry, *Culture and Equality* (Cambridge, MA: Harvard University Press, 2001), 136–37.
[44] Barry, *Culture and Equality,* 107.
[45] Ibid., 67, 32.
[46] Barry, for instance, talks about acculturation as a precondition of assimilation. Ibid., 72–73; see also 104 and 81.
[47] Ibid., 107.

somehow differently (less "irrationally") attached to their language than are linguistic minorities or that the language rights of majority speakers in a democracy are a priori more legitimate. In the real world of contemporary democracies, collective language loyalties exist among majority and minority language speakers, and these loyalties are embedded in a process of cultural reproduction that involves multiple self-defined communities, each of which may claim democratic rights to language use in the public domain.

Universalist liberalism provides a powerful normative call for equality and inclusion, yet in political practice this ideology often serves to legitimize the collective territorial and cultural interests of national majorities. The realization that strong and multiple collective identities coexist in contemporary democratic societies has led a number of liberal theorists to redefine the liberal framework on behalf of minority language rights. Alan Patten, for instance, proposes to "rehabilitate" the core liberal notion of government neutrality while making a case for minority language rights. In his view, neutrality—defined as evenhandedness through "roughly equivalent form[s] of assistance or recognition"—can work in favor of minority languages. "The task of language policy is not to realize some specific language outcome but to establish fair background conditions under which speakers of different languages can strive for the survival and success of their respective languages."[48] Joseph H. Carens goes further to argue that "it is often morally permissible and sometimes morally required to adopt policies to promote minority languages" in a liberal democracy.[49]

The most influential (and controversial) departure from universalism is the school that argues for the institutional accommodation of group-based cultural diversity. Prominent theorists like Will Kymlicka, Charles Taylor, and Crawford Young have criticized the individualist liberal position for being unable to provide equal and just treatment for various cultural communities that define themselves differently from the "cultural personality" of the state. They argue that the worldwide parallel processes of democratization and the forceful articulation of collective identities attest to the need for the state to recognize that cultural communities represent legitimate democratic interests. They further claim that the only way democratic regimes can accommodate these interests is by creating pluralist institutions that help reproduce diverse cultures. Instead of "difference-blind" liberalism, the

---

[48] Alan Patten, "Liberal Neutrality and Language Policy," paper presented at the American Political Science Association Annual Conference, Boston, Massachusetts, August 29–September 1, 2002, 16, 12.

[49] Joseph H. Carens, "Justice and Linguistic Minorities," paper delivered at the 2002 meeting of the American Political Science Association, Boston, MA, August 29–September 1, 2002.

democratic state should pursue "the politics of difference" or "the politics of recognition."[50] In this vision of plural democracy, political community is founded not on cultural assimilation but instead on the shared political value of toleration—which allows both for the reproduction of cultural differences and for coexistence in the same state and under the same democratic regime. In Ingrid Creppell's words, "Toleration then is the capacity to hold both conflict and mutuality together at the same time."[51]

The debate between the two perspectives outlined above centers on divergent definitions of democratic inclusion and equality. The liberal idea of equal opportunity led theorists like Barry to advocate inclusion in the form of integration. In terms of language relations, assimilation into a common official language constitutes the ideal form of integration. The pluralist idea of equity, by contrast, led prominent scholars of multilingualism like Tove Skutnabb-Kangas to advocate the institutional recognition of language differences as a more democratic way of regulating language use.[52]

For those who believe that stable democracy requires linguistic integration, the question remains how such integration can come about in a democratic fashion. For those who advocate "the politics of recognition," the question is how to ensure long-term political cohesion and stability in societies where language policies reproduce multiple group loyalties. States that democratized in the nineteenth century used aggressive, at times violent, methods of language assimilation to transform diverse people into unified "nations." The French elite, for example, pursued aggressive linguistic assimilation and still emerged as a successful example of the modern democratic nation-state.[53] In the contemporary world, however, where governmental accountability is considered essential to democratization, political elites who attempt to institutionalize a democratic political system while simultaneously imposing a dominant "national language" on minority language groups encounter a host of domestic and international political problems.

Proponents of "the politics of recognition" can point to numerous historical and contemporary examples of institutional language pluralism.

---

[50] Arguably the most influential of these authors has been Will Kymlicka. See in particular his *Multicultural Citizenship* (Oxford: Clarendon Press, 1995). See also Amy Gutmann, ed., *Multiculturalism and "The Politics of Recognition"* (Princeton, NJ: Princeton University Press, 1992); Crawford Young, ed., *Ethnic Diversity and Public Policy* (New York: MacMillan Press, 1998); Crawford Young, ed., *The Rising Tide of Cultural Pluralism* (Madison: University of Wisconsin Press, 1993); Crawford Young, ed., *The Accommodation of Cultural Diversity* (New York: St. Martin's Press, 1999).

[51] Ingrid Creppell, *Toleration and Identity* (New York: Routledge, 2003), 4.

[52] Robert Phillipson, ed., *Rights to Language* (Mahwah, NJ: Lawrence Erlbaum Associates, 2000).

[53] Eugen Weber, *Peasants into Frenchmen* (Stanford, CA: Stanford University Press, 1976); A. Zolberg, "The Formation of New States," *Annals of the American Academy of Political and Social Sciences* 467 (1983), 24–38; Barry, *Culture and Equality,* 60–61.

There were no ethnolinguistic "segments" in Norwegian society, but Norwegian elites recognized two written standards in the 1930s in order to forge a broad cross-class alliance in society.[54] In the hopes of preventing political division, the Canadian and Belgian governments chose pluralistic language policies that preserved and reproduced linguistic cleavages. In these societies, speakers of different languages live in demarcated linguistic zones, where linguistic identity roughly coincides with ethnic identity.[55] Similarly, the Indian government abandoned its earlier pursuit of language dominance in the 1950s in favor of language pluralism in a federalist state. Political scientists sometimes argue for such pluralist policies as methods of peacemaking.[56] Yet a number of scholars have also described such language policies as potential problems for democratic consolidation.

The question that remains unanswered is whether the territorial democratic state can find a commonly accepted principle for resolving the dilemmas of sovereignty in a multilingual (and in some cases multinational) context in a way that satisfies the requirements of equality and inclusion. This debate continues throughout Europe, and it reflects the difficulties of resolving dilemmas that have been at the center of the process of integration from its beginnings: how to establish a common European political space while preserving national diversity, and how to design shared norms of democratic inclusion and equality while preserving state sovereignty as an international principle.

Dilemmas of Multilingualism and Lessons from Post-Communism

Clearly, the unresolved dilemmas that new members of the European Union bring with them are not unique to post-Communist societies. Still,

---

[54] A prominent tendency exists in social science literature to treat language contestations as identical with ethnic conflicts. See Joshua Fishman, ed. *Handbook of Language and Ethnic Identity* (Oxford: Oxford University Press, 1999). The Norwegian case instructs us otherwise. There are no ethnolinguistic "segments" in Norwegian society as there are in the so-called plural societies of Belgium, Switzerland, and Canada. See Harry Eckstein, *Division and Cohesion in Democracy* (Princeton, NJ: Princeton University Press, 1966). Nonetheless, democratic political elites in Norway made language use a significant part of the social contract. See Gregg Bucken-Knapp, *Elites, Language, and the Politics of Identity* (Albany: State University of New York Press, 2003) For a discussion of how language structures socioeconomic (rather than ethnic) differences, see Pierre Bourdieu, "The Economy of Linguistic Exchanges," in Pierre Bourdieu, *Language and Symbolic Power* (Cambridge: Harvard University Press, 1991).

[55] For a description of the pluralist model represented by Belgium, Switzerland, and Canada, see Karklins, *Ethnopolitics and Transition,* 13.

[56] Horowitz discusses this type of ethnic conflict management in "Ethnic Conflict Management for Policymakers" in *Conflict and Peacemaking in Multiethnic Societies,* ed. Joseph V. Montville (Lexington, MA: Lexington Books, 1990), 122. Laitin proposed that satisfying the language demands of minorities in the newly independent republics of the former Soviet Union might serve the stability of these new democracies. See Laitin, *Identity in Formation.*

the divisiveness of these questions is more apparent in post-Communist Europe. In this region, the collapse and formation of states, together with the fall of Communist regimes and the emergence of new democracies, had already placed sovereignty issues at the center of intense debate among newly emerging political parties. The question of language use became a significant source of division in this context, complicating already difficult processes of democratization. Linguistic territoriality presented great challenges. Some members of ethnically conceived national groups viewed democratization as an opportunity to finally achieve or consolidate *national sovereignty* over territories they claimed as their "national homelands," but ethnopolitical patterns in the region made the pursuit of unitary nation-states highly problematic. Most of the states there incorporate sizeable ethnic and national minorities interested in maintaining their cultures. Both majority and minority speakers expected their respective languages to mark the spaces and institutions they associated with sovereignty and insisted on the use of their language in public education as a means of reproducing the national culture.

Debates over language rights became especially prominent in states newly established or reestablished after the collapse of former multinational federations (the Soviet Union, Yugoslavia, and Czechoslovakia). Of the eighteen countries that make up Central and Eastern Europe, thirteen are successor states, and most of these states incorporate sizeable linguistic minorities. Only five countries continued within their existing borders, and of these Bulgaria and Romania also began the difficult process of regime change by reasserting themselves as "nation-states" against the aspirations of national minority groups.[57] Significant conflicts over minority language use emerged in all of these states. Ultimately, language contestations were debates about the right to pursue cultural reproduction and sovereignty—as a spatial projection of authority (reflected in territorial sovereignty) and as the organization of political power in society (reflected in self-government).[58]

Where majorities and minorities hold separate notions of the right to cultural reproduction, the nation-state model can lock them into a "structural" conflict, and language contestations can become resistant to compromise.

---

[57] The question of which countries belong to Central and Eastern Europe is an emotionally charged one in the region. In the broadest definition of the region, the list of newly established or reestablished countries, from west to east, is the following: the Czech Republic, Slovenia, Bosnia-Herzegovina, Slovakia, Serbia, Montenegro, Macedonia, Estonia, Latvia, Lithuania, Ukraine, Belarus, and Moldova. Those continuing within existing borders are: Poland, Hungary, Albania, Romania, and Bulgaria.

[58] For the importance of analytically distinguishing between state and regime, see Valerie Bunce, *Subversive Institutions* (Cambridge: Cambridge University Press, 1999).

Minority notions of entitlement to cultural equality challenge majority notions of entitlement to cultural dominance. Most of these minorities have kin-states in the neighborhood where their ethnic kin comprise a majority. Although European norms and security arrangements have made irredentist conquest virtually impossible, linguistic territoriality can drive kin-states to take an interest in the fate of their "external kin," designing policies to reproduce a common cultural "nationhood" across borders. Most kin-states in the region have indeed developed policies aimed at encouraging their kin abroad to maintain the language and strengthen cultural relations across state borders.[59]

The conditions under which debates over language use unfolded in Romania and Slovakia highlight the significance of these constraints particularly well. In both states, the issue of language use triggered significant tensions, as national majority and Hungarian minority groups articulated different visions of the democratic state and also generated active engagement by the governments of neighboring Hungary, which at various times triggered fears about regional security. Neither the more recent history of interdependence (as "brotherly" states of the Soviet bloc) nor the shared desire to "return" to a common European space appeared sufficient to render the earlier legacies of state- and nation-building irrelevant in a region where the memories of Hungarian dominance followed by dramatic reversals of fortune fostered a culture of national competition. Romania and Slovakia incorporate large Hungarian communities that view themselves as homeland communities. Hungarian-speakers constitute a large share of the linguistic minorities scattered across Europe. From the beginning of the post-Communist transformation, the leaders of Hungarian minorities in various countries have consistently demanded substate institutional guarantees for reproducing their culture, and language use in the domains of self-government and education has been at the center of political debates among majority and minority parties in both countries.

At the same time, Romania and Slovakia represent different instances of post-Communist institutionalization. Although both states emerged from Communism, the institutional conditions under which the language debates unfolded varied in the two cases. Slovakia is a new state, established in 1993 after the breakup of Czechoslovakia. Romania continued its statehood within existing territorial boundaries after the collapse of the Communist dictatorship in 1989. Dominant political elites in both cases pursued unitary nation-states, and Hungarian minorities in both cases challenged this state

---

[59] Csergo and Goldgeier, *Nationalist Strategies and European Integration;* and Charles King, *The Moldovans.*

model, but Hungarian parties organized themselves differently—at least at the beginning of the process. In Slovakia, a minority population that numbered approximately six hundred thousand formed four political parties.[60] The Hungarian minority in Romania, which numbered about 1.7 million, formed a single political party. The prospects for European Union accession were also different in the two cases. Slovakia—an economically stronger country with a small population located between two "front-runners" of EU accession (the Czech Republic and Hungary) had much better chances than Romania—a country with a significantly weaker economy, a larger population, and a less advantageous location. Indeed, as soon as the consensual government came to power after the 1998 elections, Slovakia rejoined the queue, becoming an EU member in 2004. Although the democratic shift occurred two years earlier in Romania, the EU decided in 2002 to delay the country's accession until 2007.

Romania and Slovakia presented similarly tough challenges to international actors that aimed to bring about change in interethnic relations. The prospects of EU membership and the increased emphasis in international norms on minority protection provided a context in which governments found an incentive to adopt minority-friendly policies. Yet even authors who otherwise emphasize the effectiveness of European influence point out the difficulties that these cases presented. Kelley, for instance, argues that lack of consistency and credibility in the way the EU applied membership conditionality in Slovakia and uncertainty about the prospect of Romania's EU membership were primary causes for the weakness of external influence on minority policies.[61] Vachudova similarly points to the significance of the credibility of future membership, noting that influencing Romania remains particularly difficult for the EU.[62]

These conclusions about membership conditionality leave an important question unanswered: If even the European Union, the international institution that held out the promise of significant rewards to aspiring new members, has succeeded in effecting change only through consistent enforcement of credible membership conditionality, and if this strategy has worked only weakly in countries like Romania and Slovakia, then what lessons can conditionality provide for places outside the reach of the EU? (The tepid enthusiasm that western European populations have expressed for EU expansion further highlights the limitations of any future use of

---

[60] Although these parties formed a single parliamentary bloc early on, the story of their emerging unity makes for an interesting comparison with the Romanian case.
[61] Kelley, *Ethnic Politics in Europe,* 156–59, 136–39.
[62] Vachudova, *Europe Undivided,* 220–21.

EU conditionality.) What role can outside influence play in circumstances where international institutions have far less to offer?

The limitations of international influence render the lessons that Romania and Slovakia offer all the more valuable. They demonstrate that international influence can only achieve substantive and lasting change when it matches domestic interests and strategies.[63] Only those majority and minority political elites and parties that take the democratic process seriously are able and willing to work with international actors toward shared goals. In other words, specific *internal* conditions are necessary for external conditionality to claim success. The role of domestic political actors in the process is not merely that of "compliance" with international requirements or "effectiveness" in responding to external pressure. Rather, domestic actors are the key agents of change in a democratic process that unfolds primarily in parliaments, party headquarters, electoral campaigns, and voting booths. As this book will demonstrate, it has been primarily the ongoing debate in these spaces about the most divisive issues that has created the conditions for change in these countries.

The normative implications of this argument are no less significant than those offered by studies that shed light on the conditions under which international actors can play a role in achieving peace and stability. If we can better understand the ways in which majority and minority actors can make democracy work under adverse domestic conditions, we can also improve the way international institutions can continue to participate in the process without the specific tools of membership conditionality.

The salience of the issue of language use continues today in these societies, because "national" cultural reproduction remains significant for both majority and minority populations. The nation-state model, which emerged in Europe and remains the most powerful international norm within the EU, continues to constrain the choices that majority and minority elites make in the process. The complex ethnopolitical map of the region—which involves multiple nation-building ambitions not only within states but also across state borders—continues to complicate interethnic reconciliation. Yet, less than fifteen years after the collapse of Communism, these majorities and minorities had built lasting electoral and governing coalitions and had found acceptable resolutions to these highly divisive issues.

The chapters that follow trace the process of the language debate in Romania and Slovakia in the contexts of post-Communist institutional transformation, European accession, and relations with the Hungarian

---

[63] See also Jeffrey Checkel, "Why Comply?" *International Organization* 55, no. 3 (2001): 553–88.

kin-state. Chapter 2 explains the language conflicts of the first years after Communism as embedded in a larger debate about sovereignty—a debate made possible by democratization and shaped by the strategies and choices of majority and minority elites, which, in turn, were powerfully influenced by domestic and international legacies. Chapter 3 explores the participation of key international actors (European institutions and the governments of Hungary) and explains how majority and minority political elites and parties used the opportunities of the international framework to reach consensus under conditions of continued nationalist competition. Chapters 4 and 5 lay out the three models that emerged in the debate concerning the relationship between languages in key domains of contestation: public spaces and self-government (chapter 4) and education (chapter 5). Chapter 6 explores the broader implications of the lessons learned from these countries, especially about the options that democratic governments have for regulating language relations and about the implications of these options for democratic legitimacy and stability. Although the link between language and the territorial state in the European context has a pronounced tendency to lock elites representing majority and minority populations into conflicts with each other, the cautiously optimistic conclusion is that strong commitment to the democratic process helps political elites to create possibilities for cooperation that cross cultural divides and ultimately to find common ground even on issues as hotly contested as the right to cultural reproduction on mutually claimed homelands.

Chapter 2

Language, Sovereignty, and Cultural Reproduction

The debates over language rights in post-Communist Europe attest to the persistence of competitive nation-building in the region grounded in competing notions of sovereignty. One of the fundamental principles of political organization, sovereignty is highly contested because it takes different forms in changing domestic and international conditions, forms that are at times incompatible with one another.[1] As Barkin and Cronin observe, "There has been a historical tension between state sovereignty, which stresses the link between sovereign authority and a defined territory, and national sovereignty, which emphasizes a link between sovereign authority and a defined population."[2] This tension became particularly apparent by the middle of the nineteenth century, as multiple groups sharing the same state defined themselves in national terms and began pursuing self-government on the basis of the same (national) principle of sovereignty yet in opposition to one another—in many cases through fierce debates over the same "national homeland." Nationalist conflicts over sovereignty also emerged in other parts of the world that had adopted the European nation-state model. Notions of sovereignty became even more divisive where political actors attempted to reconcile state and national sovereignties in culturally diverse societies while simultaneously trying to adopt the democratic principles of

---

[1] Stephen Krasner, ed., *Problematic Sovereignty* (New York: Columbia University Press, 2001), chapter 1.
[2] Barkin and Cronin, "The State and the Nation."

self-government: inclusion and equality. The question of who constituted "the people" and under what terms became fundamental for defining both national and democratic citizenship all over the world. Through this process of definition, national sovereignty and popular sovereignty (especially where the latter emphasized individual rights and freedoms over group-based cultural rights) evolved into distinct concepts. As Greenfeld observed, the original relationship between nation and democracy changed substantively, as an exclusive idea of "the nation" replaced the originally inclusive idea of "sovereign people": "Nationalism was the form in which democracy appeared in the world. . . . But as nationalism spread in different conditions and the emphasis in the idea of the nation moved from the sovereign character to the uniqueness of the people, the original equivalence between it and democratic principles was lost. . . . As it did so, the nature of sovereignty was inevitably reinterpreted."[3]

After 1989, the post-Communist states were reconstituted on the basis of this changed concept of sovereignty, in which "the people" meant "the nation" defined in cultural terms, and "national sovereignty" replaced "popular sovereignty" as the basic principle of democracy. As Central and Eastern European (CEE) countries emerged from the Soviet sphere of dominance, all three federations in the region collapsed, and new states were established on the basis of the national principle. The same principle was also dominant in the unitary states that remained in place. In Mark Beissinger's words, "The belief that post-communist states should represent the aspirations of the ethnic groups which gave them their names—even if their elites claim that these states are seeking to incorporate other groups living on their territories, and even if elites openly define these states as 'civic' rather than 'ethnic' politics—is fundamental to ethnic majorities throughout the region."[4] At the same time, most states in the region, whether new or old, wanted to join the EU—a process that required surrendering significant aspects of their newly acquired sovereignty.

Under such conditions, minority articulations of *multinationalism* create particularly acute sovereignty dilemmas. Many states in the CEE incorporate not only diverse populations but also more than one group claiming "nationhood," that is, the right to institutional forms for cultural reproduction on a "homeland." A great number of national minorities in the region also have kin in neighboring states. National majority and minority political elites and publics share the idea that governments should facilitate national cultural reproduction. However, from the perspective of majority elites who

---

[3] Greenfeld, *Nationalism,* 10.
[4] Beissinger, "How Nationalisms Spread," 135.

seek to adopt the nation-state model with its emphasis on cultural homogenization, a minority that demands institutions as a "national community" constitutes a problem. Minority elites, in turn, define their institutional demands not as problems but as legitimate democratic interests that a new social contract ought to include. The majority asserts "titular" rights to all institutions of the state, while the minority claims institutional spaces that would guarantee its share of popular sovereignty. The majority places emphasis on the interests of the sovereign state; the minority stresses the need for community sovereignty within a pluralist institutional structure.

The complex matrix of competing and complementary self-defined national entities raised fundamental issues for the political actors that designed the institutions of the new democracies. The first years of post-Communist transformation were critical in this process. The political leaders and elites that dominated the process in this period were in effect the "founding fathers" of the new institutions. With an unprecedented opportunity to create new social contracts for the twenty-first century, majority elites in power throughout the region opted for the traditional nation-state model that had been dominant in Europe throughout the nineteenth and twentieth centuries.

Ernest Gellner famously defined this form of nationalism as "primarily a political principle, which holds that the political and the national unit should be congruent."[5] This ideology became dominant in the newly independent states of Croatia, Estonia, Latvia, Lithuania, Macedonia, Serbia, and Slovakia, and also in the older states of Bulgaria and Romania. In most of these cases, national minorities whose ethnic kin constituted the majority in a neighboring state challenged the unitary nation-state model and articulated alternative institutional forms for cultural reproduction. In most majority-minority debates, language policy became a central issue. Whether the issue was language competency requirements of citizenship (as in the Baltic states), comprehensive legislation about language rights (Slovakia), or specific clauses of legislation concerning public administration and education (Romania), one of the fundamental questions was whether minority cultural communities should gain access to the same institutional forms available to majority cultures in order to perpetuate themselves and pass their "story" and traditions to the next generation. This was a question that democratizing governments in all multilingual societies in the region had to answer.

The choices that majority and minority participants made in this debate were bound by the powerful constraints of the Westphalian territorial nation-state model as well as by the legacies of competitive state- and nation-building in the region. As Romania and Slovakia demonstrate, however, the debate

---

[5] Gellner, *Nations and Nationalism*, 1.

over competing notions of sovereignty created divisions not only between but also within national groups. Ultimately, these divisions over sovereignty made possible the cross-national alliances that helped majorities and minorities to move from conflict to significant consensus on divisive issues.

Shaping the Future with Faces Turned toward the Past

In an effort to establish a new "national state" (Slovakia) and to consolidate an already existing unitary state (Romania), the main architects of post-Communist transformation in Slovakia and Romania opted for the traditional unitary nation-state model and pursued centralized territorial-administrative control as well as centralized control of the institutions of national reproduction (education and culture). A key element of this strategy was the choice to exclude minority languages from the institutional spheres considered most important for national reproduction: government, territory markings, and the educational system.

From the beginning of the 1990s, Hungarians in both states voted overwhelmingly for Hungarian minority parties. These parties consistently challenged the unitary nation-state model by defining the Hungarian minority as a "national community"—a homeland community with claims to institutionalized cultural reproduction rather than an ethnic group. It is important to note, however, that in neither country did Hungarians pursue secession and reincorporation into Hungary or a separate state. Rather, they asked to be recognized as state-constituent entities in their respective states—in ways reminiscent of the "politics of recognition" discussed in the first chapter. Although Hungarians in both states were largely bilingual, they demanded the right to use their language not only in the individual or civil (nongovernmental) domains but also in the official domain, the markings of the public spaces in the settlements they inhabited, and all levels of public education. Throughout the 1990s, they engaged in heated language contestations with each state's respective "titular" majority.

The legacy of past relations of dominance between ethnic groups continued to influence the competition over language rights. The Romanian population of Transylvania, today constituting the western region of Romania, lived for centuries under Hungarian rule. Similarly, the Slovaks lived under Hungarian domination for much of their history. It was only after the end of World War I that the current borders of Hungary were drawn, to the bitter resentment of the Hungarians who fell under the domination of Romanians and Slovaks in the newly created states of Romania and Czechoslovakia. Language hierarchies were suddenly reversed. Hitler redressed Hungarian resentments in World War II when he returned the northern part of Transylvania and southern Slovakia to Hungary. With Hitler's defeat, the contested borders were drawn once again, largely along the same lines that had been created after World War I, and Eastern Europe fell under the influence of the Soviet Union. The evolving patterns of domination and subordination in territories and institutions led to conflicting majority-minority representations of institutional history and adversely impacted Romanian-Hungarian and Slovak-Hungarian relations.

The pursuit of modern nation-states by nationalist political elites and counter-elites began in the second part of the nineteenth century, and the dynamics of these aspirations highlighted the fundamentally competitive character of modern nationalism.[6] Whether in the framework of the multinational Habsburg state (reconstituted after 1867 as the dualist Austro-Hungarian monarchy) or its successor states, the nationalist policies that a dominant ethnic group adopted invariably triggered resentment and engendered conflicting nationalist aspirations on the part of other groups. It was in this process that national literatures emerged in vernacular languages, that national historiographies were written and became justifications for nationalist demands.

Despite sharing similarities in this history, the dominant majority elites in the two states shaped opportunities provided by the international system and reacted to their respective minorities differently. Austria-Hungary was a single empire from 1867 to 1918, yet minority and language policies were distinct in the two units of the Dual Monarchy. On the Austrian side, the government was formally committed to language equality, with a fairly liberal policy allowing the use of local languages for both administrative and educational communication—even though this policy was by no means uniformly applied. On the Hungarian side, the political elites were significantly more interested in creating Hungarian language dominance than their Austro-German counterparts. Aggressive policies of assimilation and increasing urbanization contributed to high levels of linguistic assimilation in the Hungarian-dominated part of the monarchy.[7]

The interwar Czechoslovak state sought to provide equal status for the two dominant ethnic groups, the Czechs and the Slovaks. The educational system was expanded in order to solidify the foundations of Slovak culture and language, and the state initiated a relatively aggressive program to encourage

---

[6] Miroslav Hroch, "From National Movement to the Full-Formed Nation," *New Left Review* 198 (1993): 3–20; Hugh Agnew, *The Czech and the Lands of the Bohemian Crown* (Stanford, CA: Hoover Institution Press, 2004).

[7] Robin Okey, *The Habsburg Monarchy* (New York: St. Martin's Press), 285–303.

a flourishing Slovak press and other cultural activities. Unfortunately, the migration of Czech government agents to Slovakia to implement these programs left the Slovak people feeling vulnerable and had the effect of aggravating national consciousness more than ameliorating it.[8] Although the new state established some of the most inclusive democratic institutions in the region, the two dominant groups were reluctant to accommodate minority demands. In the new state, Czechs composed 50.4 percent of the population, Germans 23.4 percent, Slovaks 15 percent, Hungarians 5.6 percent, Carpatho-Rusyns 3.5 percent, and Jews, Poles, and Roma together 2.1 percent.[9] Discontented with their status, many members of the two most sizeable and formerly dominant minorities, Germans and Hungarians, joined political parties that challenged the legitimacy of the Czechoslovak republic. These groups felt vindicated when in 1938 Hitler dismembered Czechoslovakia, occupied the Czech lands, and helped to redraw contested political borders throughout the region. As a result of Hitler's policies, the Hungarian government, which had consistently pursued revisionism during the interwar period, was able in November 1938 to re-annex the southern region of what is now Slovakia, which had a majority Hungarian population. The reassertion of Hungarian political and cultural control was a traumatic experience for Slovaks in this region.

In interwar Romania, the dominant political elites were largely xenophobic, especially toward the Hungarians as the formerly dominant nation and toward the Jews, many of whom were also Hungarian-speakers. In the newly expanded state, the primary focus of administrative, economic, and educational policies was on shifting the ethnic hierarchy in Transylvania in favor of Romanian dominance.[10] The ineffectiveness of the state bureaucracy, however, helped to attenuate the effects of discriminatory policies.[11] Hungarian irredentism resulted in the return of northern Transylvania to Hungary between 1940 and 1944 under conditions that were similarly traumatic to Romanians in this territory, as had been the Hungarian reoccupation of southern Slovakia. Nevertheless, the Communist-dominated Groza government in post–World War II Romania was much better disposed toward Hungarians than was the Beneš government in Czechoslovakia.[12]

---

[8] Joseph Rothschild, *East Central Europe between the Two World Wars* (Seattle: University of Washington Press, 1974), 119–20.

[9] Paul Robert Magocsi, "Magyars and Carpatho-Rusyns," in *Czechoslovakia 1918–88,* ed. Gordon H. Skilling (Oxford: Macmillan, 1991), 105.

[10] Irina Livezeanu, *Cultural Policies in Greater Romania* (Ithaca: Cornell University Press, 1995).

[11] Rothschild, *East Central Europe,* 288.

[12] Bennett Kovrig, "Peacemaking after World War II," in *Hungarians: A Divided Nation,* ed. Stephen Borsody (New Haven: Yale Center for International and Area Studies, 1988), 69–88.

The Communist regimes were built on the ideology of internationalism, and many members of minority communities saw Communism as an attractive alternative to nationalist government. Nevertheless, nationalism remained an organizing principle throughout the Communist bloc, including Romania and Czechoslovakia.[13] The spectrum of minority policy in the region ranged from the pursuit of aggressive and often violent policies of assimilation (Bulgaria) and the denial of the existence of national minorities (Poland) to the creation of substate territorial units in which certain national minorities were recognized as "titular" groups (Czechoslovakia, Yugoslavia, and the Soviet Union).[14]

Although part of the same Soviet-dominated region for decades, the interethnic experiences of the people of contemporary Romania and Slovakia differed in important ways during the Communist period. The role of the Soviet Union in the evolution of majority-minority relations in postwar Czechoslovakia and Romania also differed significantly. To secure its interests in establishing Communist regimes in the two states, the government of the Soviet Union supported the Beneš government in Czechoslovakia and undermined the monarchy of King Michael in Romania. Consequently, the Soviet government on the one hand gave its full support to President Beneš's idea of eliminating challenges to Czechoslovak sovereignty by expelling the German and Hungarian minorities, and on the other hand it facilitated the establishment of regional autonomy for Hungarians in Transylvania.

After the defeat of the Axis powers at the end of World War II, the government of the reestablished Czechoslovakia declared Germans and Hungarians collectively guilty of destroying the state during 1938 and 1939, and gained international approval for their expulsion.[15] Based on the so-called Beneš decrees, Czechoslovakia expelled a large percentage of the Hungarian population, including much of the Hungarian educated class, to Hungary.[16] By 1948, a third of the Hungarian population, over 200,000 people, had left the country. Approximately 60,000 emigrated voluntarily to Hungary, and the rest were forcibly expelled. In the latter group, approximately 73,000 were exchanged for an equal number of Slovaks in Hungary who had volunteered to move to Czechoslovakia. (About 41,600 Hungarians were forced to work in the depopulated Sudeten region from which the German population had been expelled.)[17] Hungarians in Slovakia commonly call the

---

[13] Katherine Verdery, *National Ideology under Socialism* (Los Angeles: University of California Press), 1991; and Sharon Wolchik, *Czechoslovakia in Transition* (New York: Pinter, 1991).
[14] Liebich, "Ethnic Minorities," 120–21.
[15] Kovrig, "Peacemaking after World War II," 69–73.
[16] Vojtech Mostny, "The Beneš Thesis," in *The Hungarians,* ed. Borsody, 231–43.
[17] Magocsi, "Magyars and Carpatho-Rusyns," 115–16.

period between 1945 and 1948 "the years of homelessness" and refer to it as the most traumatic time in their history.[18] Slovaks in Hungary who had declined to participate in this population exchange and remained in Hungary also consider this period to have been traumatic.[19]

The Beneš decrees in Czechoslovakia denied citizenship to ethnic Hungarians, closed all Hungarian institutions, and prohibited the use of the Hungarian language in all public places. Declaring Hungarians in Slovakia to be "ethnic Slovaks" who had assimilated to Hungarian culture during centuries of Hungarian domination, the government began a process of forced "re-Slovakization."[20] It was only after the Communist coup of 1948 that Hungarians gained full citizenship rights and began reestablishing their educational and cultural institutions. Their efforts, however, remained seriously limited by Slovak policies of linguistic assimilation. These policies included the consolidation of Hungarian into Slovak language schools and the manipulation of school administrations and curricula to promulgate the Slovak language at the expense of Hungarian.[21]

In Romania, Soviet interests placed constraints on minority policies during the first decade of Communism. Because Hungarian Communists were instrumental in the Communist takeover of the country, they received Moscow's support in achieving full citizenship rights, participation in the government, and the right to maintain cultural and educational institutions. At least partly due to Soviet pressure, the Romanian government created a Hungarian Autonomous Region in the middle of Transylvania in 1952.[22] As the influence of ethnic Hungarian leaders in the Communist Party weakened, however, the government launched a nationalizing strategy that gradually eliminated Hungarian regional autonomy and severely weakened the political status and social structure of the Hungarian community in Transylvania.[23] After 1956, the Romanian government began pursuing an integrationist policy toward minorities with a focus on merging Hungarian-language schools with their Romanian counterparts. This process culminated in the

[18] Kálmán Janics, *A hontalanság évei* (Budapest: Hunnia, 1989); and Štefan Šutaj, "A Beneš-dekrétumok a magyar kisebbségek történeti tudatában," *Régió* 1–2 (1995): 185–91.
[19] Anna Gyivicsán, anthropologist, author interview, Budapest, Hungary, April 4, 1996.
[20] P. Hunčík and F. Gál, "The Historical Background to the Formation of Slovak-Hungarian Relations," in *The Hungarian Minority in Slovakia*, ed. Pavol Frič et al. (Prague: Institute of Social and Political Science, Charles University, 1993), 22–28; Katalin Vadkerty, *A reszlovakizáció* (Bratislava: Kalligram, 1993).
[21] Robert R. King, *Minorities under Communism* (Cambridge: Harvard University Press, 1973), 111–14.
[22] Stefano Bottoni, "The Creation of the Hungarian Autonomous Region in Romania (1952)," *Regio* (2003): 71–93.
[23] George Schöpflin, "Transylvania," in *The Hungarians,* ed. Borsody, 129–44.

merger of the historic Hungarian-language Bolyai University in Cluj with the Romanian-language Babeş University.[24] The increasingly aggressive language policies of the Ceauşescu regime signaled that integration in Communist Romania required linguistic assimilation.[25]

With the collapse of Communism came the promise of change; for majorities and minorities alike, change brought a chance to redefine old ideas of government. The process of redefinition, however, remained bound by old concepts of sovereignty and past institutional practice. It was not inevitable that nationalism remain the dominant organizing principle of post-Communist transformation. At the beginning of the process, most societies in the region experienced a unifying spirit of euphoria over the collapse of Communism, the end of Soviet dominance, and the possibility of "returning" to an integrating and prosperous Europe.[26] Soon, however, majority and minority political elites began forcefully articulating competing notions of sovereignty. In the process, collectivist ideas of national sovereignty gained dominance.

During the Communist period, liberal intellectuals in Warsaw, Budapest, and Prague had articulated universalist desires to expand individual freedoms and opportunities, and their informal networks acted in many ways as transnational communities. Thanks at least in part to these voices, influential Western democratization scholars expected free elections throughout the post-Communist world to prove the triumph of liberal democracy over all other political ideologies in the region. Francis Fukuyama's famous piece on "the end of history" captures the spirit of this expectation.[27] Yet in the realities of post-Communist electoral competition, former dissident circles and movements were capable of articulating successful liberal alternatives to the electorate only in the Central European countries of Hungary, Poland, and Czechoslovakia—and even in these cases primarily in the first years of democratization. In Czechoslovakia, dissident circles formed the core of the organizations Civic Forum (centered in Prague) and Public Against Violence (centered in Bratislava), which cooperated closely in the ousting of the Communist government in November 1989. These organizations also helped create the post-Communist government of Czechoslovakia. In the Slovak part of the federation, Public Against Violence (VPN) was the largest party in the first democratically elected coalition government. The VPN

---

[24] Nándor Bárdi, ed. *Autonóm magyarok?* (Csíkszereda: Pro-Print, 2005); Gábor Vincze, *Illúziók és csalódások* (Csíkszereda: Státus, 1999).

[25] King, *Minorities under Communism,* 146–53.

[26] Vladimir Tismăneanu, *Fantasies of Salvation* (Princeton, NJ: Princeton University Press, 1998).

[27] Francis Fukuyama, "The End of History?" *National Interest* 16 (Summer 1989): 3–35.

also formed an alliance with the Independent Hungarian Initiative (FMK), the leadership of which also espoused liberal ideas of citizenship.

Although represented by prominent figures in the government during the federalist period (November 1989–July 1992), the liberal democratic approach to sovereignty quickly became marginalized in Czechoslovakia. Emerging leaders of VPN, many of them former reform Communists, opted for a collectivist national strategy. The most successful of these leaders, Vladimír Mečiar, elected Slovak prime minister after the June 1990 elections, became confrontational with the Czechs, downplayed the urgency of economic restructuring, and elevated national issues above the other "pillars" of the VPN's program. In 1990 the VPN leadership called for a new contract between two equal state-forming nations, the Czechs and the Slovaks.[28] By early 1991, a deep rift developed in VPN, and in March Prime Minister Mečiar split the party in half by creating a new faction called Public Against Violence—For a Democratic Slovakia. Political developments soon confirmed the weakness of the liberals in the competition over the institutions of the new democracy. In April 1991, Mečiar's faction became a new political party, Movement for a Democratic Slovakia (HZDS), a powerful new rival of VPN.[29] The Slovak-Hungarian alliance broke, and by the 1992 parliamentary elections the opportunity that VPN had represented for an ethnically inclusive political party disappeared together with the party itself. The former (Slovak) liberal core of the VPN became the Civic Democratic Union, and Mečiar's HZDS emerged as the dominant political force for the coming years, with an image as the defender of Slovak sovereignty against internal and external enemies.

What began as a debate about the right approach to democratic sovereignty in post-Communist Czechoslovakia turned into a question of Slovak independence. A growing distance emerged between the Hungarian minority and the Slovak majority elite from early 1990 to June 1992, as the issue of sovereignty became "ethnicized" in the process of political competition. It appeared as though there had emerged degrees of "Slovakness," measurable by one's level of support for the idea of an independent state. The Hungarian minority ranked at the bottom of the scale of "good Slovakness," although Hungarians were not the exclusive recipients of "anti-Slovak" charges. Slovak critics of the Mečiar government also found themselves under attack as enemies of independence.[30] Although the prominent winners of the

---

[28] *Program vlády Slovenskej republiky* (Bratislava: June 1990).
[29] Abby Innes, "The Breakup of Czechoslovakia," *East European Politics and Societies* 11, no. 3 (Fall 1997): 393–435.
[30] Daniel Butora, "Meciar and the Velvet Divorce," *Transition* 5, no. 8 (August 1998): 75.

1992 parliamentary elections had not campaigned for statehood before these elections brought them to power, soon after the elections the peaceful separation of Czechs and Slovaks was put on a fast course by the new political leadership in both parts of the federation.[31] Independent Slovakia was declared on July 17, and the Slovak constitution was adopted on September 1, 1992.

By January 1993, the Slovak majority in its new state was facing a different side of the question of national equality. They had to respond to demands by a politically resourceful Hungarian minority that also defined democratic sovereignty in national terms and proposed that "the declaration [of independence] contain the following statement: the equality of national minorities and ethnic groups will be established in the constitution of the Slovak Republic and guaranteed in international treaties."[32] The drafting of the new constitution, designed without the participation of the Slovak and Hungarian parliamentary opposition, foretold deep problems for the new state. This constitution declared that Slovakia was the state of the Slovak nation, Slovak was the state language, and minority rights must not be enforced at the expense of the state's integrity or of other citizens.[33] Excluded from the constitutional process, Hungarian deputies proposed "changing the [draft] text of the constitution to define the Slovak Republic as the state of the sovereign citizens of Slovakia."[34] The largest Hungarian minority party stated in a press release that the constitution treated national minorities as an appendix to the Slovak nation. The deputies of the two largest Hungarian parliamentary parties walked out during the final vote on the constitution.[35] The presidents of all four Hungarian parties declared in a written statement that "once again, we find ourselves participants in an antidemocratic process."[36]

The Slovak nation-state design challenged Hungarian minority political organizations to formulate a response, and their response, unsurprisingly enough, was unanimous rejection of the homogeneous nation-state strategy. Rejection, however, did not reflect unity in political ideology among the

---

[31] Martin Bútora and Zora Bútorová, "Political Parties, Value Orientations, and Slovakia's Road to Independence," in *Party Formation in Central Eastern Europe*, ed. G. Whitman and M. Waller (Cheltenham, UK: Edward Elgar Publishing, 1994).
[32] *A Magyar Kereszténydemokrata Mozgalom az Autonómiáért* (Bratislava: MKDM, 1995), 9.
[33] Constitution of the Slovak Republic, available online at www.nrsr.sk/sub/language_free/ustava_sk.doc, accessed July 18, 2004.
[34] A Magyar Kereszténydemokrata Mozgalom az Autonómiáért, 9.
[35] "Dangers of Disadvantageous Discrimination of National and Ethnic Minorities in the Constitution of the Slovak Republic," Coexistence press release, September 12, 1992.
[36] "Statement on the Circumstances Surrounding the Dissolution of Czechoslovakia," December 5, 1992.

Hungarian parties. Significant differences remained, especially between the liberal Hungarian Civic Party (heir to FMK) on the one hand, and the Hungarian Christian-Democratic Movement (MKDM) and the Coexistence Political Party (Coexistence) on the other. In contrast to the MPP's liberal individualism, MKDM and Coexistence embraced the idea that government should reflect the sovereignty of nations. The 1992 electoral coalition agreement between MKDM and Coexistence expressed the essence of this minority nationalism: "The right for self-determination, as a group right of persons of the same identity, applies to both majority nations and minority groups."[37] A July 1992 statement delivered to the Slovak National Council by MKDM deputy Pál Csáky on behalf of the MKDM-Coexistence deputies, expressed the same idea:

> [We] fully recognize the right of nations for self-determination. Based on this principle, we understand the current emancipatory aspirations of the Slovak Republic. Considering that the self-determination of every society is derived from the sovereignty of the citizen, we stress that all citizens of the same identity, cultural, historic, and social heritage are entitled to the right for self-determination. This means that national minorities and ethnic groups are also entitled to assert this right in the form of self-administration, in order to preserve their identity, just as it is natural in the democratic states of the world.[38]

The leader of Coexistence—the party that claimed the largest support base among Hungarian voters at this time—articulated the idea that the Hungarian community should be an equal "partner-nation" in Slovakia: "We must establish our institutionalized equality with the majority nation. . . . If a nation or part of a nation lives in a community of equality and partnership with another nation or part of nation, in a politically and legally defined framework, the relationship that develops between them is one of partner-nations."[39] The Coexistence leadership defined the Hungarians in Slovakia as a "national community living in numerical minority."[40] Coexistence publications emphasized that the Hungarians formed a "compact" national community in southern Slovakia not only in a cultural sense

---

[37] *Közösségünk szolgálatában* (Bratislava: Hungarian Christian-Democratic Movement, 1990–1995), 93.
[38] Ibid., 62.
[39] "Duray Miklós elnöki beszámolója az Együttélés IV. országos kongresszusán 1993 február 27-én, Komáromban (részlet)," in *Az Együttélés kézikönyve,* Coexistence publication, 8.
[40] "Duray Miklós," 5–10.

but also territorially: "Ninety-nine percent of the Hungarians of Slovakia live in 13 districts and 2 large cities in Southern Slovakia. The settlements populated by ethnic Hungarians compose an almost continuous linguistic territory in Southern Slovakia, from Bratislava (Pozsony) to the Slovakian-Ukrainian border."[41] Based on this approach, in February 1993, one month after the creation of independent Slovakia, the Coexistence leadership proposed territorial self-government for the Hungarian minority as a peaceful solution to the problem created by the establishment of the Slovak national state.

After the declaration of Slovak national sovereignty in July 1992, the MKDM leadership also began advocating ideas of Hungarian *community sovereignty.* An August 1992 leadership statement declared that "the future solution to the problems of our national minority lies in the realization of an educational and cultural self-administration that could be complemented later by a territorial-regional arrangement that would assure our legal standing in our homeland."[42]

Although both Coexistence and MKDM actively sought institutional solutions for multinationalism after January 1993, they disagreed on important issues. Key sources of disagreement were the Coexistence "partner-nation" concept and territorial autonomy. MKDM leaders considered territorial autonomy as desirable but inappropriate for the Slovak situation.[43] Both parties, however, shared the view that democratic government had to be based on a political contract between the Slovak nation and the Hungarian minority. In July 1993, the Coexistence and MKDM deputies jointly submitted to the Slovak parliament a proposal for such a contract, arguing that "in a multi-national state such as the Slovak Republic, the status of minority communities must be fixed by law [and] their rights and obligations, as well as [those] of the state, must be precisely determined."[44]

The Mečiar government showed no inclination to consider the idea that Slovakia should be a pluralist democracy rather than a unitary Slovak "nation-state." The Coexistence-MKDM proposal was never put on the Slovak parliament's agenda. Instead, the government aggressively began to establish the institutions of a centralized unitary state with full control over the institutions of national reproduction.

---

[41] *Hungarians in Slovakia,* Coexistence document, 6.
[42] Statement published in *Közösségünk szolgálatában,* 63.
[43] Pál Csáky, "Introduction," in *A Magyar Kereszténydemokrata,* 2.
[44] Hungarian Christian Democratic Movement—Coexistence, "Draft of Fundamental Principles of a Constitutional Law of the National Council (Parliament) of the Slovak Republic about the Legal Status of National and Ethnic Minority Communities in the Slovak Republic," 1.

In Romania, collectivist nationalism was dominant from the beginning of post-Communist transformation, and it represented a direct link to the pre-1989 political practice. The Romanian intellectual tradition provided few resources for the emergence of liberal democratic thought. The particularly repressive nature of the regime had led to an almost complete absence of organized liberal dissident activity during Nicolae Ceauşescu's totalitarianism. As a consequence, liberal groups were unable to formulate a powerful alternative to the collectivist ideologies rooted in the experience of nationalist Communism.[45]

The broad political movement that toppled the Ceauşescu dictatorship and established its successor government promised the possibility of an inclusive political society. The National Salvation Front (FSN or "the Front") formed in Bucharest during the revolution comprised many former Communists but also some dissident intellectuals. An ethnic Hungarian served as one of the Front's vice presidents, and the Democratic Alliance of Hungarians in Romania (RMDSZ) actively participated in the legitimization of the Front as the "salvation movement" that would lead Romanian society's exit from the Communist era. Rather than liberal democratic notions of citizenship, however, cross-ethnic alliance was based on an early consensus that post-Communist social organization should be based on a national collectivist principle. Immediately after the bloody revolution, FSN created a separate Ministry for Nationality Affairs (headed by Károly Király—an ethnic Hungarian and former Communist who turned dissident) and issued a declaration recognizing the *collective* rights of national minorities and supporting the establishment of an institutional structure that would guarantee the exercise of these rights, above all the unrestricted use of the Hungarian language.[46]

Soon, shared majority-minority interest in nationalism became the source of deep division, as the leadership of the Front opted to continue the centralizing policies of the previous period. Tismăneanu notes that "Romania has presented scholars of the post-communist transition with a striking paradox: the most abrupt break with the old order seemed to have resulted in its least radical transformation."[47] Ion Iliescu, a former ranking Communist official

---

[45] Andrei Marga, "Cultural and Political Trends in Romania before and after 1989," *East European Politics and Societies* 17, no. 1 (Winter 1993): 14–32. Alina Mungiu, "Intellectuals as Political Actors in Eastern Europe," *East European Politics and Societies* 10, no. 2 (Spring 1996): 333–64; and Vladimir Tismăneanu and Ondrejovič Pavel, "Romania's Mystical Revolutionaries," *East European Politics and Societies* 8, no. 3 (Fall 1994): 403.
[46] Sándor Vogel, "Kisebbségi dokumentumok Romániában," *Regio* 5, no. 1 (1994): 158–59; and Democratic Alliance of Hungarians in Romania, *Documents* (Cluj, 1994), no. 1, 21.
[47] Vladimir Tismăneanu, "Tenuous Pluralism in the Post-Ceausescu Era," *Transition* (December 27, 1996), 6.

was elected president in 1990 and reelected in 1992. During its first seven years in power (1990–1996), his regime demonstrated little desire to foster an inclusive society. Iliescu alienated democratic political forces by employing authoritarian methods reminiscent of the Ceauşescu period and by courting the Romanian ultra-nationalist forces.[48]

These conditions affected all of the defining events of the Romanian democratic transition, guaranteeing that the process of preparing and conducting the first multi-party elections after forty years would be flawed.[49] Like Slovakia, the drafting of the new constitution and other important legislation, which established the new rules of democratic process, was marked by exclusionary practices. Drafted by the FSN leadership, the constitution adopted in November 1991 defined Romania as a "unitary nation-state" and stipulated that the basis for the Romanian state was the unity of the Romanian "*popor*," which in colloquial Romanian means people in the ethnic sense, similar to *Volk* in German.[50] The Hungarian minority party rejected this state model and began articulating a pluralist response based on the notion that Romania was a multinational state. Insisting that the Hungarian minority composed a separate national community within the Romanian state, the RMDSZ leadership submitted a nationality statute proposal to parliament—a proposal that was essentially ignored.[51] After the 1992 reelection of the nationalist government, the RMDSZ leadership responded by declaring the need for the "internal self-determination" of the Hungarian community. This declaration (known as the "Declaration of Cluj") caused an uproar within the Romanian majority political elite, as it was a clear articulation of a desire for Hungarian community sovereignty (Hungarian community self-government): "Accepting our [community as a] national

---

[48] H.-R. Patapievici, "Regimul Iliescu," in H.-R. Patapievici, *Politice* (Bucharest: Humanitas, 1997), 141–53; Juliana Geran Pilon, *The Bloody Flag* (New Brunswick, NJ: Transaction Publishers, 1992); Katherine Verdery and Gail Kligman, "Romania after Ceausescu," in *Eastern Europe in Revolution,* ed. Ivo Banac (Ithaca: Cornell University Press, 1992); Michael Shafir, "Government Encourages Vigilante Violence in Bucharest," *Report on Eastern Europe* 1, no. 27 (1990): 32–39; and Vladimir Tismăneanu, "Romania," *East European Reporter* 4, no. 2 (1990). The term *ultra-nationalist* is used here for political actors who advance extremely exclusivist nationalist ideas, including the banning of national minority political organizations, the exclusion of minority national markers from the public sphere, or the expulsion of national minorities from the territory of the state. In Romania, the three main ultra-nationalist parties were the Greater Romania Party (PRM), the Socialist Labor Party (PSM) and the Party of Romanian National Unity (PUNR).

[49] *May 1990 Elections in Romania,* 61. Washington, DC: The National Democratic Institute for International Affairs and the National Republican Institute for International Affairs an International Delegation, 1991.

[50] Constitution of Romania, Article 1, paragraph 1, and Article 4, paragraph 1. Available at domino. kappa.ro/guvern/constitutia-e.html, accessed August 31, 2006.

[51] This bill was titled "Draft Law on Nationality" and was signed by Géza Szőcs, at the time co-president of the RMDSZ.

entity, we do not want either to secede or to emigrate, as we consider our native land our home. Nor do we wish, however, to assimilate to the Romanian nation. The Hungarian community in Romania constitutes a political subject, it is a state-constituting factor, and as such it is an equal partner of the Romanian nation. . . . We proclaim that internal self-determination is the path [leading to a solution]."[52] Thus, the majority-minority division over sovereignty that emerged in both Romania and Slovakia during the defining first years of post-Communism reflected both the continuing appeal of the territorial nation-state model and the constraints this model placed on democratization in multilingual societies.

Differences in the stages of state development had important consequences for nationalist strategy. For Slovak nationalists, the goal was to gain national independence. The question of independence became the primary arena of conflict in which state-seeking elites pursued a strategy of centralized control over cultural reproduction. After a period of decentralization during the Czechoslovak federalist government, the state-seeking Slovak nationalists chose to *re-centralize* institutions and reinstitute authoritarian methods of government reminiscent of the Communist regime. In Romania, where the goal was to maintain and strengthen control over an existing state, unwillingness on the part of the dominant elites to break with Communist practices of centralization and the use of authoritarian methods was the initial arena of conflict. This conflict brought to the fore the state-consolidating elite's continued preference for the cultural policies of a unitary nation-state.

Language and Constructing the Nation-State: Slovakia

The choice of dominant majority actors to frame the question of language use in terms of the independence of an ethnically defined Slovak nation pressured all other political actors to articulate their positions in relation to this framework. Consequently, the liberal approach to language rights and citizenship faded away, Hungarian minority positions converged on a pluralist nationalist response, and the Slovak political actors outside the nationalist coalition were eventually compelled to articulate a separate position. In this process, a pattern of divisions emerged that manifested conflicting visions about the new social contract in Slovakia.

The two organizations that defined the terms of the debate most vocally were the Matica slovenská and its parliamentary ally, the Slovak National

---

[52] "A Romániai Magyar Demokrata Szövetség Ideiglenes Intéző Bizottságának kiáltványa," *Magyar Kisebbség* 1, no. 1 (May 1995): 15; and "Az RMDSZ nyilatkozata a nemzeti kérdésről," *Magyar Kisebbség* 1, no. 1 (May 1995): 17.

Party (SNS). Established in early 1990, SNS claimed to be the heir of the historic Slovak National Party—the only political party the Slovaks had in Hungary until 1918. A cultural institution of long standing, Matica slovenská was important for nurturing Slovak culture in Hungary before the end of World War I. The Matica movement was revived after the 1968 federalization of Czechoslovakia, and after the 1989 revolution Matica leaders forcefully reasserted the scope of the organization as a defender of Slovak national interests.[53] After 1994, the activities of the Matica became increasingly intertwined with those of state institutions.

By elevating the cause of the "national language" to the status of a key political issue, the Slovak nationalist elite followed a traditional nationalist strategy, with the goal of creating majority language dominance in all official domains on the state's territory. Just months after the Communist collapse, Matica slovenská proposed a language law to codify one literary Slovak standard as the exclusive language used in all official interactions in the Slovak part of Czechoslovakia, where Hungarians comprised about eleven percent of the population. This so-called Matica law, submitted to parliament under SNS sponsorship in March 1990, proposed to exclude minority languages from official use in all state, social, political, and economic organizations and institutions.[54] Accordingly, the Hungarian language could only be used informally, for instance within a Hungarian cultural institution or church, but all formal interactions, even between Hungarian institutions or between an individual and a Hungarian cultural institution, had to occur in Slovak. Supporters argued that such a law was necessary to protect Slovaks against the threat of linguistic assimilation to the Hungarians in southern Slovakia and thereby guarantee the integrity of Slovak territory. As SNS deputy V. Miskovsky stated during the parliamentary debate, "It is clear for all of us that the battle is waged not only for the language. The stake is to preserve the integrity of Slovakia."[55]

This reasoning allowed the nationalists to place all major political actors in the "pro-Slovak language" or "anti-Slovak language" camp. Throughout the summer of 1990, there were no unified Slovak or Hungarian responses to the Matica proposal, and liberal views (in favor of no regulation, allowing informal norms to govern linguistic interaction) had significant representation among both the Slovak and Hungarian elites. Soon, however, three

---

[53] Miroslav Kusý, "Slovak Exceptionalism," in *The End of Czechoslovakia,* ed. Jiří Musil (Budapest: Central European University Press, 1995), 142.

[54] For the original Slovak text of the bill and a comprehensive account of the Matica campaign, see József Berényi, *Nyelvországlás* (Bratislava: Fórum, 1994), 47–66 and appendix 2.

[55] Quoted in ibid., 69.

positions emerged that revealed conflicting notions of the social contract. The ruling Slovak nationalists were adamant on the exclusion of minority languages. An increasingly united Hungarian minority elite demanded domestic and international legal guarantees for the unrestricted use of Hungarian in all domains they considered important for the reproduction of their culture. Slovak moderates were inclined to comply with international recommendations for language liberalization but were not ready to accept the notion of language equality that the Hungarians demanded.

The liberal idea of a culturally neutral state, where informal norms and the free individual's rationality govern language choice, received a spotlight only at the beginning of the language debate. In early 1990, the liberal core of VPN-FMK, including the leaders of the Independent Hungarian Initiative, represented the predominant position within the governing coalition. From their perspective, the specifics of language use needed no regulation, as the constitution and other laws already provided sufficient legal framework, while informal rules could regulate linguistic interaction in mixed communities. Due to intensifying nationalist pressure, however, VPN changed its course of action from rejecting the idea of an official language law to refusing to support the exclusionary "Matica law" and eventually to participating in the drafting of the coalition government's language bill in October 1990.

The process of drafting the language law tested the strength of the liberal democratic alternative in the Slovak part of the federation and seriously affected the relationship between Slovak and Hungarian liberals. Although the liberal approach had provided a source of agreement between the FMK and the VPN leadership at the beginning of the language debate, the consensus failed to withstand the nationalist pressure inside and outside the coalition. First, responding to perceived social pressure to enact language legislation, the Slovak and Hungarian liberals in the government drafted a bill containing general statements that Slovak was the official language, Czech could also be used in official interactions, and the use of national minority languages would also be allowed in the districts they inhabited.[56] As the Matica-led campaign intensified and nationalist voices in the government increased in volume, however, the initial VPN-FMK proposal became less liberal with each draft. The final version submitted by the coalition government to the Slovak parliament was so unlike the first draft that FMK leader László A. Nagy refused to sign it.[57]

---

[56] For the original Slovak text of the law see ibid., appendix 3.
[57] However, all but one FMK deputy voted in favor of the "coalition law" on October 25, 1990, to prevent the passing of the Matica bill and in order not to threaten the stability of the coalition.

The debate over this law contributed significantly to the emergence of Hungarian minority unity and to the crystallization of a pluralist nationalist response. At the beginning of the post-Communist period in Czechoslovakia, the Hungarian minority did not organize itself as a unified ethnic bloc. Instead, four Hungarian parties were formed, the first of which was the Independent Hungarian Initiative (FMK), the liberal party that allied itself with Public Against Violence (VPN). The failure of this alliance to prevent minority language exclusion affected the character and strength of the other Hungarian minority parties that emerged in the spring of 1990. Already the elections of June 1990 indicated that the less consensual Hungarian minority parties (those less accepting of Slovak perspectives on the language issue) had stronger electoral appeal among Hungarian voters (see table 2.1).

Although unanimous on the rejection of minority language exclusion, Hungarian minority parties initially followed diverse approaches to the issue of language legislation. The leadership of FMK participated in the drafting of the first, liberal version of the government's proposal. The leader of MKDM, Béla Bugár, argued against a language law as late as one month before the parliamentary debate of the law: "We consider the language law unnecessary; citizens should freely decide what language to use with whom and in what situation."[58] Coexistence was the only Hungarian party to stand for language legislation consistently. Instead of the negative (restrictive) language law proposed by Slovak nationalists, however, Coexistence leaders demanded a positive minority language law guaranteeing the right to use minority languages in all spheres of public life. As Slovak nationalist pressure grew for an exclusive official language law, the two Hungarian opposition parties coordinated their positions and submitted a proposal that guaranteed the use of Hungarian in all public institutions and public spaces (including the display of geographic names) and official bilingualism in the districts in which Hungarians composed at least 10 percent of the population.[59] Official bilingualism would have meant coequal status for the minority language in administrative districts where the minority composes a given percentage of the local population. This proposal never passed beyond the committee debates.

By late October 1990, the Hungarian elite from all parties felt compelled to join forces despite their differences.[60] After the parliamentary vote, the FMK leaders (at the time still members of the governing coalition) published an optimistic but unambiguously critical evaluation of the language law in

---

[58] Cited in Berényi, *Nyelvországlás,* 115.
[59] See Coexistence-MKDM proposal published as ibid., appendix 5.
[60] See ibid., 105.

TABLE 2.1
Relative popularity of Hungarian minority parties among the Hungarian minority electorate in local elections, 1990 and 1994

| | 1990 | | | | 1994 | | | |
| | Mayors | | Local council members | | Mayors | | Local council members | |
	Numbers	Percent	Numbers	Percent	Numbers	Percent	Numbers	Percent
FMK＝MPP	27	16.5%	482	11.9%	62	24.9%	812	18.5%
Coexistence	102	62.2	2,416	59.7	131	52.6	2,215	50.4
MKDM	35	21.2	1,151	28.4	56	22.5	1,367	31.1
Total	164	99.9	4,049	100.0	249	100.0	4,394	100.0

Sources: Öt választás Szlovákiában 1990–1994 [Coexistence publication], 7, 15–16; *Közösségünk szolgálatában: A Magyar Kereszténydemokrata Mozgalom öt éve* (Pozsony: MKDM, 1995), 201.

which they made conciliatory gestures toward the Hungarian parties in opposition.[61]

Besides contributing to the alienation between the Slovak and Hungarian liberal elite and to rapprochement among the Hungarian minority elite, the language debate also led to deepening divisions within the majority political parties. When on October 25, 1990, "the nationalist wave reached its climax" in the parliamentary debate over the language law, the main actors facing each other were not Slovak deputies on one side and Hungarian deputies on the other.[62] Rather, the principal battle took place between Slovak deputies who favored greater democratic pluralism than their counterparts, who in turn preferred an exclusive majoritarian Slovak polity, including institutionalized Slovak linguistic dominance. Eventually, the "coalition law" won out over the "Matica law," albeit with added limitations on minority language use: geographic names and the names of cities, towns, streets, and squares could be displayed in Slovak only. Under enormous nationalist pressure, many coalition deputies also voted for the "Matica law." Those who argued for the "coalition law" over the "Matica law" ended up having to leave through the back door of the parliament building, to evade a crowd of angry demonstrators.[63]

The language law finally adopted in 1990 (No. 428/1990) was less restrictive regarding the use of Hungarian than the draft proposed by Matica slovenská and SNS but more restrictive than the draft proposed by the Coexistence-MKDH faction. The law guaranteed the dominance of the Slovak language in all spheres of public life and allowed the display of bilingual signs only in places where minorities composed more than 10 percent of the local population (leaving the 20 percent hurdle open as an alternative). The use of minority languages in official business was allowed, but only on a voluntary basis (that is, if both parties in the interaction agree) and only in administrative districts in which the minority composed at least 20 percent of the population. Citizens of Slovak ethnicity were *required* to use the Slovak language in their communications with public officials. Official bilingualism, demanded by the Hungarian minority parties in opposition, was not allowed in any part of southern Slovakia.[64]

Seemingly a reasonable middle-of-the-road solution between the total exclusion of Hungarian and the legalization of official bilingualism, the law nevertheless failed to end the vehement debate over language use. The Slovak nationalists demanded the law's reversal and called for civil disobedience

[61] *Új Szó*, November 9, 1990.
[62] Kusý, "Slovak Exceptionalism," 143.
[63] Berényi, *Nyelvországlás*, 67–72, 84–85.
[64] Ibid., 80.

against the government.[65] Hungarians were also dissatisfied, although most Hungarian deputies had voted for it in order to prevent the passage of a more restrictive bill. Slovak and Hungarian politicians interpreted the scope of the law differently. The most heated issue in the continuing controversy concerned the display of place names in the Hungarian language in southern Slovakia. The Slovak nationalists showed particular interest in the banning of Hungarian place names and considered the display of the historical Hungarian place names as tantamount to the revival of Hungarian oppression in southern Slovakia.[66] The Hungarian counterargument was that the Slovak renaming of many localities after the creation of Czechoslovakia (Decree No. A311/16–II/e in 1948) had been undemocratic, and the new democracy had to rectify such abuses. Hungarian leaders argued that many Slovak names had been forced on the Hungarian inhabitants of those localities and that democratization should allow Hungarians to use their settlements' old names, many of which went back to the thirteenth century. Public referenda demonstrated that the inhabitants of these settlements overwhelmingly demanded the right to use traditional Hungarian names.[67]

The Slovak nationalists could claim some success when a law on local administration adopted on November 22, 1990, provided a long list of circumstances in which the use of the Slovak names was mandatory.[68] The Hungarian elite, in turn, looked for loopholes and argued that "anything that the law does not explicitly prohibit, is allowed."[69] The Hungarian deputies claimed, for instance, that the law did not explicitly prohibit the display of minority language place names near the Slovak names. Hungarian names appeared behind the official Slovak display, on a smaller board in a different color. Slovak opponents found this solution unacceptable. The Slovak moderates in the governing coalition set up a broad parliamentary committee to investigate the implementation of the law. After a lengthy inquiry, the committee concluded that the display of Hungarian place names violated the language law, and the controversy over the law worsened Slovak-Hungarian relations in the mixed settlements of southern Slovakia.[70]

The differences that emerged during the debate over language use also contributed to the restructuring of political alliances and oppositions, both among majority Slovak and minority Hungarian parties and between Slovak

---

[65] "Ulica kontra parlament," *Pravda,* October 27, 1990.
[66] See Matica slovenská evaluation of the execution of the language law, cited in Berényi, *Nyelvvországlás,* 123.
[67] Interpellation by Coexistence deputy Edit Bauer in Zsigmond Zalabai, *Mit ér a nyelvünk, ha magyar?* (Bratislava: Kalligram Könyvkiadó, 1995), 44–70.
[68] Berényi, *Nyelvvországlás,* 118.
[69] See interpellations and letters of Hungarian deputies in Zalabai, *Mit ér a nyelvünk, ha magyar?* 14–18.
[70] Berényi, *Nyelvvországlás,* 118–26.

and Hungarian parties. Although the liberal VPN leadership could claim immediate victory in the legislative battle over the 1990 language law, it lost the long-term political competition with the nationalists. The political elites that had worked for a consensual resolution of the language issue (the Slovak and Hungarian liberals) remained outside the Slovak parliament after the 1992 elections that brought the Mečiar-led HZDS to power. Neither the Civic Democratic Union (ODU, formerly VPN) nor the Hungarian liberals (MPP, formerly FMK, renamed in January 1992) exceeded the necessary threshold for representation in parliament (see table 2.2).

The period between 1992 and 1998 was dominated by Prime Minister Vladimír Mečiar and his HZDS. Mečiar's consecutive governments pursued a nationalist, centralizing, and increasingly authoritarian political strategy that Slovak moderate and Hungarian minority parties in parliamentary opposition continuously challenged. The only intermezzo in this dynamic occurred in March 1994, when the Slovak moderates in opposition, with the help of the Hungarian parties, brought down the Mečiar government. During the six months of the Moravčik government, the moderates liberalized the use of Hungarian personal names and allowed the unofficial display of bilingual signs in southern Slovakia. The September 1994 elections, however, brought Mečiar and the HZDS back to power and sent the Slovak moderate bloc back to its accustomed role as part of the parliamentary opposition.[71]

The reconstituted nationalist coalition launched a series of policies that followed even more aggressively the traditional nationalist strategy of establishing centralized control over a culturally monolithic Slovak society. The State Language Act adopted in November 1995 required citizens of Slovakia to use one literary Slovak standard in virtually all areas of social life. A 1996 law elevated the openly anti-Hungarian Matica slovenská to the status of Slovakia's supreme cultural, social, and scientific institution. The Law on Territorial-Administrative Division of the Slovak Republic, adopted in March 1996, limited the self-government of Hungarian communities in southern Slovakia and the use of Hungarian in official business. Amendments to the law on school administration and a series of ministerial orders limited the authority of local communities over schools and aimed to restrict the use of Hungarian as a language of instruction. The Law on the Organization of Local State Administration reinforced the authority of a strong central government over weak local government.[72]

---

[71] Dušan Leška and Viera Koganová, "The Elections 1994 and Crystallization of the Political Parties and Movements in Slovakia," in *Slovakia,* ed. Soňa Szomolányi and Grigorij Mesežnikov (Bratislava: Interlingua Publishing House, 1995), 86–102.
[72] Grigorij Mesežnikov, "Domestic Political Developments and the Political Scene in the Slovak Republic," in *Global Report on Slovakia,* ed. Martin Bútora and Péter Hunčík (Bratislava: Sándor Márai Foundation, 1997), 11.

TABLE 2.2
Slovak parliamentary elections, 1990, 1992, 1994, 1998, and 2002

	1990		1992		1994		1998		2002	
	Percent	Seats	Percent	Seats	Percent	Seats	Percent	Seats	Percent	Seats
VPN/FMK	29.34%	48								
KDH	19.20	31	8.88%	18	10.08%	17	(SDK)		8.3%	15
SNS	13.94	22	7.93	15	5.4	9	9.07%	14		
SDĽ[1]	13.34	22	14.70	29	10.41	18	14.66	23		
KSS									6.3	11
MKP[2]	8.66	14	7.42	14	10.18	17	9.12	15	11.2	20
DS	4.39	7					(SDK)			
SZ	3.48	6					(SDK)			
HZDS			37.26	74	34.96[3]	61	27.0	43	19.5	36
DÚ[4]					8.57	15	(SDK)			
ZRS					5.40	13				
SDK[5]							26.33	42		
SDKÚ[6]									15.1	28
SOP							8.01	13		
Smer									13.5	25
ANO									8.0	15
Others	7.65	0	23.8	0	15.0	0	5.81	0	18.1	0
Total	100.0	150	100.0	150	100.0	150	100.0	150	100.0	150

Sources: For 1990, Grigorii Mesežnikov, "Domestic Political Developments and the Political Scene in the Slovak Republic," in Global Report on Slovakia: Comprehensive Analyses from 1995 and Trends from 1996, ed. Martin Bútora and Péter Hunčík (Bratislava: Sándor Márai Foundation, 1997), 11. For 1992, Jiří Pehe, "Czechoslovakia's Political Balance Sheet, 1990 to 1992," RFE/RL Research Report, 1, no. 25 (June 19, 1992), 29. For 1994, Dušan Leška and Viera Koganová, "The Elections 1994 and Crystallization of the Political Parties and Movements in Slovakia," 87. For 1998, Statistical Office of the Slovak Republic at volby98.statistics.sk/ArcGeo/table3.asp and table4.asp. For 2002, Statistical Office of the Slovak Republic at www.statistics.sk/volby2002/webdata/engl/tab/tab4.htm.

Note: The first two elections (1990 and 1992) occurred in the Czecho-Slovak federation. This table contains results for the Slovak National Council.

[1] In 1990, SDĽ formed the electoral coalition Social Democracy (SD), which included also SDSS. In 1994, SDĽ was the largest party in the 1994 electoral coalition Common Choice (SV), which included also SZS, HP and SDSS.

[2] The Hungarian Coalition (MK) was composed in 1990 and 1992 of Coexistence and MKDM. In 1992, MNP candidates ran on the MK list. In 1994, MK also included MPP. In 1998, MK became MKP.

[3] HZDS participated in the 1994 elections in alliance with RSS.

[4] The Democratic Union was formed by the HZDS splinters AD and APR in summer 1994. In 1995, the SNS splinter NDS-NA also merged with DÚ.

[5] The Party of the Slovak Democratic Coalition (SDK) was formed in 1998 by KDH, DÚ, DS, SDSS, and SZS.

[6] The Slovak Democratic and Christian Union (SDKÚ) was formed in 2000 by leaders of SDK.

Contestations over these policies further reinforced unity among Hungarian minority political parties and led to a crystallization of their pluralist nationalist response to the unitary nation-state design. The debates also revealed a significant cleavage in majority notions of sovereignty, which became a source of majority-minority cooperation toward the end of the decade.

Although differences in political ideology among the Hungarian parties remained, unanimous rejection of the unitary nation-state model and of minority language exclusion from public institutions brought together formerly liberal elites with those calling for collective minority rights. From 1990 to 1992, Coexistence President Miklós Duray had believed that the Hungarian voters in Slovakia wanted unified political representation in the form of a single Hungarian minority party. By contrast, the MKDM leadership had been more interested in an electoral and parliamentary coalition of equal partners. Before the 1992 elections, the Hungarian liberals—although unable to continue their electoral alliance with the Slovak liberals—had continued to reject the idea of monolithic Hungarian representation and had refused to join the Hungarian electoral coalition.[73] The 1992 elections, however, forcefully demonstrated that Hungarian voters favored the proponents of unity in minority politics: the Coexistence-MKDM coalition was successful, while the Hungarian Civic Party (MPP, formerly FMK) shifted from a place in the previous Slovak government to no representation in the new parliament (see table 2.3).

Although their party was excluded from parliament, MPP leaders joined leaders of other Hungarian parties after 1992 in a unified effort to secure domestic and international pressure on the Slovak government to lift restrictions on minority rights. The 1994 MPP program still reflected some of the distinctness of the party in attempting to match minority rights issues with civic values as well as a more pronounced emphasis on economic matters. After the 1994 elections, MPP became a full member of the Hungarian Coalition (MK), which Coexistence and MKDM had formed in 1990. By the end of 1994, the Hungarian parties together set the concept of community sovereignty (articulated as a demand for national-minority self-government within a pluralist state) against the Slovak government's concept of Slovak national sovereignty (expressed in the Slovak nation-state). Language rights remained the touchstone of the sovereignty debate. The Hungarians aimed at maintaining substate territorial districts in southern Slovakia where Hungarians could use their language in government, territory markings, and public education.

---

[73] Darina Malová, "The Development of Hungarian Political Parties during the Three Election Cycles (1990–1994) in Slovakia," in *Slovakia,* ed. Szomolányi and Mesežnikov, 201.

TABLE 2.3
Relative popularity of Hungarian minority parties among the Hungarian minority electorate in parliamentary elections, 1990, 1992, and 1994

	1990			1992				1994		
	Percentage of all votes	Seats	Preferences*	Percentage of all votes	% votes to Hungarian parties	Seats	Preferences*	Percentage of all votes	Seats	Preferences*
FMK=MPP	**			2.29%	23.60%	0			1	9.39
Coexistence			69.7			9	66.0		9	45.81
MK	8.66%	14		7.42	76.05	(14)		10.18%	(17)	(100–0.85)
MKDM			30.3			5	30.0		7	43.95
MNP							4.0			0.85
Total	8.66	14	100.0	9.71	99.65	14	100.0	10.18	17	100.00

Sources: For the sources of official parliamentary election data, see table 2.1. Data on preference votes were compiled from MKDM statistics in *Közösségünk szolgálatában: A Magyar Kereszténydemokrata Mozgalom öt éive* (Pozsony: MKDM, 1995), 200 (for 1990 and 1994); and Coexistence statistics in *Öt választás Szlovákiában 1990–1994*, 11, 15 (for 1992 and 1994). The MKDM source shows 9.5% for MPP and 46.6% for Coexistence.

Notes: **Bold numbers** indicate official election results of MK and MPP and parliamentary representation. In 1990 and 1992, the Hungarian Coalition included Coexistence and MKDM. MNP candidates ran on the MK list in 1992. In 1994, MK also included MPP.

* Voters were allowed to mark a maximum of four candidates on the party (or coalition) electoral list as their "preferences." These marks can be used as measures of the popularity of various parties within an electoral coalition.

** FMK participated in the 1990 elections in alliance with VPN-FMK. The alliance won 29.34% of the votes. It is difficult to estimate the percentage of FMK votes. We know that the Hungarian minority comprised 10.67% of the population of Slovakia according to the 1991 official census and that the Coexistence-MKDM coalition won 8.66% of the votes. Assuming that the ratio of Hungarian minority voters was similar to that of the Slovak voters, FMK could not have received more than 2% of the votes even if all ethnic Hungarian voters had cast their votes for Hungarian parties.

Slovak elites and parties occupied different places along two different axes of the sovereignty debate, one of which had to do with *state sovereignty* and the other with *popular sovereignty*. Valerie Bunce, in her discussion of the collapse of Communism, distinguishes between questions of state and regime, that is, between questions related to the spatial projection of authority and those related to the organization of political power in society.[74] In Slovakia, the debate over questions of state focused on whether the post-Communist decentralization of authority could allow for substate territorial entities that empowered national minorities in certain regions or localities. On this question, Slovak political actors in government and opposition agreed. They unanimously rejected Hungarian proposals that would have preserved or created districts where Hungarians comprised a regional majority. The question of regime concerned democratization, that is, the degree to which newly gained popular sovereignty meant departure from the previous political and economic system and methods of government. The most divisive issue in this respect was whether the new political regime should organize political power in such a way as to guarantee governmental accountability and empower lower levels of government. On this question, Slovak parties in government and opposition were engaged in vehement battles.

Agreement on the question of state sovereignty and disagreement on the question of popular sovereignty created a flexible pattern of division and alliance between majority and minority political parties. Fear of the Hungarian minority's potential to weaken Slovak state sovereignty motivated Slovak parties in government and the opposition to join together against the Hungarian parties. Fear of the Mečiar government's authoritarian strategies that excluded the opposition from institutional design created a deep division in the Slovak majority political spectrum and pushed Mečiar's opposition into alliance with the Hungarian parties.

Their support for increased popular sovereignty eventually allowed Slovak moderates to accept Hungarian demands for increased control over local institutions in the spheres of culture and educational policy. Their concern for state sovereignty, however, prevented the same moderates from articulating a markedly different alternative to the government's nation-state strategy. Many among the Slovak elites in opposition shared the view that the government's blatant nationalism engendered dangerously divisive politics that threatened to steer Slovakia away from "standard" (Western European) democratic development. In contrast, Slovak opposition leaders perceived themselves as the "consensual and pro-reform elite" that aimed at the genuine democratization of Slovakia. They opposed a government that intended

[74] Bunce, *Subversive Institutions*.

to maintain a high level of centralization in the institutional structure, prevent the separation of powers, and considerably delay economic restructuring.[75] Yet few openly criticized the Slovak nation-state project. Miroslav Kusý was the only prominent Slovak intellectual in this period who explained Hungarian minority demands for "ethnic autonomy" as a reaction to the Slovak nation-state strategy. Kusý wrote a critique of the nation-state with the intention of sparking a debate among the Slovak moderate elite. His efforts failed, however, as even the editors of the moderate Slovak periodical *Národná obroda* hesitated to publish his articles.[76]

In the context of ongoing electoral competition, Slovak moderates were regularly labeled "anti-Slovak." Under those circumstances, keeping silent on "the Hungarian question" appeared to be the safest strategy.[77] The Slovak opposition did take part, however, in the creation of institutional and legislative policies that shaped the relationship between the Hungarian minority and the Slovak state. Although many Slovak deputies in opposition were critical of the government's pursuit of nationalist centralization, many of the same deputies voted for the laws embodying that goal. The Slovak opposition voted overwhelmingly for the 1995 language law, the 1996 territorial redistricting act, and the 1996 legislation empowering Matica slovenská.

The Slovak opposition's choice of silence on the main issues that the Hungarian Coalition raised, coupled with its pattern of voting for legislative acts that pursued centralized and Slovak-controlled institutions for cultural reproduction manifested both electoral calculations and wariness of Hungarian demands for self-government.[78] Many among the Hungarian minority elite recognized the divisiveness of the concept of territorial autonomy and instead emphasized decentralization, self-administration, and self-government as democratic goals favorable to *all* Slovak citizens. As elsewhere in the region, however, Hungarian propositions with a potential for territorial autonomy remained highly explosive, and the fissure between "titular" majority and minority nationalist concepts of territoriality hindered Slovak-Hungarian cooperation against the Mečiar government.

The intense debates over policies of nationalist centralization in the late 1990s revealed the influence of differences along the two axes of sovereignty

---

[75] Soňa Szomolányi, "Does Slovakia Deviate from the Central European Variant of Transition?" in *Slovakia,* ed. Szomolányi and Mesežnikov, 16.

[76] Miroslav Kusý, "Národný štát a etnická autonómia," *Národná obroda,* March 20, 1996; Kusý, "Dvojitá identita národnostnej menšiny," *Národná obroda,* February 22, 1996; Kusý, author interview, Bratislava, Slovakia, April 23, 1996.

[77] These expressions appeared with high frequency, for instance, in the HZDS publication *Slovensko do toho!* during 1997 and 1998.

[78] Leška and Koganová, "The Elections 1994," 97.

described above on divisions and potentials for cooperation on language rights. The State Language Act adopted in November 1995 was a major landmark in these debates. The return of the nationalists to power had created an opportunity for Matica slovenská and SNS to reverse the 1990 law and codify language as an instrument for establishing a culturally homogeneous society. The new law declared: "The Slovak language is the most important characteristic of the Slovak nation, the most valuable part of its cultural heritage, [the] expression of Slovak sovereignty, and the general means of communication of its citizens, guaranteeing them freedom and equality in dignity and rights on Slovak territory."[79]

This comprehensive language law aimed to accomplish the dual goals of "status planning" and "corpus planning." Language planning always seeks to bring about deliberate change in the ways language is used in society. Status planning changes the norms according to which particular languages are allowed in certain institutions and settings. Declaring one language in a multilingual state as official, for instance, elevates that language over others. Corpus planning entails official policies that establish a standardized (literary) form for a particular language by selecting one of alternative forms in a written or spoken code, creating new forms, or modifying old ones.[80] The usual consequence of corpus planning is that other forms of the same language, such as dialects, become associated with lower status. Besides declaring Slovak as the only official language in the state, the new law authorized the Ministry of Culture to identify certain books as official dictionaries and grammar books to serve as the basis for *correct* Slovak. A council of language inspectors was established to supervise the observance of the law. The law also stipulated that, beginning in January 1997, fines would be issued to violators of the language law.

Supporters argued that the law was intended to purify and strengthen the Slovak language and that a separate law would soon be adopted to regulate minority language use. The government, however, never presented a minority language law to the parliament, and on a number of occasions government officials stated that there was no need for such a law.[81] The Hungarian Coalition submitted a minority language law in June 1996, but this draft was never put on the parliament's agenda.[82] The Hungarian minority elite

---

[79] "Zákon Národnej Rady Slovenskej Republiky o štátnom jazyku Slovenskej Republiky," 1995, no. 270 in *Zbierka zákonov Slovenskej republiky* (Collection of Laws of the Slovak Republic).
[80] Robert L. Cooper, *Language Planning and Social Change* (Cambridge: Cambridge University Press, 1989).
[81] Ján Stena, advisor to President Michal Kováč, author interview, Bratislava, Slovakia, April 12, 1996.
[82] "Törvényjavaslat a nemzeti kisebbségek és etnikai csoportok nyelvének használatáról a Szlovák Köztársaságban," document of the Hungarian Coalition, April 1996.

considered the 1995 language law and the failure to adopt a law legitimizing minority language use as evidence that the ruling Slovak political elite had no desire to accommodate the Hungarian community in the Slovak state. The Hungarian Coalition argued that the 1995 law, by guaranteeing "freedom and equality in dignity and rights on Slovak territory" only to Slovak speakers, in fact institutionalized second-class citizenship for speakers of other languages.[83]

Many Slovak moderates also criticized the government's bill, but primarily for its "corpus planning" aspects: They worried about the law's interference with the evolution of the Slovak language. KDH president Ján Čarnogurský charged that the law imposed "bureaucratic limitations" on language development.[84] Some Slovak linguists considered it to be an unnecessary intrusion into the "natural" evolution of linguistic exchanges in society. Slavo Ondrejovič, for example, argued that although the regulation of the relationship between Slovak and minority languages was necessary in the new state, the wide use of literary Slovak in society made language standardization unnecessary.[85] Some Slovak analysts also opposed the law for its restrictions on Hungarian language use.[86] Given the heightened nationalist pressure during the parliamentary debate, however, even those opposition deputies who had previously promised to reject the government's version of the bill ended up voting with the coalition. Although the drafting of the language law was highly secretive, the roll-call vote was broadcast live on Slovak television. As an example of the tone of the debate, one HZDS deputy argued that "anyone who votes against that bill is against the fulfillment of the Slovaks' desires and deserves public contempt."[87] A task force formed in April 1996 by the Hungarian Coalition and Slovak opposition parties to prepare a minority language bill produced no results. The Slovak opposition refused to support the Hungarian draft, and in the end the Hungarian deputies submitted their proposal independently to parliament in June 1996.[88]

[83] "A Szlovák Köztársaság államnyelvéről szóló törvény, melyet a Szlovák Köztársaság Nemzeti Tanácsa 1995. november 15-én hagyott jóvá (A Magyar Koalíció párjainak elemzése)," November 23, 1995, document of the Hungarian Coalition.

[84] Author interview, Bratislava, Slovakia, April 24, 1996.

[85] Author interview, Bratislava, Slovakia, April 26, 1996. See also articles in *Domino,* February 23–29, 1996.

[86] Sociologist Vladimir Krivy, quoted in Sharon Fisher, "Making Slovakia More 'Slovak,'" *Transition* 2, no. 24 (November 29, 1996): 16. Also Miroslav Kusý in interview by author, Bratislava, Comenius University Department of Political Science, April 23, 1996.

[87] Fisher, "Making Slovakia More 'Slovak,'" 14–15.

[88] Coexistence President Miklós Duray, interview by author in Bratislava, Slovakia, April 18, 1996.

The plan for Slovakia's territorial redistricting triggered similarly vehement debate. Territorial redistricting became a central issue after Slovak independence, and the Hungarian minority elite viewed the government's plan as a deliberate attempt to break up existing substate boundaries of a relatively "compact" Hungarian community. Reacting to the preparation of this plan, in 1993 the Association of Towns and Villages of Zitny Ostrov (in Hungarian, Csallóköz, a region in southern Slovakia in which the Hungarians are the majority) called a general assembly of Hungarian minority local councilors, mayors, and members of parliament to discuss local and regional self-government.[89] This event caused substantial commotion in Slovakia, as Slovak politicians discouraged Hungarian parties from participating, and Matica slovenská organized an intense anti-Hungarian campaign.[90] The meeting took place in Komarno on January 8, 1994, with the sponsorship of the Coexistence and MKDM leadership and—contrary to Slovak fears—without manifestations of Hungarian separatism.[91] The assembly forcefully rejected the government's redistricting plan as undemocratic and proposed three alternative administrative maps for Slovakia, each preserving majority-Hungarian districts. The "Komarno declaration" carefully avoided terms like "autonomy" or "collective rights" and referred instead to "local self-government" and "community rights."[92]

No matter how tame the vocabulary was, however, from the Slovak perspective the Komarno declaration was a call for ethnic Hungarian autonomy—an idea that all Slovak parties unanimously rejected. The Mečiar government showed no inclination to discuss the Hungarian proposals. During the parliamentary debate over the government's territorial redistricting bill at the beginning of 1996, the Hungarian Coalition again presented two alternatives.[93] One would have united southern Slovakia into one large territorial unit in which the Hungarians composed a majority. The other would have established three larger territorial units with ethnic Hungarians in majority. In the end, the Hungarian Coalition's proposals received no consideration, and the government's version of the Administrative Territorial law was adopted in March 1996 without significant changes, replacing the existing

[89] Pál Csáky, "Introduction," *Közösségönk szolgálatában,* 108–9.
[90] Sharon Fisher, "Meeting of Slovakia's Hungarians Causes Stir," *RFE/RL Research Report* 3, no. 4 (January 28, 1994): 43. and Árpád Duka Zólyomi, "A szlovák-magyar kiegyezés felé?" in *Önkormányzat az önrendelkezés alapja,* 22–25.
[91] Slovak Television news broadcast, January 9, 1994, cited in Erzsébet Pogány et al., "A komáromi nagygyűlés sajtóvisszhangja," in *Önkormányzat az önrendelkezés alapja,* 201.
[92] Duray, "A komáromi nagygyűlésen elfogadott állásfoglalás rövid elemzése," in *Önkormányzat az önrendelkezés alapja,* 198.
[93] These proposals had been included in the Komarno document, which became part of the Hungarian Coalition agreement of 1994.

administrative structure in Slovakia with eight new regions (*kraje*) and seventy-nine districts (*okresy*). For the Hungarian minority, the law was more than a matter of administrative change, although it raised administrative questions as well. (Because the districts in which Hungarians lived were larger than the ones in northern Slovakia, Hungarian inhabitants would live farther away from district government offices than would citizens in the other regions.) The greater concern was that the plan broke up traditional districts and drew new regional boundaries in such a way that ethnic Slovaks composed a significant majority in all eight larger territorial units. Consequently, Hungarian minority proposals for community self-government, most importantly the official use of the Hungarian language in regional government and local authority over Hungarian schools, as well as ideas about the voluntary association of local governments to form larger regional units, would be circumvented completely.[94]

Although the preparation of the Mečiar government's redistricting plan triggered criticism from all opposition parties as well as from the Union of Cities, the Association of Slovak Cities and Municipalities (ZMOS), and other organizations outside parliament, Slovak and Hungarian opposition parties were unable to reach consensus on an acceptable design. The Slovak opposition's main concern was that the government's plan did not genuinely pursue devolution of central power to regional and local governments, as it lacked specifics on the powers that would be transferred to lower levels. The Hungarian Coalition shared this concern, but the alternative proposals it advanced were unacceptable to the Slovak opposition, because they claimed collective rights to minority self-government in southern Slovakia.[95] Unable to agree on an alternative design, Slovak deputies overwhelmingly voted in favor of the government's bill.[96]

The dynamics of the debate over policies affecting cultural and educational institutions manifested similar tensions between competing notions of sovereignty. The government's preference for a unitary centralized Slovak culture was evident in the institutional changes it instituted, such as the consolidation in 1996 of a broad range of cultural institutions under regional cultural centers, which would make administrative, financial, and policy decisions for individual museums, art galleries, and other cultural

---

[94] MPP Vice President Kálmán Petőcz, author interview, Bratislava, Slovakia, April 16, 1996; Coexistence President Miklós Duray, author interview, Bratislava, Slovakia, April 18, 1996; "László Szarka, Közigazgatási reform és kisebbségi kérdés," *Kisebbségkutatás 2* (2001): 208–22.
[95] KDH President Jan Čarnogurský, author interview, Bratislava, Slovakia, April 24, 1996.
[96] Vladimír Krivý, "Slovakia and Its Regions," in *Slovakia 1996–1997,* ed. Martin Bútora and Thomas Skladony (Bratislava: Institute for Public Affairs, 1998), 55–56.

institutions.[97] Beginning in 1996, regional centers asserted their power over Hungarian minority institutions. Funding for CSEMADOK, the largest Hungarian cultural institution, was severely reduced, and financial support was allocated to foundations and periodicals close to the government with marginal roles in Hungarian cultural life. Hungarian minority leaders challenged these policies vocally, and the Slovak moderate elite was critical as well. Slovak intellectuals and artists organized several manifestations of dissatisfaction with activities of the Ministry of Culture, such as the consolidation of theaters.[98]

The coalition government charged the Matica slovenská organization with shaping and overseeing the development of Slovak national culture, and in 1996 it introduced legislation declaring the organization to be "the most significant institution of the Slovak nation in cultural, social, and scientific activities" (superseding universities, the Slovak Academy of Sciences, and other research institutions) and endowing it with extremely generous resources to perform a broad range of activities aimed at "strengthening Slovak patriotism" and "deepening relations between citizens and the state." To enhance centralization of the Slovak national canon, the coalition attempted to place two institutions of the Slovak Academy of Sciences, the Historical Institute and the Institute of Slovak Literature, under Matica's authority. After strong expressions of opposition from the academic community, the latter changes were eventually dropped from the law adopted in early 1997.[99] Throughout 1996, many Slovak opposition members expressed disapproval with the law empowering Matica.[100] Nonetheless, in the end not a single Slovak opposition deputy voted against it in parliament.

The strategy of nationalist centralization was also evident in the sphere of education. An amendment to the Act on School Administration in Education in April 1995 gave the state the authority to appoint and recall school principals, and this law was used to remove several ethnic Hungarian principals who failed to implement Ministry of Education directives on bilingual education. In an effort to control educational activities at every level, the Education Ministry issued numerous regulations, directives, and decrees that did not always correspond to the provisions of legislative acts

---

[97] Ladislav Snopko, "Culture," in *Slovakia: 1996–1997,* ed. Bútora and Skladony, 202.
[98] See Snopko, "Culture," 201–4.
[99] See Vladislav Rosa, "Education and Science," in *Slovakia 1996–1997,* ed. Bútora and Skladony, 157.
[100] Peter Hunčik, conversations with the author, April 1996; Slovak linguist Pavel Onrejovič, author interview, Bratislava, Slovakia, April 26, 1996; Miroslav Kusý, author interview, Bratislava, Slovakia, April 23, 1996.

on education. The territorial redistricting act passed in March 1996 further expanded the powers of the central state in the sphere of education. School councils were incorporated into the state administration, and the Interior Ministry took over much of the executive and financial authority formerly in the hands of the Ministry of Education.[101] The Hungarians responded to these policies with demands for greater local authority over schools and the devolution of financial resources to local communities. The Slovak opposition was also critical of efforts to re-centralize the institutional structure, but they were suspicious of the Hungarian elite's desire for educational autonomy.[102]

After 1995, the government accelerated the introduction of the so-called alternative instruction plan, a form of bilingual education used in formerly Hungarian language schools. The goal, according to the Ministry of Education, was to improve the Slovak language proficiency of Hungarian students, thereby enhancing their chances for future employment. The Union of Hungarian Educators, Hungarian linguists, and Hungarian parties vehemently opposed the plan as another manifestation of what they considered the systematic attempt to establish Slovak majority control over Hungarian minority education in order to assimilate the Hungarians in Slovakia. Although participation in alternative instruction was not considered mandatory but an option for parents of Hungarian students to choose voluntarily, several directors of Hungarian schools were dismissed for their lack of support for the plan.[103] The Slovak moderates in favor of Slovak-language education did not support the vehement Hungarian criticism of the government's alternative instruction plan.

Despite disagreement on minority institutional autonomy, shared rejection of the government's centralizing authoritarianism provided the Slovak and Hungarian opposition sufficient common ground to oust the Mečiar government in the 1998 elections and to form a governing coalition that promised to break Slovakia away from nationalist isolation and integrate it into Euro-Atlantic institutions. Because this coalition also included the (by then united) Hungarian Coalition Party for the first time, the new consensual government could create the potential for renegotiating the terms of language relations in Slovakia.[104]

---

[101] Ondrej Dostál, "Minorities," in *Global Report on Slovakia,* ed. Bútora and Hunčík, 66; Rosa, "Education and Science," 152–53, 189.
[102] Author interview with KDH President Ján Čarnogurský, Bratislava, Slovakia, April 24, 1996.
[103] "Hungarians in the Slovak Republic," Coexistence analysis.
[104] László Szarka, A szlovákiai Magyar Koalíció Pártjának kormányzati szerepvállalásáról, *Régió* 11:4 (2000): 122–49.

Language and Strengthening the Nation-State: Romania

The key issues of the debate over multilingualism in Romania were the same as those in Slovakia. As in Slovakia, these issues demonstrated the powerful consequences of the continuing links connecting language, sovereignty, and cultural reproduction that the Westphalian nation-state model perpetuates. The dynamics of the debate also indicated that linguistic territoriality remained a highly salient factor in the democratization of the CEE multilingual states that were not newly created after the Communist collapse. Nonetheless, differences in state development influenced the forms that the language debate took in the two cases. In Slovakia, where national independence became the primary arena of conflict, both majority and minority nationalists explicitly tied the language issue to notions of sovereignty. The state-seeking elites in Slovakia were more vocal than their state-consolidating counterparts in Romania in calling for a comprehensive official language act to establish the rules of linguistic ownership over the newly independent territory and its institutions. In Romania, where achieving independence was not a concern, instead of designing comprehensive language legislation, dominant political actors formulated language policy as part of the legislation concerning public administration and the educational system.

Nationalism had been a prominent driving force of state-society relations and a dominant elite ideology throughout the Ceaușescu period.[105] Rather than moving away from that ideology, the first post-Communist leadership formed alliances with ultra-nationalist parties of the left and right and instituted minority-policies that were more restrictive than their counterparts during the Ceaușescu dictatorship. The new constitution affirmed that Romanian was the only official language on Romanian territory.[106] Although it advocated the principle of self-government and the decentralization of public offices, the constitution also established the institution of the prefecture to maintain central control over locally elected administrative bodies. A law on local public administration (No. 69/1991) made Romanian the exclusive language at all levels of government, and a law on education (No. 48/1995) restricted education in minority languages. From the perspective of national minority rights, these two laws were throwbacks to the Ceaușescu period and became sources of intense controversy between the Romanian government and the Hungarian minority party.[107]

---

[105] Verdery, *National Ideology Under Socialism.*
[106] Constitution of Romania. In Article 1, paragraph 1, the state was defined as a "unitary nation-state." Article 4, paragraph 1 stated that the basis of the Romanian state was the unity of the Romanian people. Article 13 stated that the Romanian language was the sole official language of the Romanian state.
[107] "Az RMDSZ és az adminisztratív önkormányzatok," *Szabadság,* November 15, 1993.

The main patterns of the debate over language rights in Romania were remarkably similar to those in Slovakia and were rooted in similar divisions over competing notions of sovereignty. During the defining first Iliescu period between 1990 and 1996, the dominant political elites placed primary emphasis on state stability and territoriality and aggressively sought to preserve a centralized unitary nation-state with its traditional emphasis on majority language dominance. Disagreement over continued unitary nation-state strategies placed the Romanian majority and Hungarian minority political actors on opposite sides. Although broad majority consensus on the need to control all territorial and institutional spaces prevented moderate Romanian parties in opposition from formulating a consistently minority-friendly approach to the social contract, shared opposition to the Iliescu government's authoritarianism enabled moderate Romanian and Hungarian parties to form a series of alliances that became sources of a more pluralist consensus toward the end of the 1990s.

Like the situation in Slovakia, as the broad political movements of the first years of post-Communism differentiated into narrower political parties that engaged in fierce electoral competition, the main participants of the sovereignty debate in Romania were governmental coalitions that included or cooperated with expressly ultra-nationalist anti-minority parties and, of course, the opposition. By January 1995, the Iliescu leadership found itself in an ominous governing coalition described effectively by Michael Shafir:

> The chauvinist Greater Romania Party (PRM) and the Socialist Labor Party (PSM), the heir of the defunct Romanian Communist Party, formalized their relationship with the ruling coalition. . . . The fourth signatory to the protocol, the extreme nationalist Party of Romanian National Unity (PUNR), had already joined the government. . . . At the signing of the protocol, Ilie Verdeţ a former premier under Ceauşescu and now PSM chairman; Adrian Păunescu, PSM first deputy chairman and a "court poet" of the Ceauşescu family; Corneliu Vadim Tudor, another Ceauşescu "court troubadour" and now the overtly anti-Semitic PRM chairman; and the staunchly anti-Hungarian Funar were immortalized in photographs alongside the PDSR leadership.[108]

The partnership between these ultra-nationalist parties and the Iliescu party was based primarily on an agreement concerning the relationship between the Romanian state and national minorities. On other salient

---

[108] Michael Shafir, "Ruling Party Formalizes Relations with Extremists," *Transition* 1, no. 5 (1995): 42. PDSR stands for the Party of Social Democracy in Romania.

political questions, the three ultra-nationalist parties covered the left-right spectrum of political ideology and policy preferences.[109]

The Hungarian minority elite formed a strategic unity to challenge the government's unitary nation-state design. Unlike the Hungarians in Slovakia, the Hungarians in Romania from the beginning of the post-Communist transformation overwhelmingly supported a single Hungarian political organization. The Democratic Alliance of Hungarians in Romania (RMDSZ) claimed to represent the collective interests of the Hungarian national community and was remarkably successful in commanding the overwhelming majority of the Hungarian minority votes in every parliamentary election after 1989. RMDSZ leaders were also effective in persuading Hungarian voters how to vote in presidential elections. (This was especially important in 1996, when the Hungarian votes contributed significantly to the election of opposition candidate Emil Constantinescu as president.)

Ethnicity in itself was no more likely to create ideological unity among Hungarians than it was among Romanians. It was primarily the ruling regime's adversarial nationalism that helped the RMDSZ maintain a united constituency after 1989. Nonetheless, early divisions between "radicals" and "moderates" and disunity between the collectivist and liberal approaches to Hungarian identity led to the formation of so-called political platforms within the RMDSZ. The RMDSZ leadership made great efforts to preserve the umbrella character of the organization, allowing organized channels for the articulation of a spectrum of political views while maintaining the unified character of the party in the Romanian parliament.

The RMDSZ consistently defined the Romanian state as multinational and the Hungarian minority in Romania as a "national community." From 1993, the term most frequently used for this self-definition was "the national community of Hungarians in Romania." Based on this concept, the RMDSZ asked for the constitutional guarantee of collective political rights, which centered on the right to unrestricted use of the Hungarian language in the institutions of self-government and those of cultural reproduction. The aim was to establish institutions in which Hungarians could live their social and public life *in Hungarian.*[110]

To achieve legal guarantees for maintaining a substate "national community," the RMDSZ made three basic institutional demands: a pluralist constitution, a contract between the state's Romanian majority and the Hungarian

[109] Marian Preda, "Partidele politice in România: clasificare şi relaţii parlamentare," *Revista de cercetări sociale* 3 (1994): 7–10.

[110] RMDSZ, "Law on National Minorities and Autonomous Communities (Draft)," *Documents* (Cluj: Democratic Alliance of Hungarians in Romania, 1994), no. 1, 37–54; "A Romániai Magyar Demokrata Szövetség Ideiglenes Intéző Bizottságának kiáltványa," 15.

minority (a so-called nationality statute), and a Ministry of Nationalities to oversee the protection of the rights contained in the nationality statute. From the perspective of the RMDSZ leadership, the Iliescu regime failed on all three counts: it adopted a constitution unacceptable to the Hungarian minority, it refused to discuss the RMDSZ proposals for a nationality statute, and—in the RMDSZ interpretation—it corrupted the idea of a Ministry of Nationalities.[111]

Thus, the Romanian ruling elite and the Hungarian minority elite had significantly different conceptions of sovereignty in the post-Ceaușescu Romanian state. The dominant Romanian majority accepted the idea of a collective national entity as valid only for the Romanian majority and rejected the idea of a collective Hungarian minority. The Hungarian elite called for a Romanian state in which the sovereignty of *multiple* national communities would be reflected in the constitutional, legislative, and institutional framework. These two major points of contention—Romania as a "unitary nation-state" versus a multinational pluralist state, the supremacy of the Romanian language versus institutionalized multilingualism in the territories inhabited by national minorities—captured the core of the conflicts between the Romanian majority and the Hungarian minority throughout the Iliescu period.

Besides the battle over the new constitution, the first important legislative conflict that reflected the importance of linguistic territoriality took place over the 1991 Law on Local Public Administration, which empowered the state to modify territorial administrative units and excluded minority languages from local government.[112] Unsuccessful in challenging this strategy, the RMDSZ leadership submitted to the Romanian parliament a proposal for a comprehensive majority-minority contract, the "Draft Law on National Minorities and Autonomous Communities."[113] This bill, considered the "official RMDSZ program," proclaimed that "all national minorities [that] declare themselves [as] autonomous communities are entitled to internal self-determination and [to] the right to have [their] own system of institutions."[114] As to the meaning of "autonomous communities" and

---

[111] Zsuzsa Csergo, "Beyond Ethnic Division," *East European Politics and Societies* 16, no. 1 (Winter 2002): 1–29.

[112] *Documents* (Cluj: Democratic Alliance of Hungarians in Romania, 1994), no. 1, p. 24.

[113] The RMDSZ leadership considered this document the best articulation of the organization's political goals. RMDSZ President Béla Markó expressed this view in interview conducted by the author, Tîrgu-Mureș, Romania, June 26, 1996.

[114] "Law on National Minorities and Autonomous Communities (Draft)," *Documents*, no. 1, p. 38.

the forms of "internal self-determination," the RMDSZ bill provided the following explanation:

> Article 2.
> National identity is a fundamental human right and both individuals and communities are equally entitled to it.
> It is the inalienable right of each national minority to define itself as an autonomous community.
> The national minorities and autonomous communities together with the Romanian nation are political subjects and state-forming communities.
> Internal self-determination is the inalienable right of autonomous communities and it manifests itself in various forms of autonomy.
> National minorities [that] define themselves as autonomous communities shall have the right to *personal autonomy* based on the minority rights of persons belonging to them, as well as to *local self-government* and *regional autonomy.*[115]

"Autonomy" quickly became the central metaphor of the division between the Romanian and Hungarian political elites. According to RMDSZ President Béla Markó, "Autonomy is not an end, but a means of maintaining a separate [Hungarian] language, culture, and national identity."[116] But for the Romanian government, autonomy was unacceptable, because it presented a fundamental challenge to the idea of a unitary national state. As Senate Education Committee chairman Gheorge Dumitraşcu (PDSR) summarily stated, "Romania is a unitary state. An ethnically based territorial autonomy can never happen."[117] The RMDSZ leadership considered the autonomy concept articulated in the "Draft Law on National Minorities and Autonomous Communities" to be an expression of strong consensus within the organization.[118] Yet some members of the Hungarian minority elite questioned the way in which the RMDSZ used the terms "internal self-determination" and "autonomy." In fact, the November 1992 "Declaration of Cluj" and the talk about autonomy surrounding the publication of the November 1993 RMDSZ nationality bill helped articulate differences in political ideology that eventually led

---

[115] Ibid., 39, emphasis added.
[116] Béla Markó, author interview, Tîrgu-Mureş, Romania, June 26, 1996.
[117] Gheorghe Dumitraşcu, chairman of the Senate Education Committee, author interview, Bucharest, Romania, May 21, 1996.
[118] "Törvénytervezet a nemzeti kisebbségekről és autonóm közösségekről—Az RMDSZ dokumentum vitája," *Hitel—Erdélyi Szemle* (May–August 1994), 96.

to the formation of the liberal and conservative/Christian platforms within the RMDSZ.[119]

The sharpest difference emerged between those in the RMDSZ who used a national-collectivist line of argument and those who articulated a civic-individualist approach. Those who fully identified with the collectivist view emphasized the historical (or natural) rights of the Hungarian minority as an artificially severed part of the Hungarian nation. Their primary concern was to "repossess" institutions, land, and property confiscated by the Romanian government from the Hungarian community after 1945. In the words of Hungarian journalist László Pillich, these RMDSZ politicians conducted their activities "with their face turned toward the past." For them, "instead of the creation of institutions, the repossession of institutions became the goal; instead of an economic strategy, [they] compiled a list of losses and demands."[120]

Those who articulated a civic argument for Hungarian minority rights followed a different logic. According to this logic, any autonomous individual is entitled to choose between alternative ethnic and linguistic identities. In a well-functioning civil society, autonomous individuals may voluntarily join communities and exercise certain rights through these communities. For such communities, regardless of nationality, self-administering autonomous political institutions are the most efficient and democratic organizations.[121] These institutions have to be created anew and given a flexible structure. This approach was articulated in the founding documents of the Liberal Circle, the liberal "platform" within RMDSZ.[122] The members of this group did not challenge the idea of community rights but derived these rights differently from their counterparts and emphasized the need for continuous redefinition of what the Hungarian community was and what kinds of institutions and political organizations were necessary for its development.[123]

The first concern of the advocates of the civic approach was to create a framework within which a meaningful discussion of the issues related to minority politics could take place. Because the one-party structure of

---

[119] As an example of the intense preoccupation with the idea of autonomy, the November 1993 issue of a prestigious Hungarian-language periodical in Romania, *Korunk,* took as its theme "Speaking about Autonomy."

[120] László Pillich, "Pótcselekvéseink kora lejárt," *Hitel—Erdélyi Szemle* (March-April 1994), 10.

[121] Éva Cs. Gyimesi, RMDSZ educational specialist in the early 1990s, author interview, Cluj, Romania, May 13, 1996.

[122] See "A Szabadelvű Kör Kokumentumai," *Hitel—Erdélyi Szemle* (March–April 1994), 94; Gábor Kolumbán, "Autonómia törekvések és konszociáció, a szövetségi demokrácia esélyei Romániában," *Hitel—Erdélyi Szemle* (March–April 1994), 3–9.

[123] See Pillich, "Pótcselekvéseink kora lejárt," 10–13.

Hungarian minority political organization was not conducive to such a discussion, various Hungarian intellectuals established virtual round tables (in the form of polemical essays and reactions to these essays published in prominent Hungarian-language journals) to address questions such as the meaning of autonomy and the collectivist strategy of the RMDSZ leadership.[124] The best-developed articulation of an alternative approach was the "Proposed Bill on the Rights Concerning National Identity and the Fair and Harmonious Co-existence of National Communities" authored by Sándor N. Szilágyi, a linguistics professor at the Babeş-Bolyai University in Cluj. The main difference between the "official" RMDSZ draft and the Szilágyi proposal was that the latter defined national equality not as a primordial (natural) right of a collectivity but as a civic right that a democratic state had to make available and that members of nationality groups had to claim in order to possess.[125]

Instead of allowing a parliamentary debate of Hungarian proposals, the government soon reinforced its exclusivist strategy by first appointing members of the anti-Hungarian Party of Romanian National Unity (PUNR) to cabinet positions strategically important to Hungarians (for example, the Ministry of Education) in August 1994, then formally including the ultra-nationalist parties in the government in January 1995.[126] In October 1994, the government proposed a law on education that restricted the use of minority languages and therefore became a major source of friction with the Hungarian minority.

It was against this backdrop that the RMDSZ introduced territorial autonomy into the alliance's political program in May 1995.[127] Although the concept of institutional autonomy in the form of a separate system of Hungarian institutions, especially in the area of education and culture, had been an integral part of the RMDSZ program since the December 1989 formation of the organization, the call for territorial autonomy was clearly the outcome of a process in which the nationalizing Romanian government refused to discuss Hungarian minority preferences. Shafir observes that the RMDSZ "adopted a program based on a quest for autonomy . . . gradually— as a result of seeing its less radical demands rejected by the political establishment."[128] Paralleling developments in Slovakia, the government's adversarial

---

[124] Levente Salat, "A bénultság természetrajza," *Korunk* 3 (1994), 23–27.

[125] Sándor N. Szilágyi, "Tervezet," *Korunk* 5, no. 3 (March 1994), 131.

[126] Aurelian Crăiuţu, "A Dilemma of Dual Identity," *East European Constitutional Review* 4, no. 2 (1995): 48.

[127] See text of the 1995 RMDSZ Program as an appendix to Gabriel Andreescu and Renate Weber, *Evolutions in the D.A.H.R. Conception on Hungarian Minority Rights* (Bucharest: APADOR-CH, 1994), 49.

[128] Michael Shafir, "A Possible Light at the End of the Tunnel," *Transition* 2, no. 19 (September 20, 1996): 30.

approach to minority policy strongly influenced the increasing unity of Hungarian minority nationalism in Romania.

The significance that majority and minority political actors attributed to language for their community's cultural reproduction was most evident in the contestations over language use in education. When the government codified the limitation of minority language use in education in the 1995 Law on Education, this legislation—like the 1991 local administration law that had been drafted with similar intent—became the center of fierce institutional debate between Romanian and Hungarian political forces. The education law was debated in parliament for more than a year. In the process, the RMDSZ submitted a proposal calling for a comprehensive and separate educational system, but the government refused to bargain. The Hungarians gathered almost a half a million signatures to support the proposed RMDSZ bill—an impressive achievement for a group that according to official statistics numbered approximately 1.7 million—but the government used procedural inertia to kill the RMDSZ effort.[129] Despite the extraordinary Hungarian opposition, expressed not only in the Romanian parliament but also in RMDSZ letters to international organizations, and massive demonstrations by Hungarian parents, teachers, and students, the government's restrictive bill became law in July 1995.[130]

The strategy of minority language exclusion in the 1991 Law on Local Public Administration, the inclusion of ultra-nationalists in the government in 1994, and the adoption of the 1995 Law on Education served as powerful external unifying conditions that enabled the RMDSZ leadership to hold the Hungarian alliance together. Although there were important disagreements within the organization, a strong consensus emerged about the need for a separate, autonomous institutional system for the Hungarians.[131] Questions of disagreement concerned the appropriate forms of autonomy as well as the ways in which these forms should be articulated for the Hungarian constituency, the Romanian majority, and the international political actors from whom the RMDSZ repeatedly called for assistance. The debate within the Hungarian minority elites focused primarily on the principle

---

[129] RMDSZ President Béla Markó, "Közakarat és érdekképviselet," *Romániai magyar szó* (October 11, 1994).

[130] RMDSZ statements published in *Romániai magyar szó,* June-July 1994. The RMDSZ leadership went so far as to declare the law "the most recent and serious evidence of an intention of cultural genocide and of its gradual accomplishment." RMDSZ appeal signed by the Council of Representatives, *Cronica Română,* July 3, 1995.

[131] See Zoltán Biró, "A restaurációs kísérletektől a pragmatikus modellekig," manuscript, 1996, for the evolution of ideas on institutional autonomy. For an explanation of RMDSZ unity as primarily the result of the perceived need for "self-defense," see Károly Vekov, "A romániai magyarság tömbszerveződésének okairól," *Regio* 2, no. 1 (1991), 101–2.

by which national communities were composed ("naturally" or voluntarily), the logic by which the right to language use and the meaning of autonomy were derived, and the methods by which community self-government could be achieved within the Romanian state. Some among the RMDSZ leadership were ready to search for common ground even with the nationalizing Romanian government in order to move gradually toward an autonomous system of Hungarian institutions. Others refused to seek consensus with the government and also distrusted the moderate Romanian elite. The most vocal critic of the "pragmatic" leaders within the RMDSZ was the party's honorary president, Bishop László Tőkés.[132]

The framework provided on the one hand by the Iliescu leadership's nation-state policies and on the other by Hungarian demands for institutional autonomy shaped the dynamics of relations between the RMDSZ and the Romanian anti-Iliescu opposition. In the latter camp were the revived interwar parties—the National Liberal Party, the National Christian and Democratic Peasant Party, and the Social Democratic Party—as well as incipient new political organizations. These parties were unwilling to join the Iliescu alliance, yet they were also incapable of presenting a coherent alternative to the electorate. Rather than a shared commitment to democratic values, the main basis for consensus was shared consideration of Iliescu as a "crypto-Communist."[133]

On the key issue concerning departure from the old political and economic system, the Romanian democratic opposition and the Hungarian minority party were in partnership against the Iliescu regime. The RMDSZ was one of thirteen opposition parties and organizations that formed the Democratic Coalition to represent common electoral and parliamentary interests. A study in 1994 showed that the Democratic Convention agreed with the RMDSZ even on the need for some (unspecified) degree of "community autonomy."[134] Yet the RMDSZ demands for institutional autonomy remained divisive. Although the Romanian democratic opposition strongly criticized the Iliescu regime for allying with the ultra-nationalist parties, the "dual identity of the RMDSZ" as a member of the Democratic Convention that was at the same time primarily an ethnic party remained problematic.[135] The Romanian democratic opposition disapproved of the

[132] László Tőkés, "Az RMDSZ pere," *Erdélyi napló* 3, no. 111 (October 14, 1993): 10.
[133] Tismăneanu, "Tenuous Pluralism," 7. On the similarities and differences between the parties in the Romanian opposition, see Preda, "Partidele Politice in Romania."
[134] Preda, "Partidele Politice in Romania," 17.
[135] Crăiuțu, "A Dilemma of Dual Identity," 43; Andrei Pleșu, "Vadim cel rău și Funar (Verdeț) cel bun," in *Chipuri și măști ale tranziției* (Bucharest: Humanitas, 1996), 202–4; and Mungiu, *Românii după '89,* 44.

RMDSZ deputies' refusal to vote for the new Romanian constitution in 1991—although this opposition was also critical of the method in which the constitution had been drafted and of the failure of this fundamental document to guarantee the effective separation of powers.[136] The Romanian moderates criticized the RMDSZ for its "all or nothing" approach.[137]

The call for "internal self-determination" was especially divisive.[138] Although the RMDSZ leadership tried to package the demand for institutional autonomy into terms that would not provoke fears of Hungarian secessionism, as in Slovakia, this strategy did little to thwart majority suspicions. The expression "internal self-government" in the November 1992 Cluj Declaration emphasized the idea that Hungarian community self-government would be internal to Romania. The "Draft Law on National Minorities and Autonomous Communities" submitted by the RMDSZ carefully derived minority sovereignty as a "three-level" autonomy (personal, local, and regional) based ultimately on the idea of individual freedom.[139] But the Romanian opposition found the logic of the three-level design unclear and remained suspicious of the whole idea of minority self-determination.[140] The leader of the Democratic Convention (and, after November 1996, president of Romania), Emil Constantinescu, stated at a citizens' forum in October 1994 in the Transylvanian city of Oradea that he found all forms of minority autonomy unacceptable.[141] When the RMDSZ held a conference on self-government and created the Council of Mayors and Local Councilors in January 1995, members of the Democratic Convention (of which the RMDSZ was still a member) criticized the RMDSZ's "conception of autonomy and the formation of the new Council as aspects of an overall drive to carve out some kind of territorial autonomy based on ethnic criteria."[142]

No matter how it was phrased or justified, the demand for an autonomous institutional structure (including an autonomous system of education in the Hungarian language) raised suspicion even in liberal Romanian intellectual circles.[143] A primary source of fear was that the concept of

---

[136] Alina Mungiu-Pippidi, "Problema democraţiei transetnice," *Sfera politicii* 37 (April 1996), 41.

[137] Crăiuţu, "A Dilemma of Dual Identity," 43.

[138] Ibid., 45.

[139] The logic of the three-level design is not entirely clear in the RMDSZ draft. The individual right to "adhere to a national minority" is a personal right, yet "personal autonomy" is defined as the right of national minorities who define themselves as autonomous communities. See "Law on National Minorities and Autonomous Communities (Draft)," Articles 13, 18, and 51.

[140] Gabriel Andreescu, head of Romanian Helsinki Committee, author interview, Bucharest, Romania, June 29, 1996.

[141] István Wagner, "Nesze neked autonómia!" *Erdélyi napló* 4, no. 162 (October 19, 1994): 4.

[142] Crăiuţu, "A Dilemma of Dual Identity," 49.

[143] The RMDSZ carefully supported its demands with international documents, primarily referring to the European Charter of Local Self-Government.

minority rights might lead to "the fragmentation of the sovereignty of the Romanian state."[144] Thus, the concept of autonomy marked a division not only between the nationalizing government and the Hungarian minority elite but also between the RMDSZ and the Iliescu regime's most vocal critics in the Romanian opposition. Senator Ticu Dumitrescu, leader of the Prisoners' Association (a group that vehemently demanded that Iliescu and other former Communists in the government be held accountable for their past), noted that the demand for autonomy "spoiled everything" between the RMDSZ and the anti-Iliescu Romanian opposition and made the prospect for future cooperation "very difficult."[145] Senator Matei Boilă, one of the leaders of the National Christian Democratic Peasant Party, claimed that the question of autonomy created the only significant dividing line between the RMDSZ and his party: "We believe that our state has favorable conditions for [becoming] a unitary state with administrative decentralization . . . that would be based on the principle of subsidiarity and would solve nationality problems on the local level, allowing all possible freedoms for minorities. The Hungarians, on the other hand, want some kind of federalism, in other words territorial autonomy, or 'personal autonomy'—as they call it at times. . . . But even they don't understand what they are talking about."[146] For this reason, the Romanian opposition was unable to provide unequivocal support for the Hungarian challenge to the government's policy of continued administrative centralization and increased minority language exclusion in local government and education.

Romanian opposition parties did not develop a coherent position concerning the issue of language use. In 1992, at the time of pre-election negotiations between the Romanian opposition and the RMDSZ, the program of the strongest party in the Romanian Democratic Convention, the National Christian–Democratic National Peasant Party (PNȚCD), stated its commitment to the freedom of linguistic identity. But the education bill this party proposed was not altogether liberal. Minority language education was allowed from preschool to high school but not in professional schools and other higher educational institutions. The draft also required that Romanian history, geography, and civic education be taught in Romanian.[147] By contrast, the

---

[144] Gabriel Andreescu, Valentin Stan, and Renate Weber, "Două proiecte de lege privind drepturile minorităților naționale," *Legislația în tranziție* (January 1995), 78; Alina Mungiu-Pippidi, "Problema democrației transetnice," *Sfera Politicii* (April 1996), 37.
[145] Dumitrescu, author interview, Bucharest, Romania, May 20, 1996.
[146] Boilă, author interview, Cluj, Romania, May 10, 1996.
[147] For an analysis of PNȚCD approach to language use, see Vogel, "Kisebbségi dokumentumok Romániában," 162.

approach expressed in the program of the liberal Civic Alliance (AC) was the closest to that of the Hungarian minority elite. It declared that national, linguistic, and religious minorities had individual and collective rights and called for a minority law corresponding to European norms, one allowing the right to use the mother tongue in public administration, justice, and education on all levels. The attitude expressed in the party program, however, was not supported unanimously by the leadership of the party, nor was it reflected in the votes of the AC constituency.[148]

Differences in the approach to Hungarian language use in education strongly contributed to tensions between the Hungarian alliance and the Romanian opposition parties, leading to the formal departure of the RMDSZ from the Romanian Democratic Convention in 1995.[149] The Romanian opposition did not support the Hungarian campaign against the education law. The Democratic Convention disapproved of the RMDSZ leadership's protests and appeals to international bodies. The leadership of the major opposition parties, PNȚCD and PNL, disagreed with the Hungarian contestations of the law, while the Civic Alliance was also reluctant to support the Hungarian position.[150]

Only Romanian liberals at the Center for Human Rights in Bucharest expressed strong discontent with the education law. This group criticized the bill especially for preserving the extremely centralized structure of the Romanian educational system. Weber also points out that the term used in the law is "state education" rather than "public education" and that a disproportionate emphasis on certain subjects—for instance, Romanian geography or history—revealed the strong nationalist principle underlying Romanian educational policy. At the same time, analysts at the Center for Human Rights disagreed with the RMDSZ claim that the 1995 education law was a tool of "cultural genocide."[151]

---

[148] Ibid. Alina Mungiu-Pippidi notes that during the 1992 local elections, in many cases the electorate of the Democratic Convention voted for the extreme nationalist PUNR candidate against the Hungarian candidate of the Convention. See Mungiu-Pippidi, *Romananii dupa '89,* 44.

[149] Michael Shafir, "Agony and Death of an Opposition Alliance," *Transition* (May 26, 1995), 23–28. Prominent Hungarian intellectual Éva Gyimesi, former RMDSZ education specialist and chair of the Hungarian literature department at Babeș-Bolyai University, expressed the view that the alienation between the RMDSZ and the Romanian opposition was not inevitable and that the RMDSZ leadership was partly responsible for the lack of understanding between these groups. Author interview, Cluj, Romania, May 13, 1996. See CDR statement signed by Emil Constantinescu, *Cronica română,* July 22, 1995.

[150] See Vasile Radu of PNȚCD, quoted in *Curierul național,* July 25, 1995; interview with Emil Tocaci, PNL, *Curierul național,* August 15, 1995. See also Tom Gallagher, "Nationalism and the Romanian Opposition," *Transitions* 2, no. 1 (January 1996): 30–32.

[151] Renate Weber, "Legea învățământului," *Revista română de drepturile omului* (May–June 1995): 16.

Although unable to agree on a mutually acceptable alternative to the unitary national strategy of the ruling regime, the Romanian and Hungarian anti-Iliescu opposition found sufficient common ground to defeat the Iliescu government in the November 1996 elections (see table 2.4). Based on a shared desire to change the direction of the country from "crypto-communism" to democratization and Euro-Atlantic integration, the former opposition parties formed a consensual governing coalition, including the Hungarian minority party.[152] This coalition created possibilities for revisiting the debate over language use in the domains all sides considered fundamental to sovereignty and cultural reproduction. The two pieces of legislation that marked the relationship of the Romanian state and its Hungarian community in the first years after Communism, namely, the laws on public administration and education, remained central to the language debate that continued in the consensual period that began in Romania in 1996.

In an interview in April 1996, Slovak journalist and political analyst Juraj Alner began his description of Slovak politics by drawing a fence on a piece of paper and marking "government" on one side and "opposition" on the other.[153] This image of a deeply divided political arena surfaced in various ways in virtually all of my interviews with Slovak and Hungarian political elites during 1996.[154] By the 1998 parliamentary elections, the division between government and opposition had grown into vehement opposition. In Romania, similarly fierce antagonisms between the Iliescu regime and its opponents created such enmity that by the 1996 elections political analyst Horia-Roman Patapievici was prompted to characterize Romanian society in terms reminiscent of Alner's in Slovakia: "Half of Romania hates the other half."[155] Rather than "ethnic division," the fissures that Slovak and Romanian analysts so bleakly described actually marked lines of opposition between political actors that dominated the design of new institutions after the Communist collapse and those left outside this process. Yet the divisions and alliances in the first defining years after Communism reveal a

---

[152] Zoltán Kántor and Nándor Bárdi, "The DAHR (Democratic Alliance of Hungarians in Romania) in the Government of Romania from 1996 to 2000," *Regio* 13 (2002): 188–226.

[153] Juraj Alner, Slovak journalist, author interview, Bratislava, Slovakia, April 25, 1996.

[154] Author interviews: Ján Stena, advisor to the Slovak President, Bratislava, Slovakia, April 12, 1996; KDH President Ján Čarnogurský, Bratislava, Slovakia, April 24, 1996; Zuzana Magurová, legal representative of the "Gremium" of nonprofit organizations, Bratislava, Slovakia, April 22, 1996; Juraj Alner, journalist at *Národná obroda,* Bratislava, Slovakia, April 25, 1996; Ondrej Dostál, journalist at *Sme,* Bratislava, Slovakia, April 19, 1996; Miklós Duray, Coexistence president, Bratislava, Slovakia, April 18, 1996; Béla Bugár, MKDM president, Bratislava, Slovakia, April 25, 1996; and Kálmán Petőcz, MPP vice president, Bratislava, Slovakia, April 16, 1996.

[155] Patapievici, "Regimul Iliescu," 141–53.

TABLE 2.4
Romanian parliamentary elections, 1990, 1992, 1996, and 2000

	1990		1992		1996		2000	
	Chamber of deputies	Senate	Chamber of deputies	Senate	Chamber of deputies	Senate	Chamber of deputies	Senate
PDSR[1]	66.3	67.0	27.7	28.3	21.5	23.1	36.6	37.1
CDR[2]			20.0	20.2	30.2	30.7	5.0	5.3
PNL[3]	6.4	7.1					6.9	7.5
PNTCD[4]	2.6	2.5						
USD[5]			10.2	10.4	12.9	13.2	7.0	7.6
PUNR[6]	2.1	2.2	7.7	8.1	4.4	4.2		
RMDSZ	7.2	7.2	7.5	7.6	6.6	6.8	6.8	6.9
PRM[7]			3.9	3.8	4.5	4.5	19.5	21.0
PSM			3.0	3.2	2.1	2.2		
Others	15.4	14.0	20.0	18.4	17.8	15.3	18.2	14.6
Total	100.0	100.0	100.0	100.0	100.0	100.0	100.0	100.0

Sources: For 1990, National Republican Institute for International Affairs and National Democratic Institute for International Affairs, *The May 1990 Elections in Romania* (Washington, D.C.: 1990), 129. For 1992, Petre Datculescu, "Cum a votat România: O analiză a alegerilor generale și prezidențiale de la 27 septembrie 1992," *Revista de cercetări sociale* 1 (1994), 43–60. For 1996, Rompress. For 2000, see the International Foundation for Election Systems (IFES) website at www.ifes.org/eguide/resultsum/romaniares.htm. For 1996 and 2000, "Political Transformation and the Electoral Process in Post-Communist Europe," www2.essex.ac.uk/elect/database/aboutProject.asp, accessed November 30, 2006.

[1] Ran as National Salvation Front (FSN) in 1990 and as Democratic National Salvation Front (FDSN) in 1992, after splitting from the original FSN. Changed to Party of Social Democracy (PSD) in 2001.

[2] The Democratic Convention of Romania was an electoral alliance formed by major opposition parties; in 2000, after the withdrawal of PNL, it was reinstituted as "CDR 2000."

[3] Having left the Democratic Convention of Romania (CDR) before the general elections in 1992, the National Liberal Party (PNL) lost much of its support, failed to meet the necessary 3% hurdle and remained unrepresented in the parliament. Before the 1996 elections, PNL rejoined the CDR.

[4] The Christian Democratic National Peasant Party (PNȚCD) joined the CDR before the 1992 elections.

[5] The Social Democratic Union (USD) was formed in 1996 to include the Democratic Party–National Salvation Front (PD-FSN) and the Social Democratic Party of Romania (PSDR). PD-FSN (registered under this name in May 1992) was a splinter of the original National Salvation Front (FSN), ran as FSN in 1992 (after FDSN split from FSN), and—with changed composition—as Democratic Party (PD) in 2000.

[6] Ran as Romanian Unity Alliance (AUR) in 1990.

[7] The Greater Romania Party (PRM) was formed as a political party in May 1991.

more complex and dynamic political arena than what such pronouncements might suggest. In both countries, the institutional and legislative strategies of dominant political actors engendered dividing lines both between and within national groups.

The principle framers of the debate about the new social contract, that is, those in power during the first years of post-Communist transformation, were nationalist elites who established the new institutions with their faces turned toward the past. They opted for a traditional unitary nation-state, employed methods of government reminiscent of the Communist period, and approached linguistic diversity as a threat to the stability of their desired state model. They forced both majority and minority actors in opposition to formulate their positions in relation to this strategy. In the process, liberal approaches emphasizing individual language choice and informal norms were overshadowed by both "titular" and minority strategies that reflected the strong influence of linguistic territoriality on the part of majority and minority actors alike.

The preference of these governments for a traditional unitary nation-state with full majority control over the institutions of government and cultural reproduction triggered vehement opposition on the part of the sizeable and politically well-organized Hungarian minorities that *also* defined themselves in "national" terms. In response to the government's strategy, Hungarian parties in both cases articulated notions of community sovereignty and demanded rights to autonomous institutions in the spheres they considered most important for cultural reproduction. Equally important, the strategy of majority nationalism also failed to unite the Romanian and Slovak "titular" majorities. By weakening newly established democratic institutions and hindering the emergence of alternative sources of power, the dominant political elites contributed to sharp divisions within the majority.

The axes of agreement and disagreement reflected conflicting notions about sovereignty and national cultural reproduction. In every case, the majority placed primary emphasis on state sovereignty and opposed minority demands for institutional autonomy that had the potential for weakening majority national control throughout the state's territory. At the same time, national majority actors in both states disagreed vehemently with each other over questions of popular sovereignty, that is, to what extent government should empower regional and local levels of government, be accountable to the people, and generally decrease its control over society. On these questions, the Slovak and Romanian democratic opposition and their Hungarian counterparts found themselves on the same side of the debate (see figure 2.1).

Although nationalist governments in the two cases pursued different aims—independence in Slovakia, the strengthening of the nation-state in

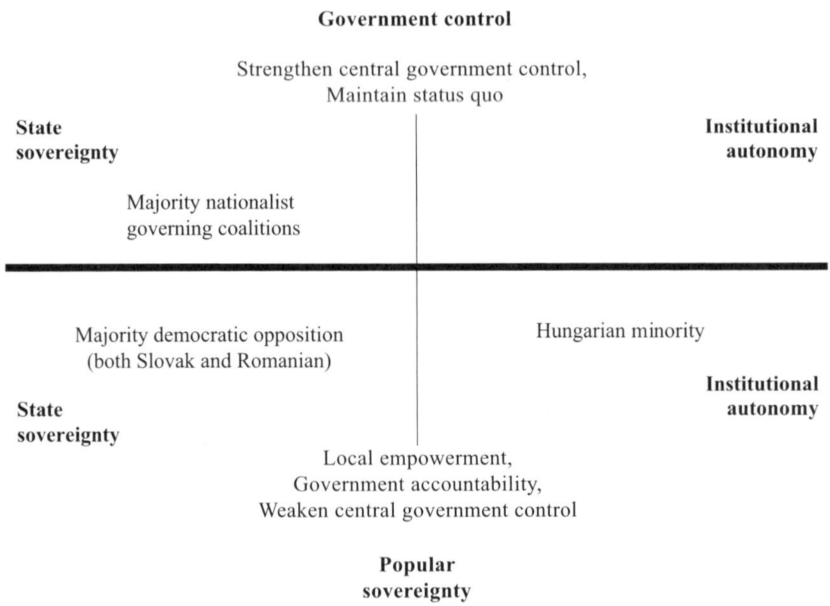

Government control

Strengthen central government control,
Maintain status quo

**State
sovereignty**

**Institutional
autonomy**

Majority nationalist
governing coalitions

Majority democratic opposition
(both Slovak and Romanian)

Hungarian minority

**State
sovereignty**

**Institutional
autonomy**

Local empowerment,
Government accountability,
Weaken central government control

**Popular
sovereignty**

Figure 2.1: State sovereignty versus institutional autonomy

Romania—their common emphasis on a centrally controlled national development ultimately engendered similar contestations over sovereignty that manifested themselves in (1) national minority unity on the pluralist challenge to the nation-state; (2) a national majority alliance on the rejection of minority demands for substate institutional autonomy; and (3) division within the national majority over democratic change and governmental control over society. As the next chapter will demonstrate, these divisions within the national majority enabled majority-minority strategic alliances that in turn compelled participants to negotiate mutually acceptable resolutions to the language debate.

The absence of a dichotomous ethnic standoff defied the logic of so-called divided society arguments about majority-minority conflicts. At the same time, the difficulties of reaching consensus in the debate over language use also demonstrated the extraordinary challenges of achieving an inclusive social contract in multilingual societies where majority and minority alike define themselves in national terms and regard language as a fundamental link between people and a national space. Language served as a touchstone for defining the terms of sovereignty and rights to cultural reproduction in the newly democratic state.

The choices that majority and minority political actors made reflected the continuing power of the territorial nation-state model. As Walker argues, "contemporary thinking about democracy cannot go much beyond the attempt to sustain or revitalize practices that have been associated with at least some states for a significant period without coming to terms with the limits of that historically specific understanding of political community under present historical conditions."[156] Clearly, the legacies of past relations between national groups influenced their approaches to the language question. Memories of Hungarian dominance in southern Slovakia and Transylvania heightened Slovak and Romanian notions of entitlement. For members of the Romanian and Slovak majority—who viewed themselves as victims of centuries of Hungarian domination followed by decades of Communist totalitarianism—the right to assert national sovereignty by marking their states' territory and institutions with the national language, and to assure the reproduction of the majority national culture on every piece of the land—were seen as matters of entitlement. Similarly, from the perspective of members of the Hungarian minority—who saw themselves as victims first of World War I and II peace agreements, then of totalitarian dictatorships, only now emerging as potential agents of democratic change—the same right to language and cultural reproduction was also a question of entitlement.

In summary, the dominant "titular" majorities in the state viewed their own demands for cultural ownership as a right and minority claims as privileges, and national minority elites mirrored that perception. Nonetheless, majority and minority political actors that rejected the dominant institutional strategy during the first Iliescu regime in Romania and the Mečiar period in Slovakia were able to form electoral alliances that defeated the traditional nationalist governments. As the twentieth century reached its end, shared interests in democratic government coupled with Euro-Atlantic integration created incentives in both countries for a consensual approach to the continuing debate over multilingualism. The next chapter will explore the sources of this emerging majority-minority consensus by examining the participation of key international and domestic actors in the debate.

---

[156] J. B. Walker, *Inside/Outside* (New York: Cambridge University Press, 1993), 154.

Chapter 3

Sovereignty and International Integration

The first years of post-Communism in Romania and Slovakia demonstrated the continuity of competitive nation-building and the continuing divisiveness of linguistic territoriality within the constraints of the traditional Westphalian nation-state. By the middle of the 1990s, the governments of Ion Iliescu in Romania and Vladimír Mečiar in Slovakia had instituted a series of policies that seriously restricted minority language rights, triggering vehement parliamentary battles as well as significant international engagement. The year 2000 witnessed remarkable change in both states toward more inclusive language policies. This chapter explores the question of what drove the emerging majority-minority consensus in the deeply divisive debate over multilingualism by examining interactions between the key domestic and international participants of the debate. The international actors most actively engaged in the language battle were European institutions and Hungary (as the active kin-state of Hungarian minorities in the region).

Increasing interest among students of nationalism and ethnic issues in the influence of international actors and the role of kin-states in majority-minority dynamics has resulted in a growing literature on these themes in recent years. Much of this literature, however, treats the two themes separately. The literature regarding international influence on minority policy examines the international-domestic relationship mostly in a linear manner, concentrating primarily on the efforts of prominent institutions—such as the European Union and its related institutions, NATO, and international nongovernmental organizations (such as the Soros Foundation)—to achieve change in various domestic environments in Central and Eastern Europe (CEE).[1] Although scholars usually note that domestic "receptivity" is an important factor in the effectiveness of international influence, few systematically explore the domestic side of the relationship, that is, the varying degrees of willingness on the part of "host" governments to yield to Western influence and the actual policies that would reflect changes in political practice—not just exhortative norms—as a result of international influence.[2] The argument that emerges from this chapter is that the primary source of interethnic reconciliation is the domestic political process. International influence is effective only when it matches the interests of dominant domestic political elites.

As the majority of the national minorities in Central and Eastern Europe have kin-states that pursue various policies toward them, the engagement of kin-states in nationalist dynamics has attracted the attention of scholars and policymakers interested in nationalism. A 1996 study by Rogers Brubaker titled *Nationalism Reframed* was especially influential on later scholarship on such nation-building processes.[3] This study popularized a "triadic nexus" model involving two neighboring states (a "host state" and an "external homeland") and a national minority that lives in the "host state" and is linked through ties of kinship and culture to an "external homeland." Given the influence of this model in the literature about kin-states, it is important to explain why its terms are not adoptable. First, the triadic nexus leaves out the international framework without which nationalism in the post-Communist world cannot be properly understood. European integration has fundamentally changed nationalist strategies throughout the region, and a fuller and more dynamic account of nationalist debates must include the agents of European integration.[4] Second, the vocabulary of the triadic model is inadequate for this project. Calling the state in which minorities live a "host state" implies that the members of a minority community are guests on someone else's land; calling kin-states "external homelands" obfuscates the notion of the homeland, which is fundamental to minority nationalism and is understood here as the idea of the territory on which a national minority (or majority) pursues institutional forms for perpetuating its culture. As explained in the first chapter, homeland territoriality is a key

[1] Linden, ed., *Norms and Nannies;* McMahon, "Managing Ethnicity in Eastern Europe"; Kelley, *Ethnic Politics in Europe;* Dan Reiter, "Why NATO Enlargement Does Not Spread Democracy," *International Security* 25, no. 2 (2001): 41–67; and Harvey Waterman and Dessie Zagorcheva, "Correspondence: NATO and Democracy," *International Security* 26, no. 3 (2002): 221–35.
[2] Judith Kelley is one of the few authors who focus on the domestic side of European Union conditionality. See her *Ethnic Politics in Europe.*
[3] See Brubaker, *Nationalism Reframed.*
[4] Csergo and Goldgeier, "Nationalist Strategies."

element of the debate over multilingualism. Both majority and minority national groups are "homeland" communities in the sense that they attribute great significance to the perpetuation of their cultures where they live, and part of the debate over cultural reproduction in these cases is that the "homeland" is contested.

The influence of European institutions and Hungary on policies concerning multilingualism in the region cannot be understood linearly, in terms of causal relationships. International influence is sifted through domestic lenses, and domestic calculations change according to international opportunity structures.[5] European norms themselves evolve in the process. Thus, the analysis in this chapter proposes a more dynamic approach and presents international agents as participants in a broader debate about cultural reproduction. European officials that took part in this debate represented the EU as an evolving institutional framework with its own dilemmas regarding multilingualism. The successive Hungarian governments that also engaged actively in these debates represented changing approaches to kin-state "obligations."

As the main participants of the debate over cultural reproduction, the dominant political elites in Hungary, Romania, and Slovakia as well as the Hungarian minority elites sought membership in the European Union and NATO, yet they had different visions about and expectations from these institutions—especially the EU. Hungarian minorities wanted to weaken the control of their states over minority cultural reproduction and aimed at internationalizing (Europeanizing) minority policy. Partly through the Hungarian government as a mediator, they pressed for a comprehensive European legal regime that would recognize minority rights and enforce them throughout a unified Europe. The Hungarian government supported this strategy and indeed acted on the behalf of Hungarian minority parties at international fora. Simultaneously, Hungary actively pursued a transsovereign strategy of nation-building to maintain institutional links with Hungarian communities in the neighboring countries. The Romanian and Slovak governments were highly reluctant to give up control over contested institutions and sought Western assurance that states' sovereignty over cultural policy would not suffer in the process of integration. European institutions opted for flexibility over coherence in their policies.[6] The absence of EU-level policies significantly constrained the potentials of external influence, despite the historic opportunity that membership conditionality offered. Although all sides participating in the multilingualism debate sought

---

[5] Checkel, "Why Comply?" 553–88.
[6] For an argument in favor of ambiguity, see Brusis, "The European Union and Interethnic Power-Sharing Arrangements in Accession Countries."

international legitimization for their positions, they were able to interpret "Western norms" differently according to their own domestic strategies.

Europe and the Flexibility of Westphalia

From the beginning of the post-Communist transformation, European institutions demonstrated a strong interest in preventing nationalist conflicts in the region. Concerns for the continent's peace and security placed minority issues at the top of the European agenda, and the outcome was a remarkable growth in minority protection documents. Already at the beginning of the 1990s, the Conference on Security and Cooperation in Europe (CSCE, predecessor of the OSCE), the Council of Europe, and the United Nations began adopting a set of principles on national minority protection. In 1990, the CSCE issued the so-called Copenhagen Document—known also as the European Constitution on Human Rights—which included a chapter on the protection of national minorities. Two years later, the Council of Europe (CE) adopted a European Charter for Regional or Minority Languages calling on signatories to foster the use of minority languages in a broad spectrum of public life. By June 2006, twenty-two governments had signed and ratified this charter.[7] In 1995, the CE adopted the Framework Convention for the Protection of National Minorities—commonly considered a major achievement as the first legally binding European instrument for minority protection. Of the twenty-five members of the European Union, France is the only country that has not signed this convention.[8] In 1998, the OSCE issued the Oslo Recommendations Regarding the Linguistic Rights of National Minorities, designed to serve as a reference for the implementation of such policies.[9]

As most CEE countries lined up to join the Council of Europe, NATO, and the European Union, these institutions were in the best position to pressure governments in the region to adopt accommodative minority policies

[7] Of the pre-2004 EU members, Belgium, Greece, Ireland, and Portugal have neither signed nor ratified it; France and Italy signed but did not ratify it. Of new members from CEE, Estonia, Latvia, Lithuania have not signed it; Poland signed but did not ratify. Of the two CEE states that entered in 2007, Bulgaria did not sign; Romania signed but did not ratify it. Available on the Council of Europe mainframe website on Conventions at conventions/coe.int, accessed January 2007.
[8] Belgium, Greece, and Luxembourg have signed but not ratified. Available on the Council of Europe mainframe website on Conventions at conventions/coe.int, accessed January 2007.
[9] Available at www.osce.org/hcnm/documents/recommendations/oslo/index.php, accessed July 7, 2004.

and reconcile their differences through bilateral agreements. The EU, as the institution embodying cross-national reconciliation, had a unique opportunity to influence similar developments in the post-Communist part of the continent. To foster stability in a region where most national minorities have kin-states in the neighborhood, EU leaders designed the Stability Pact for Europe in 1993 (signed in 1995), calling on aspiring members to sign friendship (or basic) treaties that would promote "good neighborly relations, including questions related to frontiers and minorities, as well as regional cooperation and the strengthening of democratic institutions."[10] In a similar vein, the European Council declared minority protection to be a primary EU membership criterion in Copenhagen in June 1993, stating that aspiring countries must demonstrate "stability of institutions guaranteeing democracy, the rule of law, human rights and respect for and protection of minorities."[11] Accession negotiations could begin only on the basis of a favorable "Opinion" on the country prepared by the European Commission. The Commission's first comprehensive Opinions in 1997 about the CEE countries' pre-accession performance restated the criterion of "respect for minorities."[12] Western interest in ethnic conflict prevention also led to the creation of specific offices to deal with minority problems in post-Communist states. The most significant of these was the Office of the High Commissioner for National Minorities (HCNM), created in 1992 specifically for the purpose of preventing violent ethnic conflicts. This office became instrumental in monitoring and also mediating contestations over language use.[13]

Yet concerted efforts by these institutions to influence the resolution of the language debate in Romania and Slovakia were largely unsuccessful, demonstrating the weakness of external institutions against the power of linguistic territoriality in the framework of the traditional Westphalian nation-state. Due to the emphasis on state sovereignty in matters of cultural reproduction, EU integration had limited impact on majorities' asymmetrical power over minorities in defining the scope of language rights.

European documents on minority protection recognize the fundamental significance of language use for the maintenance of minority cultures.[14]

---

[10] 94/367/CFSP: Council Decision of June 14, 1994, on the continuation of the joint action adopted by the Council on the basis of Article J.3 of the Treaty on European Union on the inaugural conference on the Stability Pact. Available at europa.eu.int, accessed June 1, 2004.
[11] European Council, "Conclusions of the Presidency, Copenhagen, 21–22 June 1993," 13, quoted in Melanie Ram, "Transformation through European Integration," 336.
[12] Bruno de Witte, "Politics versus Law in the EU's Approach to Ethnic Minorities," in *Europe Unbound*, ed. Zielonka, 138–60.
[13] McMahon, "Managing Ethnicity in Eastern Europe."
[14] Kristin Henrard, "Devising an Adequate System of Minority Protection in the Area of Language Rights," in *Minority Languages in Europe*, ed. Hogan-Brun and Wolff, 47–51.

The Council of Europe's Charter for Regional or Minority Languages is particularly important in this respect, as it clearly specifies a comprehensive range of settings and institutions in which states must foster access and use of minority languages: education, courts, communication with authorities, public services, the media and other cultural activities, economic and social life, as well as cross-border exchanges. The integral role of language rights in protecting minority cultures is also evident throughout the text of the Framework Convention for the Protection of National Minorities. The EU designed institutions for protecting national minority languages, such as the European Bureau of Lesser Used Languages in Dublin and the MERCATOR network for information and documentation on minority languages.

Despite an overall norm of "complete multilingualism," the hierarchy between official "national languages" (the languages spoken by titular groups in individual member states) and minority languages remains a hindrance in minority groups' pursuit of linguistic equality in the EU.[15] Furthermore, the explicit exclusion of immigrant languages from this language protection regime reinforces the continuity of the link between language and territoriality in Europe. Scholars argue that there is a gap between the official EU rhetoric about the value of language diversity and the traditional hostility of most member states toward the minority languages within their borders.[16] Romaine observes that this ideological gap between the supranational and national levels prevents full minority language protection within the current political structures of the EU.[17] The European Charter for Regional or Minority Languages, although a significant achievement, does not provide the EU with the authority to regulate language use within individual states.[18] Rather than empowering the speakers of minority languages, the goal is to preserve linguistic diversity by focusing on languages themselves. The charter allows considerable freedom for each government to define the circumstances under which minority languages may be protected and to choose the forms of protection. The draft of the European Union constitution demonstrates the same unwillingness on the part of EU leaders to design EU-wide legislative standards for language policy. Meanwhile, member states' language policies range from Finland, where the language of the 6 percent of the population

---

[15] Patten and Kymlicka argue that Western norms are progressing towards granting increased language rights. See "Language Rights and Political Theory," 4.
[16] Romaine, "Language Contact," 15; and Donall O Riagain, "Unity in Diversity," in *Language Contact and Language Conflict,* ed. Royneland, 174.
[17] Romaine, "Language Contact," 14.
[18] Sigve Gramstad, "The European Charter for Regional or Minority Languages," in *Language Contact and Language Conflict,* ed. Royneland, 91–96.

that is Swedish is recognized as an official language, to Greece, where the government denies even the existence of linguistic minorities on its territory.[19]

The duality in the approach that promotes minority protection while upholding state rights is evident in the landmark Framework Convention adopted in 1995. On the one hand, the convention specifies a number of minority rights and requires states to preserve and support minority cultures. Although it consistently refers to "persons" and "individuals" rather than groups that would benefit from such rights, the Framework Convention refutes the notion of individualists like Brian Barry that states should be ethnoculturally neutral institutions and that cultures have no rights. On the other hand, the convention emphatically reaffirms the primacy of the principle of state sovereignty in this domain, declaring that "nothing in the present framework convention shall be interpreted as implying any right to engage in any activity or perform any act contrary to the fundamental principles of international law and in particular of the sovereign equality, territorial integrity and political independence of States."[20]

The primacy of stability and security concerns further limited EU opportunities for contributing substantively to language debates involving democratic demands for institutional autonomy. In the recommendations they carried with them to CEE capitals, the agents of European integration called on post-Communist governments to weaken centralized control over their societies and allow regional and local self-governments. At the same time, European officials were hesitant about empowering national minorities to make institutional claims against their states. EU and CE officials decidedly avoided advocating federalism and other substate versions of territorial autonomy available to national minorities in several Western states for maintaining control over their institutions of cultural reproduction. Only in extreme crisis situations, such as Kosovo and Northern Ireland, did international agents propose such solutions.[21]

In 1993, the Council of Europe issued Recommendation No. 1201, which included an article encouraging states to allow their national minorities to form substate self-governments.[22] This article became a key issue of majority-minority debate in Romania and Slovakia. While the CE repeatedly called on CEE governments to apply this recommendation in their minority policy, minority elites regarded it as a legitimization of their demands for collective

[19] Riagain, "Unity in Diversity," 174.
[20] Article 21, quoted in Bruno de Witte, "Politics versus Law," 138.
[21] John Doyle, "Challenges to the Hegemonic Image of Westphalia," paper presented at the 45th Annual ISA convention, Montreal, Canada, March 17–20, 2004
[22] The text of report on CE Recommendation 1201 (including in-text quote) is available at venice. coe.int, accessed July 7, 2004.

rights, and majority elites vehemently rejected it. Subsequent interpretation of the recommendation by the Venice Commission indicated that, on a second look, European officials viewed territorial autonomy more as a source of tension than one of resolution.[23] According to the commission's reasoning, there are no consistent Western standards for substate minority self-government for the EU to promote. Although examples for such an arrangement exist in Canada (for the Québécois), Belgium (for the Flemish), Spain (for the Catalans, Basques, and Galicians), and Switzerland (for the French-speaking and Italian-speaking minorities), in other cases federalism has been used to dilute the weight of ethnic minority cultures in substate territorial units.[24]

Still, inconsistencies in Western norm and practice cannot satisfactorily explain the reluctance of European institutions to endorse particular institutional solutions, such as minority self-governments. No consistent Western standards exist on any of the minority-related strategies that European officials actively advocated in CEE, not even on the prevention of violent ethnic conflict. In some EU member countries (Northern Ireland in the United Kingdom, the Basque country in Spain) ethnic conflicts have been more violent than in much of Central and Eastern Europe, yet this did not prevent EU officials from promoting peaceful solutions. Also, that France, one of the main engines behind European integration, as of June 2006 had not signed the Framework Convention for the Protection of National Minorities did not prevent the EU from requiring aspiring CEE governments to sign this legally binding document. All new EU members from CEE have signed and ratified the Framework Convention.

EU reluctance to legislate forms of minority protection at the European level cannot be simply explained by its respect for CEE states' sovereignty. The more than 80,000 pages of EU laws and regulations included in the *acquis communautaire* require newly acceding CEE governments to adopt major institutional changes in all areas of economic, social, and political life in ways that profoundly weaken their sovereignty. Against this backdrop, it is remarkable that the primacy of state sovereignty is asserted so forcefully with respect to minority policies. Control over policies of cultural reproduction remains fundamentally important in all European societies. Even as they transfer their powers to the European level on important domains of institutional life, EU

---

[23] The full name of the Venice Commission is the European Commission for Democracy through Law. The Council of Europe initially created the commission for "emergency constitutional engineering." Through its activities, the commission has become an internationally recognized independent legal think tank. Although its role has been expanded, the primary task of the commission remains advising relevant actors, both state and nonstate, on constitutional matters. See venice.coe.int, accessed July 7, 2004.

[24] Kymlicka, "Introduction," *Can Liberal Pluralism be Exported?* 29–30.

member states retain almost complete sovereignty over education policy in addition to the policies of defense, taxation, and spending.[25] This approach reflects the recognition that education, a primary institution over which language debates are fought, is fundamental to national reproduction and that governments in the West and East seek to maintain their control over it.

The ambiguities and inconsistencies of the messages that European officials carried with them to the capitals of post-Communist states aspiring for membership in the Western club have been documented by a number of scholars.[26] Less well explored are the consequences of these inconsistencies among the "recipients" of Western influence. The flexibility of Western norms allows majority and minority political actors to choose from a spectrum of institutional designs and policy alternatives, and these choices reflect the differences in perspectives on sovereignty and democratization discussed in the previous chapter. Accordingly, national majorities throughout the post-Communist region chose the unitary nation-state model and excluded federalism from the repertoire of democratic institutional forms. Kymlicka points out that minority autonomies were revoked in Serbia (Kosovo and Vojvodina), Georgia (Abkhazia and Ossetia), and Azerbaijan (Ngorno-Karabakh); requests to reestablish old autonomous provinces or to create new ones were rejected in Estonia (Narva), Kazakhstan (the Russian-dominated northern provinces), Macedonia (Western Macedonia), Romania (Transylvania), and Ukraine (Chernowitz and Transcarpathia). Some more aggressive nationalist majority governments went even further, redrawing internal administrative districts to weaken the self-governing potential of national minorities (Slovakia and Croatia). Of the numerous national minorities that articulated demands for substate self-government, only a handful achieved de facto autonomy—by taking control of local governments without the previous consent of the government. Such examples include Trans-Dniester in Moldova, Abkhazia in Georgia, Krajina in Croatia, Crimea in Ukraine, and Ngorno-Karabakh in Armenia.[27]

Romanian and Slovak nationalist elites were interested in examples of a minimalist interpretation of "the European norm" on minority accommodation, especially in the French model. Hungarian minority elites, in turn, looked to examples of minority institutional autonomy, such as in the case of the Catalans in Spain, Swedes in Finland, German-speakers in South Tyrol, and even, in some instances, the French- and Italian-speakers in Switzerland

---

[25] Andrew Moravcsik, "The Myth of a European Leadership Crisis in an Era of Diminishing Returns," *Challenge Europe* (March–April 2004), www.theepc.net, accessed March 26, 2004.

[26] De Witte, "Politics versus law"; and Kelley, *Ethnic Politics in Europe.*

[27] Kymlicka, "Introduction," *Can Liberal Pluralism be Exported?* 62–63.

or the Québécois in Canada.[28] Beyond interpreting "the Western norm," majority and minority political actors also made efforts to influence this norm. Minority politicians lobbied the European Union to formulate comprehensive rules that would guarantee minority protection. Majority elites wanted to see the EU reinforce the sovereignty of member states over their minority populations.

In the absence of consistent EU policies on minority language rights, the primary significance of the EU integration on the language contestations in Romania became that it provided incentives for majority and minority elites to form cross-national electoral alliances, defeat the nationalist governments, and negotiate more inclusive language policies.

EU Integration and Hungarians as Internal Minorities

Although both Romania and Slovakia applied for EU and NATO membership soon after the dissolution of the Soviet bloc, enthusiasm on the part of the Romanian and Slovak political actors for fulfilling admission requirements varied substantively and in correlation with their willingness to democratize and accommodate national minority demands for cultural pluralism.[29] The governments of Vladimir Meçiar and Ion Iliescu, respectively, exhibited more interest in centralized control and majority cultural dominance than in joining the club of Western democracies. As a consequence, the efforts of Western international actors to influence these governments to design more minority-friendly language policies were ultimately unsuccessful. In both cases, the political parties that presented themselves to the electorate as well as to Western policymakers as democratic forces that could take their countries into NATO and eventually the European Union were able to form alliances with the Hungarian parties and consequently adopt more accommodative language policies.

Romania

After decades of isolation during the Ceauşescu era, the new Romanian elite endeavored to connect the country to international society. One of

---

[28] In my interviews during 1996 and 1997, Hungarian minority leaders made frequent reference to these minority situations in the West. Many Romanian and Slovak elites, in turn, referred to centralized cultural policies in France. See also Andreescu, "Universal Thought, Eastern Facts," 277.

[29] Romania applied for EU membership on June 22, 1995, Slovakia on June 27, 1995. Available at europa.eu.int/comm/enlargement/negotiations/index.htm, accessed July 7, 2004. NATO invited Romania and Slovakia (together with Bulgaria, Estonia, Latvia, Lithuania, and Slovenia) to begin accession talks during the Prague Summit on November 21–22, 2002. Available at www.nato.int/docu/comm/2002/0211–prague/more_info/membership.htm, accessed July 7, 2004.

the principal goals of the Iliescu regime after 1990 was to prepare Romania for joining the Western democracies in the European Union. As a first step, the government applied for membership in the Council of Europe (CE) in March 1990. Between then and September 1993, the Council closely scrutinized Romanian national minority policies.[30] As no meaningful communication was taking place between the Iliescu governments and the Democratic Alliance of Hungarians in Romania (RMDSZ) during this time, the Hungarian minority elite directed its complaints abroad, primarily to the Hungarian government and the European Council. The Romanian leadership viewed efforts to internationalize minority issues as evidence that Hungarian minority demands constituted a challenge to Romanian state sovereignty. Perhaps the most criticized of such communiqués was the "Memorandum by the Democratic Alliance of Hungarians in Romania on Romania's Admission to the Council of Europe" signed by the president and vice president of RMDSZ on August 26, 1993. In this memorandum, the RMDSZ leaders stated that Romania would satisfy the requirements for membership in the Council of Europe only if the Romanian constitution and its legal and institutional systems were changed to include the political, cultural, and economic interests of the national minorities.[31] After a long period of bargaining that many Romanians viewed as deeply humiliating, Romania was admitted into the Council of Europe and became an associate member of the European Economic Communities in October 1993.[32] In September 1993, the Parliamentary Assembly of the Council of Europe recommended Romania's admission as a full member but amended this recommendation with a list of requirements that the Romanian government was expected to fulfill within a short period of time. According to these requirements, Romania was expected to sign the European Charter of Local Self-Government and the European Charter for Regional or Minority Languages, adopt nationality and education laws in agreement with Council of Europe Recommendation No. 1201, and use all available constitutional means to fight racism, anti-Semitism, and religious and national discrimination.[33]

Despite years of concerted efforts by the CE and the OSCE High Commissioner for National Minorities (HCNM), the Romanian government failed to fulfill its pre-admission promise to the CE to adopt a law on national

---

[30] "Application by Romania for Membership of the Council of Europe," *Romanian Journal of International Affairs* 1, no. 4 (1995): 133.
[31] See Democratic Alliance of Hungarians in Romania, *Documents* (Cluj, Romania: Democratic Alliance of Hungarians in Romania, 1994), 3–5.
[32] Vladimir Pasti, *România în tranziție* (Bucharest: Editura Nemira, 1995), 42.
[33] Note on Council of Europe Recommendation 1993, no. 176 as attachment no. 4 to Vogel, "Kisebbségi dokumentumok Romániában."

minorities. Increased CE and OSCE pressure after 1993 on the Iliescu regime to adopt specific legislation that would allow minority language use in local government and public education were similarly ineffective, as were the frequent visits by the OSCE HCNM to Bucharest.

The Romanian ruling elite allotted itself the complex task of creating a positive international image for Romania while avoiding minority-friendly legislation. While official Romanian statements about Romania's adherence to international standards were abundant, there was a simultaneous effort to sidetrack bargaining with the Hungarian minority political elite. The government signed most of the important European legal documents intended to promote liberal minority policies, including the European Convention for the Protection of Human Rights and Fundamental Freedoms, which was signed upon Romania's accession to the Council of Europe. The Romanian parliament ratified the convention on June 20, 1994. On February 1, 1995, the day that Romania's EU Association Agreement became official, Romania also signed the Framework Convention for the Protection of National Minorities, which it ratified on May 11, 1995. On July 17, 1995, the government signed the European Charter for Regional or Minority Languages, a document of primary significance to Hungarian minority elites (although the Romanian parliament still had not ratified it as of November 2006). But the signing of these framework agreements had little effect on minority policy during the same period. The habit of the Romanian government of saying one thing and doing another contributed to what one PNȚCD leader called a "terrible duplicity" between the Romanian legal framework and actual practice.[34] The Romanian government applied for EU membership in 1995, the same year that it intensified efforts to exclude minority languages from public institutions and formalized its alliance with ultra-nationalist parties. The education law adopted in 1995 and a law on public administration in 1996 restricted the use of minority languages even beyond the policies enforced under Ceauşescu.

It was only after the 1996 change in government that the Hungarian minority achieved its goal of having the language restrictions of these vehemently contested pieces of legislation revoked. The primary condition for progress in the majority-minority debate over multilingualism was the Romanian moderates' power-sharing with the Hungarian party between 1996 and 2000. The 1997 Opinions of the European Commission, which were critical of Romania's pre-accession progress, also reinforced the moderate Romanian

---

[34] Matei Boilă, author interview, Cluj, Romania, May 10, 1996; Senator Ticu Dumitrescu, author interview, Bucharest, Romania, May 20, 1996; and Petre Lițiu, PL'93 mayoral candidate, author interview, Cluj, Romania, May 9, 1996.

elites' intention to change the course of minority policy. Andreescu notes that "the will to integrate overcame the reluctance of the political class to turn Romania into a multicultural society."[35] Yet the intention to change had already been articulated in the 1996 coalition agreement between the Romanian anti-Iliescu opposition and the RMDSZ leadership, and the liberalization of language policy was the outcome of a difficult process in which the minority used the conditionality of the protocol to press for change and the majority coalition partners chose to honor the terms of the agreement.

In the eyes of most analysts of Romanian politics, the November 1996 elections represented a democratic breakthrough after six years of "proto-democratic" institutionalization under the tenure of President Ion Iliescu and his Party of Social Democracy in Romania. In the words of Vladimir Tismăneanu, "the November vote can be described as an electoral revolution meant to put an end to the creeping restoration engineered by Ion Iliescu and his supporters and revitalize the country's search for an open society."[36] The main opposition forces, the Democratic Convention of Romania (CD) in an electoral alliance with the Social Democratic Union (USD) gained 53 percent of the parliamentary votes and, together with the Democratic Alliance of Hungarians in Romania (RMDSZ), formed a coalition government that promised to move the country away from the old political order. The candidate of the Democratic Convention, Emil Constantinescu, defeated Iliescu to become the new Romanian president. "Ethnic division" was superseded by a common desire to move the country away from a regime that the main opposition forces regarded as "crypto-communist."[37]

The first democratizing Romanian government established in 1996 faced innumerable difficulties, and its tenure was remarkably ineffective in improving Romania's economic conditions. Yet the new leadership indicated strong commitment to change in interethnic relations. The 1996–2000 period became one of majority-minority power-sharing that survived a succession of serious governing crises. Although Hungarian participation in the government remained controversial, majority and minority leaders continued the partnership, demonstrating to the Romanian electorate as well as to the international community that consensual government was viable in Romania and that the Hungarian minority party was ready to participate fully in the Romanian democratic process.

[35] Andreescu, "Universal Thought, Eastern Facts," 275.
[36] Tismăneanu, "Tenuous Pluralism in the Post-Ceausescu Era," 6. See also Diana Turcone, "Pumnul opoziției," *Revista 22* 45 (November 6–12, 1996). Available at www.dntb.ro/22/1996/45/diana.htm.
[37] Tismăneanu, "Tenuous Pluralism in the Post-Ceausescu Era," 7.

The question that divided Hungarian supporters and opponents of participation was whether the RMDSZ's presence in the government meant abandonment of the goal of minority self-government. The leading proponent of an uncompromising fight for autonomy was Bishop László Tőkés, then honorary president of RMDSZ.[38] The dominant view among the organization's leaders, however, was that participation in a democratic Romanian government was a potential means of negotiating the forms of minority self-government.[39] At the same time, these parliamentarians did not view autonomy as a likely prospect in the near future. As one member noted, autonomy entailed goals that in practice could be achieved only "in decades," because "in the present context no Romanian political actor will accept [these goals], not even in a minimal form."[40] Still, the RMDSZ leaders opted for full participation in the Romanian democratic process and decided to employ the coalition agreement to negotiate for a set of "minimum conditions." These conditions centered on the use of language in education, local government, and territory markings, specifically: (1) revision of the 1995 education law to allow unlimited minority language education and the reopening of the historic Hungarian university in Cluj; and (2) legalization of minority language use in local administration and the display of bilingual place names in the localities with a significant minority population.[41]

Conditionality through coalition and cooperation agreements with Romanian parties remained a primary method that the RMDSZ employed in its negotiations for language rights. In the continued debate over multilingualism, RMDSZ leaders bargained relentlessly with their majority partners, and their majority partners were willing, despite strong electoral and parliamentary opposition, to revoke the restrictions on minority language use in education and public administration. In 1997, the government issued Emergency Decrees 22 and 36 to liberalize language use in local administration and education.

Despite the commitment of the Romanian leadership to honor the agreement with RMDSZ, lifting language restrictions became a "tearing test" of the coalition.[42] It took years for the two houses of the Romanian parliament to adopt the government's emergency ordinances into law. During this time, deputies and senators of the governing Romanian parties voted in substantial numbers against the liberalizing amendments.

---

[38] "Sikerre vinni az RMDSZ programját," *Erdélyi napló* (July 24, 1996), 6; and "Kormányzás vagy önkormányzás," *Erdélyi napló* (July 24, 1996), 4–5.
[39] "Kormányzás vagy önkormányzás."
[40] Ibid.
[41] Ibid., 4–5.
[42] József Kötő, author interview, Cluj, Romania, June 25, 1997.

Prominent Romanian intellectuals criticized the coalition for dragging its feet on the liberalization of language use.[43] RMDSZ leaders became skeptical about the ability of their coalition partners to impose the party discipline needed to pass the critical laws. As party president Béla Markó explained:

> The behavior of its coalition partners has put RMDSZ in a serious dilemma: to stay in or to leave the coalition. If it opts to end its participation in the government, it would surely lose both the institutional and legal guarantees for mother-tongue education, as there would be no one to push for the establishment of a state mother-tongue university at the high-politics level. A fresh political crisis resulting in early elections might not help the cause much either. Furthermore, the crisis could also postpone economic reforms and cause even more economic hardship for the whole population. On the other hand, if RMDSZ continues to support the current government, its coalition partners could keep on postponing the fulfillment of minority demands, thus putting RMDSZ in a more-than-awkward position vis-à-vis its constituency.[44]

Challenged repeatedly by prominent internal critics, the RMDSZ leadership continued to state its conditions forcefully, even suspending their participation in government for a short period in December 1997. They also added new emphasis to the demand for the reopening of the Hungarian university in Cluj, an issue that became a prominent source of conflict throughout 1998.[45]

Against vehement opposition among their parliamentarians, the leadership of the Romanian coalition parties continued to stand behind the 1997 emergency decrees throughout the debate. In the summer of 1999, almost two years after their promulgation, the Senate began adopting, piece by piece, the government's amendments to the two controversial laws.[46] Except for the teaching of Romanian history and geography in minority languages in upper-level classes and the establishment of an independent Hungarian university, the new legislation satisfied all important RMDSZ demands for language use in local government and education.

[43] Andrei Cornea, "Ce va fi?" *Revista 22* 34 (1998). Available at www.dntb.ro/22/1998/34/ 1edit-ac.html.
[44] Béla Markó, "Romania's Hungarians Face a Catch-22 Situation," *Transitions* 5, no. 12 (December 1998): 76–77.
[45] Minister for Minority Affairs György Tokay's statement quoted in News Mirror—DAHR MTI Press Service (Bucharest), December 19–21, 1997; statement by RMDSZ Executive President Csaba Takács, *Szabadság,* January 7, 1998; RMDSZ Communication *RMDSZ Tájékoztató,* June 10, 1998; and "Declaration" by the RMDSZ leadership, *RMDSZ Tájékoztató,* June 28, 1998.
[46] "Articolele Legii privind administrația publică locală au fost adoptate," *România liberă,* May 12, 1999, www.romanialibera.com/1POL/12s1pmin.htm.

The intensity of the debate over these pieces of legislation revealed the profound difficulties of finding acceptable institutional solutions for multilingualism, as the link between language and territoriality remained key for conceptions of cultural reproduction held by majority and minority actors alike. As Gabriel Andreescu pointed out, the use of the mother tongue in administration and education was the most sensitive area.[47] The challenge of reconciling the institutional preferences of the governing Romanian moderates with those of their coalition partners in the Hungarian minority party manifested itself most clearly in their failure to reach agreement on the Hungarian demand for coequal use of minority languages in *separate* institutional spaces (meaning separate schools, including a separate Hungarian university). The Hungarian minority's consistent demand for separate institutional spaces for cultural reproduction (that is, Hungarian schools) challenged their Romanian counterparts' ideas of inclusion and evoked fears that this demand would weaken Romanian national sovereignty over Transylvania.[48] The historian Horia-Roman Patapievici expressed frustration over the Hungarian preference for such separate institutions when he called the Hungarian minority an "imperial minority." He derided the demand for a separate Hungarian university as an outcome of past Hungarian dominance over the Romanians in the Transylvanian region.[49]

Against this backdrop, the crisis in Kosovo and international support for territorial autonomy as a resolution triggered intense alarm among Romanian politicians and intellectuals that international recognition of groups' rights to autonomous institutions might increase. A press release published by the Romanian foreign ministry in early March 1999 warned that international initiatives that recognize collective rights for minorities in Yugoslavia would endanger the stability of the entire region.[50]

The intensifying Kosovo crisis also contributed to the further articulation of differences among Romanian exclusivist, moderate, and pluralist approaches to the ongoing debate over cultural reproduction, sovereignty, and international integration. The president of the Romanian Helsinki Committee and a consistent pluralist voice, Gabriel Andreescu, challenged the new Romanian government to reconsider its approach to collective rights and autonomy. In an article reflecting on the foreign ministry's declaration,

---

[47] Andreescu, "Universal Thought, Eastern Facts."
[48] Octavian Paler, "Problema noastră," *România liberă,* May 14, 1999, www.romanialibera.com/1POL/14c2pedi.htm.
[49] H.-R. Patapievici, "Minorităţile imperiale," *Revista 22* 38 (1998), www.dntb.ro/22/1998/38/1edit-hr.html.
[50] For the full text of the release, see Andreescu, "Un comunicat al MAE sau cum face Adevărul politica externă a României."

Andreescu explained that many of the national minority rights generally recognized in the international society, such as the right to exist as a minority
and the right to language use, were in fact collective rights, regardless of what
they were called. Collective rights, said Andreescu, are "instruments that can
offer more power to people and to small communities. Their role is to improve [the human condition]. The fact that in our country certain political
forces and press organs diabolicize the idea of 'collective rights' only shows a
lack of understanding and, at times, foul political play."[51] Similarly vehement
opposition to the proposition of a small group of Transylvanian Romanians
led by Sabin Gherman, who formed a civic association called Pro Transilvania and advocated self-government for Romania's historical regions, indicated
that notions associated with autonomy, including "devolution," remained
extremely sensitive in the Romanian context at the end of the 1990s.[52]

It was under these conditions that the 2000 elections returned Ion Iliescu and the reconfigured PDSR—now called Party of Social Democracy
(PSD)—to power. These elections also marked the increased electoral appeal of nationalist parties in Romania. The moderate political parties that
had been the principal actors in the previous government (PNȚCD and
the Romanian Democratic Convention 2000) could not even gain seats
in the new parliament, while the more nationalist parties and their leaders
achieved high levels of support. Iliescu's party won a plurality of the votes,
followed by the ultra-nationalist Greater Romania Party (PRM). PRM
leader Corneliu Vadim Tudor came in second with more than 28 percent of
the votes in the first round of the presidential elections and won 33 percent
in the runoff, when Romanians had to choose between him and Iliescu.[53]
The irony of the presidential runoff (a testament to Iliescu's remarkable political fortune) was that Iliescu won the presidency with the active support
of the moderates his party had just ousted from power. In fact, the leaders
of the moderate parties found themselves campaigning for an Iliescu victory
to avert an even worse alternative—the openly xenophobic and anti-Semitic
Corneliu Vadim Tudor.[54]

The period under the second Iliescu regime in Romania signaled a consensual turn that attested to the exceptional political abilities of President
Iliescu, who after the 2000 victory reconfigured his national strategy on

[51] Ibid.
[52] *Cotidianul,* April 23, 1999; *Jurnalul National,* April 28, 1999; *Evenimentul zilei,* November 17,
1999; and "Un comunicat al MAE sau cum face Adevărul politica externă a României."
[53] See the Maxmilián Strmiska article in *Středoevropské politické studie* 3, no. 2 (Spring 2001).
Available at www.iips.cz/cisla/texty/clanky/romanian201.html.
[54] Having averted the lesser evil, the moderates rejected the idea of entering a coalition government
with Iliescu's party and remained in opposition.

the basis of electoral and legislative necessities. Having learned important lessons from the previous governing periods, primarily that the Romanian electorate was concerned about the country's prospects for Western integration and that alliances with ultra-nationalist parties would hinder Romania's integration, Iliescu now took the opportunity to present himself and his party to the West as the democratic force in comparison with the extreme nationalist alternative—Tudor and the Greater Romania Party.[55] Forming a minority government, the PSD also needed predictable parliamentary allies, and the RMDSZ had proven itself during the 1996–2000 period to be such an actor. So the post-2000 Iliescu government altered its previous adversarial strategy toward the Hungarian minority and abandoned the blatant pursuit of centralized control over society.

In the development most striking to many observers of Romanian politics, the RMDSZ leadership signed a cooperation protocol with the government. After 2000, the RMDSZ concluded similar protocols with the government at the beginning of each year. The party's leadership remained consistent in its strategy of participating fully in the Romanian parliamentary process and using terms of conditionality included in cooperation agreements to negotiate for the expansion of language rights. The governing PSD lived up to the terms of its annual parliamentary cooperation protocols with the RMDSZ despite repeated threats of a no-confidence motion on the part of PRM leader Tudor. The government refused to support a series of vigorously pursued PRM initiatives to outlaw the Hungarian party, to rescind legislation allowing minority language in public administration and education, to restrict the accreditation of Hungarian institutions of higher education, and to withdraw support from minority language liberalization in general.

This process also resulted in minority rights that were unimaginable during Iliescu's previous tenure. Despite the PRM opposition, the local administration law allowing for minority language use in settlements where the minority comprises at least 20 percent came into force in May 2001.[56] The government also agreed to amend a previously restrictive decree and allow minorities free use of their national symbols and the singing of other national anthems in public places. It also agreed to reestablish a historic Hungarian high school in the Transylvanian city Târgu-Mureş. In a more significant act, in July 2003 the Romanian Chamber of Deputies unanimously voted for amendments to the Romanian constitution, among

---

[55] Daniel Chirot, "What Provokes Violent Ethnic Conflict?" in *Ethnic Politics after Communism,* ed. Zoltan Barany and Robert G. Moser (Ithaca: Cornell University Press, 2005), 161.
[56] "Romanian Public Administration Is Difficult To Implement," FBIS-EEU–2001–0523, May 23, 2001.

which was a provision granting minority language use in courts and public administration.[57]

Clearly, the shift to more accommodative minority policies improved Romania's chances for membership in NATO and the EU, and these were primary goals for the reformed Iliescu regime. The effort to improve its image in the West was evident in the Romanian president's active international campaign. A striking testimony of his political prowess was that Iliescu managed to defeat his former democratic opponents on their own turf: Although the former anti-Iliescu opposition had portrayed itself to the Romanian electorate and Western observers as the only force that could take Romania into the Western club, the Constantinescu government failed to deliver on the promise of NATO membership and could show no real commitment on the EU's part to admit Romania in the near future. By contrast, it was the Iliescu government (which had also achieved Council of Europe membership for Romania in 1993 even without fulfilling the conditions of accession) that after 2000 not only achieved NATO membership but became NATO's favorite CEE member after the invasion of Iraq in 2003. As NATO membership was more easily achievable than EU membership, the government directed its international campaign primarily at Washington. Two editorials published under the authorship of Ion Iliescu in the *Washington Post* presented his leadership in the first years of post-Communism as a heroic democratic force that other democratizing countries should view as a model. (The editors of the *Post* made no effort to balance this misleading self-portrait.)[58]

The campaign that helped Romania secure NATO membership did not, however, improve Romania's relations with the EU. When Romania sided with the United States on Iraq, French President Chirac said Iliescu had "missed a good opportunity to shut up."[59] The low effectiveness of the Romanian government in satisfying accession requirements coupled with undemocratic practices (such as media restriction and high levels of governmental corruption) left at least some Western analysts and European leaders unconvinced that the government in the post-2000 Iliescu period had indeed changed substantively.[60] In an unprecedented expression of discontentment, in March

[57] "Romania Lifts Ban on Hungarian Flags, Anthem during National Celebrations," *RFE/RL Newsline,* June 30, 2003.

[58] Ion Iliescu, "Romania's Example," *Washington Post,* March 17, 2003, A19; and Iliescu, "Keep Russia Away From the Danube; So Says Romania, with Reason to be Wary of the Federation's Involvement," *Washington Post,* May 23, 1999, B05; both articles accessed via Lexis-Nexis on May 26, 2004.

[59] Stephen Castle and Paul Waugh, "'New Europe' Strikes Back after Vitriolic Chirac Attack," *The Independent* (London), 11. Accessed via Lexis-Nexis on July 7, 2004.

[60] Vachudova, *Europe Undivided,* 215.

2004 the European Parliament adopted a resolution to suspend accession negotiations with Romania until Romania fully implemented anti-corruption laws, guaranteed the independence of the judiciary and the freedom of the media, and stopped mistreatment of citizens by its police forces.[61]

Given the seriousness of these issues, the accommodation of minority language rights in contested institutions remains a significant achievement of this period, and it demonstrates both the importance of the language issue for majority and minority political elites and their strong commitment to conduct the debate within democratic channels. As chapters 4 and 5 will demonstrate, some elements of the language debate between the consensual majority and minority parties remain outstanding, and competing positions reflect continuing differences between majority and minority notions of sovereignty. The Hungarian minority party continues to press for substate minority autonomy, while the moderate Romanian political elites continue to stress the significance of strong state sovereignty despite their interest in European integration. In a book he authored as part of this campaign, Iliescu wrote the following: "The states still represent the cornerstones of the new European edifice. Their identity may change, but not by weakening their contents and significance, or even by dissolution, but through enhanced relevance and functional differentiation."[62]

The notion that the state should have an identity that coincides with the identity of the majority cultural nation remains dominant among Romanian political elites, even after 2000. In the debate over the amendments to the Romanian constitution adopted in 2003, Romanian parties in government and opposition were unwilling to accept Hungarian minority proposals to replace references to "the Romanian people" as the source of national sovereignty and the foundation of the state with the phrase "the citizens of Romania."[63]

Although majority-minority division remains significant on the question of substate minority autonomy, the shift to consensual government after 2000 triggered changes in the unity of the minority party. Just as the adversarial government of the first Iliescu regime had helped galvanize a unified Hungarian response within the framework of a single Hungarian party, the consensual approach of the second Iliescu regime helped weaken Hungarian unity. Internal debates within the RMDSZ focused on the question of

---

[61] Report on Romania's progress towards accession EP Document A5–0103/2004, February 24, 2004, adopted in plenary in March 11, 2004.

[62] Ion Iliescu, *Integration and Globalization: A Romanian View* (Bucharest: Romanian Cultural Foundation Publishing House, 2003), 73.

[63] Press conference by Adrian Năstase and Béla Markó on February 19, 2003. Available at www.psd.ro.

whether autonomy demands could be negotiated internally, in cooperation with the majority government, or externally, in confrontation with the
Romanian majority elite, with the latter approach depending on support
from the Hungarian state and international institutions. Despite continuing challenges from the more confrontational faction of Bishop László Tőkés,
the gradualist Markó leadership maintained a working balance: The RMDSZ
participated fully in the Romanian democratic process and also worked for
the "Europeanization" of the minority problem in Romania. Eventually, with
strong organization and electoral support and perseverance, the RMDSZ
achieved the lifting of restrictions on language use. Yet the fissure between
the confrontational and gradualist factions also led to fragmentation and, beginning in late 2003, to the creation of separate political movements and parties. In the process, two new organizations, the Szekler National Council and
the Hungarian National Council in Transylvania, have emerged as significant
challengers to the gradualist strategy of the RMDSZ, as they aim more aggressively to achieve Hungarian minority autonomy in Transylvania.[64]

Slovakia

The story of international engagement in Slovakia's multilingualism debate
is similar to Romania's. During the Mečiar period from 1992 to 1998,
European officials' efforts to influence the government to adopt minority-
friendly policies were largely unsuccessful. The Slovak government applied
for membership in the Council of Europe in 1993, signed a Europe Agreement in October 1993, and applied for EU membership in June 1995. Yet
despite extensive efforts by the Council of Europe, the OSCE High Commissioner on National Minorities (HCNM), and EU officials to influence
minority language accommodation in Slovakia, the dominant Slovak parties
remained committed to their strategy of language exclusion. It was only after
the democratic anti-Mečiar opposition came to power and formed a new
coalition government that included the Hungarian Coalition Party that the
gradual resolution of the issues concerning language use was possible.

---

[64] On different Hungarian minority approaches to the question of autonomy, see Zoltán Kántor and
Balázs Majtényi, "Autonómiamodellek Erdélyben" available at kantor.adatbank.transindex.ro/belso.
php?k=32&p=3020. Accessed on November 20, 2006. The Szekler National Council was founded
under the leadership of Bishop László Tőkés on October 26, 2003. The primary objective of this
party is the territorial autonomy of the Szekler region in Central Romania. "Romanian Politicians
Condemn Establishment of Szeklers' National Council," FBIS-EEU–2003–1028, October 28,
2003. The Hungarian National Council in Transylvania (CNMT) was established on December 13,
2003, in Cluj-Napoca. It also seeks to obtain autonomy for the Szekler region. The chairman of the
council is Bishop László Tőkés. See "Romanian Parties Reject CNMT's Ethnic Autonomy Drive,
Will Protest to Budapest," FBIS-EEU–2003–1216, December 16, 2003.

Like their counterparts in Romania, the Hungarian minority elites in Slovakia actively sought the engagement of European actors in the language debate, and the Slovak application for Council of Europe membership in 1993 provided the first opportunity. Czechoslovakia had enjoyed full membership in the CE since February 1991, but after their separation both the Czech Republic and Slovakia had to resubmit their applications for membership. The Hungarian minority elite approached the CE both directly and through the Hungarian government in Budapest, which lobbied to obtain the CE's support for what it considered legitimate demands of Hungarian minorities outside Hungary.

In February 1993, the leaders of all four Hungarian minority parties sent a memorandum to the CE, asking it to investigate the Slovak government's minority policy. Hungarian minority leaders called for European pressure on the Slovak government to harmonize Slovakia's constitution and other laws with "European norms."[65] The memorandum raised "questions of legitimacy" concerning the "nation-state" model institutionalized in the Slovak constitution and other legislation intended to restrict minority rights for self-government and the use of minority languages in government and education. The Hungarian minority elites were successful in gaining the attention of the CE. Top CE officials visited Bratislava and called on the government to lift its limitations on minority rights. On May 30, 1993, the CE recommended Slovakia's admission with a list of conditions: that Slovakia sign the European Convention for Human Rights and apply the Council of Europe's Recommendation No. 1201 of February 1993, specifically regarding the use of minority language personal names and the display of minority language place names in the localities they inhabit. The CE recommendation also stipulated that any territorial redistricting had to take into consideration the rights of minorities.[66]

Government officials repeatedly assured CE officials that Slovakia would observe these recommendations and change its policy toward the Hungarians, but the policies of linguistic exclusion continued.[67] Constitutional Court Chairman Milan Čič declared that the CE recommendations had no "legal implications for the state agencies of the Slovak Republic."[68] On June 23, 1993, the parliament issued a statement in support of Slovakia's application to CE membership and of the Council's Recommendation No.

---

[65] Text of memorandum in *Új Szó*, February 5, 1993.
[66] Published in Zalabai, ed., *Mit ér a nyelvünk, ha magyar?* 111–12.
[67] "Az MKDM és az Együttélés képviselőinek határozati javaslata," *Új Szó*, May 22, 1993. See also "Az Együttélés és az MKDM állásfoglalása a szlovák parlament határozatáról," *Szabad Újság*, June 25, 1993.
[68] *Új Szó*, September 10, 1993.

1201, the same day that the parliament rejected a Hungarian proposal to adopt legislation lifting the ban on the use of Hungarian personal names and the display of Hungarian place names. Nonetheless, the CE approved the membership applications of both the Czech Republic and Slovakia at the end of June 1993. The General Assembly attached two amendments for the protection of minority rights and established a special committee to monitor the new member countries' compliance with the CE's recommendations.[69] Paralleling events in Romania, however, by this time the CE had lost the leverage of conditionality, and post-admission monitoring was ineffective in persuading the Mečiar government to fulfill its previous promises.[70] The government made no efforts to lift existing restrictions on minority language use and was even in the process of designing means to limit minority processes of cultural reproduction.

Meanwhile, the Hungarian minority maintained its pressure at home and abroad, sending letters to the Council of Europe and organizing a large public demonstration calling for Slovakia's compliance with the CE's recommendations.[71] Hungarian efforts to involve international actors irritated the Slovak government. Foreign Minister Moravčik reprimanded the Hungarian minority party leaders for damaging Slovakia's prestige abroad with their correspondence.[72] At the same time, the problem of compliance with the CE recommendations highlighted differences between the Slovak nationalist and Slovak moderate approaches to majority-minority relations.

The moderates shared the Hungarian desire to make Slovakia more democratic and open to the international society, and they were also more open to the CE recommendations than the nationalist government. Taking advantage of the fact that the ruling HZDS found itself in the legislative minority at this time, the Slovak moderates succeeded in passing legislation bringing Slovakia into compliance with the CE recommendations. In July 1993, the parliament legalized the registration of non-Slovak Christian names and the use of non-Slovak family names in official documents. In the same month, an amendment to the law on land restitution lifted discrimination against ethnic Hungarians. In December 1993, the KDH and SDL' deputies again voted against government-proposed restrictions on the use of Hungarian personal names.[73]

---

[69] Alfred A. Reisch, "Slovakia's Minority Policy under International Scrutiny," *RFE/RL Research Report* 2, no. 49 (December 10, 1993): 39.
[70] Kelley, *Ethnic Politics in Europe,* ch. 6, 116–39.
[71] *Közösségünk szolgálatában,* 103–5; articles in *Új Szó,* August 27, 28, September 1, 1993; *Národná obroda,* August 30, 1993.
[72] *Új Szó,* September 8, 1993.
[73] Reisch, "Slovakia's Minority Policy under International Scrutiny," 38, 41.

Yet shared interest in complying with CE recommendations was not sufficient to prompt Slovak opposition parties to cooperate more boldly with the Hungarian minority parties. During the brief period in 1994 when the Slovak moderates came to power, their primary interest was in maintaining their power beyond the September 1994 elections. In the intensity of the electoral campaign that showed the continuing popular appeal of nationalism, the Slovak moderates were reluctant to adopt the two European Charters that the Hungarian minority elite found most important, the European Charter of Local Self-Government and the European Charter of Regional and Minority Languages. They adopted only minimalist measures of language liberalization, such as allowing the official use of Hungarian personal names and the unofficial display of bilingual signs in southern Slovakia.

After the adoption of the restrictive 1995 State Language Law by the reconstituted Mečiar government, the OSCE and the CE engaged in another series efforts to persuade the Slovak nationalists to put in place institutional mechanisms for the protection of minority languages. Although the government promised these institutions that it would adopt a separate law for minority language use, and European leaders extensively pressed for the adoption of such a law, the Mečiar government once again abandoned its pledge. The Agenda 2000 opinion published in July 1997 was severely critical:

> The first problem arises from the law on the national language of November 1995, which repealed the earlier provisions allowing the use of a minority language for official communications in any town or village where the minority represented more than 20% of the population. The Slovak authorities had given commitments to the European Union and the OSCE's High Commissioner for national minorities that it would adopt a new law on the use of minority languages. It should also be noted that Article 34(2) of the Slovak Constitution expressly states that minorities may use their language for official communications and that the arrangements for exercising that right should be laid down by law. Nevertheless, Slovakia has not yet passed comprehensive legislation on this point and has gone back on the commitments it gave earlier.[74]

Rejecting a draft proposed by the Hungarian parties, the government refused to budge on the matter even after an explicit demand from the EU Commission that Slovakia adopt legislation to protect its minority languages if it

---

[74] Agenda 2000—Commission Opinion on Slovakia's Application for Membership of the European Union; DOC/97/20; Brussels, Belgium, July 15, 1997; quotation in on 22. Available at europa.eu.int, accessed July 7, 2004.

entertained any hope of entering the EU. During their electoral campaign, the anti-Mečiar opposition parties were able to rely on strong support by European institution leaders.[75]

By March 1998, the desire to take charge of the democratic process contributed to the mobilization of several Slovak NGOs that launched a highly successful "get out the vote" campaign. Called Civic Campaign OK'98, this movement gained the support of trade unions, churches, and many prominent artists and mobilized a broad spectrum of Slovak society through public debates and other fora. Largely due to this campaign, 84.2 percent of voters participated in the 1998 elections, 10 percent more than in the previous elections in 1994. (This turnout was especially significant when compared with declining numbers in other post-Communist societies by the end of the decade.)[76] Although HZDS emerged from the election as the strongest party, it was unable to form a majority coalition government and went into opposition. Former Prime Minister Mečiar resigned his parliamentary seat.[77]

The ability of the former opposition to defeat the centralizing and increasingly authoritarian government of Mečiar in the 1998 elections demonstrated the inadvertently unifying effect of the adversarial strategy of the previous leadership. It was the desire to replace the Mečiar government that motivated the Slovak opposition to close ranks among themselves and with the Hungarian parties before the 1998 elections. The modified electoral law that the Mečiar government had adopted before the elections compelled Slovak and Hungarian opposition parties to form the unified Party of the Slovak Democratic Coalition (SDK) and the Hungarian Coalition Party (MKP). In October 1998, Mikuláš Dzurinda of the SDK became the prime minister of the new coalition government formed by the former opposition, which also included the SDĽ, the SOP, and the Hungarian Coalition Party (MKP).

The desire to join NATO and the European Union provided significant incentives for the Slovak-Hungarian alliance. The new Slovak leaders placed primary emphasis on changing Slovakia's image in the West and accelerating the country's inclusion in Western institutions.[78] As the resolution of "ethnic

[75] Vachudova, *Europe Undivided,* 114.

[76] Zora Bútorová, Oľga Gyárfášová, and Marián Velšic, "Public Opinion," in *Slovakia 1998–1999: A Global Report on the State of Society,* ed. Grigorij Mesežnikov (Bratislava: Institute for Public Affairs, 1999), 137.

[77] *RFE/RL Newsline,* December 7, 1998.

[78] *RFE/RL Newsline,* January 11, 19, 21, 1999; *RFE/RL Newsline,* December 8, 11, 28, 1998 and January 22, 28, 1999; *Slovak Spectator,* February 21–27, 2000; and *OMRI Daily Digest,* February 16, 2000.

conflicts" was a significant condition for achieving Slovakia's integration into the EU, the new government expressed commitment to changing the previous government's minority policies.[79]

Like Romania, the desire of the Slovak moderates to distance themselves from the previous nationalist government resulted in power-sharing with the Hungarian minority party.[80] Partnership with the Hungarian deputies was also important in securing the three-fifths majority (90 out of 150 votes) in parliament necessary to amend the constitution. The Hungarian Coalition Party received three portfolios in the cabinet, including the post of a deputy premier in charge of human rights and minority affairs.[81] As another indication of the new government's willingness to include Hungarians in the state's highest institutions, on November 25, 1999, Slovak President Rudolf Schuster appointed the first Hungarian judge to the Constitutional Court, to take office in January 2000.[82]

During the first year of consensual government, the Slovak and Hungarian coalition partners reached agreement on many contentious issues of the decade-long language debate. The coalition agreed to sign the European Charter for Regional or Minority Languages on February 20, 2001.[83] (The Charter was ratified on June 19, 2001.)[84] The government also reached consensus on a more proportional allocation of state funds to minority cultural institutions.[85]

Yet majority-minority differences over the scope of state sovereignty continued to influence the debate over the new minority language law. During the second half of the decade, Slovak moderates had agreed with Hungarian minority leaders that new legislation was necessary to fill the gap that the 1995 state language law had created in the regulation of minority language use. Yet the leaders of the Slovak and Hungarian anti-Mečiar opposition had repeatedly failed to reach an agreement to end the legislative hiatus. Sharp disagreements between these parties persisted after the formation of the new coalition government, and the minority language law finally adopted in June 1999 reflected a lack of consensus among the power-sharing elites on this critical issue.

---

[79] *RFE/RL Newsline,* November 25, 1998; *RFE/RL Newsline,* October 11, 13, 20, 1998, December 2, 3, 16, 1998; and January 26, 1999.

[80] *RFE/RL Newsline,* regularly throughout October 1998.

[81] *RFE/RL Newsline,* October 29, 1998.

[82] *Új Szó,* November 26, 1999.

[83] *Új Szó,* November 20, 1999.

[84] Advisory Committee on the Framework Convention for the Protection of National Minorities, Comments of the Government of Slovakia on the Opinion, June 5, 2001, GVT/COM/INF/OP/I(2001)001 (Council of Europe); "Slovak parliament ratifies European language charter *Bratislava TASR* (Internet Version-WWW) in English 1945 GMT 19 Jun 01 TASR Tuesday, June 19, 2001."

[85] *Új Szó,* March 2, 1999.

Primarily as a result of European pressure, the Slovak moderate leadership agreed in the summer of 1999 to draft a minority language law with the involvement of the Hungarian coalition partners.[86] The OSCE High Commissioner for Minority Affairs, Max van der Stoel, and representatives of the CE and the EU were all engaged in the language debate.[87] The coalition, however, could not agree on a mutually acceptable text for the law. Slovak cabinet members responsible for preparing the draft argued for a return to the status quo before the 1995 state language law, but they rejected Hungarian requests to reverse all of the restrictions that the 1995 law had introduced. The Hungarian Coalition pressed for a comprehensive minority language law to address all spheres of public interaction affected by the 1995 law; their Slovak partners limited the scope of the law exclusively to the regulation of language use in the sphere of government. The most contentious issue was the threshold percentage that would be required for minorities to benefit from the rights provided in the law. The Slovak coalition partners wanted to set the threshold at 20 percent, while the Hungarians demanded 10 percent. The governing coalition agreed to keep its internal debates away from the public, yet intense controversy between the Slovak moderate and Hungarian minority participants was evident from the beginning of the drafting process.[88] The leadership of the Hungarian Coalition also rejected the draft prepared by the Slovak partners and submitted to parliament a separate bill that granted rights for minority language use in all public settings.[89]

Responding to European pressure, the government's final draft took some elements of the Hungarian demands into consideration and also incorporated recommendations of the head of the OSCE HCNM, Van der Stoel, to allow greater use of minority languages in local government. The Hungarian leadership, however, charged that the Slovak coalition partners had largely ignored Hungarian preferences in the process. In the end, the parliament passed a minority language bill finalized by the Slovak moderates without the consensus of their Hungarian governing partners.[90]

---

[86] *MKP Közlöny,* April 13, 1999.

[87] Kelley, *Ethnic Politics in Europe,* 132–33.

[88] MKP parliamentary faction leader Gyula Bardos's account of the negotiations, *Új Szó,* July 19, 1999. See also "A Short Analysis of the Law on the Use of the Languages of the National Minorities," July 23, 1999, MK document; *Új Szó,* June 3, 5, 1999; *MKP Közlöny,* May 13, 1999.

[89] "Draft Bill of a Group of MP's of the national Council of the Slovak Republic on the Use of the Languages of the National Minorities," MKP document, Bratislava, June 1999. See also *FORUM News,* June 8, 10, 1999.

[90] "Zákon z 10. júla 1999 o používaní jazykov národnostných menšin" ("Law on the use of National Minority Languages") *Zbierka zákonov* 184 (1999); "Minority Language Law Passed after Emotional Seven-Day Debate," *Slovak Spectator* 5, no. 28 (July 19–25, 1999); and MK, "A Short Analysis of the Law on the Use of the Languages of National Minorities."

Despite these fissures, the Slovak-Hungarian governmental coalition survived a series of governing crises and was further reinforced after the 2002 elections. The Hungarian party continued to press for language liberalization, especially in the area of higher education, which remained more contested in Slovakia than in Romania. Whereas in Romania the issue under debate was whether Hungarians should have a separate Hungarian-language university, in Slovakia the Hungarians had a difficult time achieving the establishment of a single Hungarian department at a teacher training university.

The difficulties of parallel processes of nation-building on a mutually claimed "homeland" in the framework of a unitary state were evident in the continued debate over administrative redistricting. Slovak and Hungarian ideas remained far apart in this matter. Hungarian deputies charged that a new draft prepared by the Slovak partners continued the strategy of breaking up compact Hungarian-inhabited regions in southern Slovakia. The Hungarian party sustained its demands for an administrative design that would strengthen, rather than weaken, Hungarian representation in local and regional government.[91] In summer 2001, the MKP threatened to leave the coalition after the parliament adopted a law on public administration reform that divided the country into eight government units instead of the twelve units that the MKP had demanded. Subsequently, the government passed a law devolving state powers to self-governing bodies—the so-called power-devolution law—and the Hungarians remained in the coalition.[92]

Paralleling the situation in Romania, the danger of being left out of European integration provided strong motivation for the majority-minority alliances that changed the course of the language debate in Slovakia. The debate continued in the power-sharing context, as majority and minority participants continued to hold different positions on whether Hungarians should have control over their "own" institutions of self-government and cultural reproduction. As the next section demonstrates, the resolution of this question was further complicated by the participation of the governments of Hungary, whose nation-building strategies also involved the Hungarian minorities in the region.

Kin-State Politics and Hungarians as External Minorities

Compared to Hungary's ten million inhabitants, the approximately three million Hungarians living in neighboring states constitute a relatively large

[91] *Új Szó,* October 9, 1999. See also *Új Szó,* October 28, 30, 1999.
[92] "Slovak Minister Warns against Coalition Break-Up," *BBC Monitoring Service,* August 21, 2001; and "Slovakia's Hungarians Relax Ultimatum on Conditions for Staying in Government," *BBC Monitoring Service,* September 19, 2001. Text of report in English from Slovak commercial news agency SITA website.

segment of Hungarian-speakers in the region.[93] This latter group has consistently expressed strong interest in maintaining their cross-border social and cultural relations. Beyond a dramatic increase in informal cross-border interactions among Hungarians after 1989, consecutive Hungarian governments also demonstrated interest in assuring that Hungarian-speakers in the Carpathian basin maintain their language and Hungarian culture. Employing a complex set of indirect and direct methods, Hungarian governments sought to influence neighboring states' policies toward Hungarian minority institutions in a way that would weaken state "ownership" and strengthen the control of Hungarian minorities in the region over minority institutions of cultural reproduction. They also sought to facilitate interactions between Hungarians inside and outside of Hungary. The expression most often used for these goals in Hungarian political discourse was the "virtualization" of state borders.[94]

The distinguishing features of this indirect strategy were (a) to design a pluralist institutional system in Hungary for minority cultures as a model for neighboring states; (b) to press for the "Europeanization" of minority rights (that is, moving the question of minority protection from the state level to the European level); and (c) to use bilateral treaties with neighbors to codify guarantees for minority protection. The notable forms of this increased direct involvement were (a) the creation of a network of institutions for "Hungarian-Hungarian" relations and (b) the adoption of a comprehensive kin-state law, the so-called Status Law, for providing Hungarian state benefits for Hungarians abroad.

Aspirations for cultural reproduction across state borders are particularly problematic in an area where states place strong emphasis on maintaining their—in many cases newly acquired—territorial sovereignty. Indeed, Romania and Slovakia, Hungary's neighbors with the largest and most well-organized Hungarian minority populations, remain highly skeptical of the Hungarian trans-sovereign national project—even though both of these states also maintain kin-state policies toward national groups abroad that they consider their "own."[95]

The Hungarian political parties that took turns in government after 1990 gave varied answers to the question of how Hungary should help Hungarian minorities' efforts to maintain their language in the institutions they deemed to be significant. Although all Hungarian governments considered "care for Hungarians abroad," as articulated in Article 6, paragraph 3 of the

---

[93] For the Hungarian census, see www.nepszamlalas2001.hu, accessed July 8, 2004. For statistics on Hungarians abroad, see web.htmh.gov.hu/reports2004/west2004.htm, accessed July 8, 2004.
[94] Zsuzsa Csergo and James M. Goldgeier, "Virtual Nationalism," *Foreign Policy* 125 (July/August 2001): 76–77.
[95] Ibid.

constitution, an important goal, the question of how exactly the Hungarian state should achieve this goal was deeply divisive within Hungary.

Like political elites elsewhere in the region, these Hungarian governments faced the constraints and opportunities of post-Communist electoral competition as well as those of Euro-Atlantic integration. Hungary's engagement in multinationalism debates in the region manifested both agreement on the necessity of kin-state support for Hungarians abroad and significant variation in these governments' emphasis on the unity of Hungarian nation-building. The conservative governments of Prime Ministers József Antall from 1990 to 1993[96] and Viktor Orbán from 1998 to 2002 considered Hungarian minorities first and foremost to be part of one Hungarian cultural nation. To maintain this nation across borders, they envisioned an institutional network coordinated from Budapest as the cultural center. These governments were at least as interested in creating cross-border institutions of Hungarian-Hungarian relations as in pursuing traditional means of bilateral diplomacy with neighboring governments. The socialist-liberal coalition governments under Prime Ministers Gyula Horn from 1994 to 1998, Péter Medgyessy after 2002, and Ferenc Gyurcsány after 2004 framed their policies toward Hungarian minorities as one of the three most important pillars of Hungary's foreign policy, signaling government recognition that Hungarian minorities were primarily citizens of their respective states. To help achieve minority goals of cultural reproduction, socialists and liberals argued that Hungarians needed to invest more in negotiations with neighboring governments and less in coordination of Hungarian minority cultural strategies from Budapest.

The most indirect, least controversial, and least consequential mode of Hungarian influence on neighboring governments' minority policies was the creation of an internal institutional framework of minority self-governments in the 1993 Act on the Rights of Ethnic and National Minorities. This law recognized collective minority rights and also designed a framework for ethnic or national minority citizens of Hungary (or any Hungarian citizen who chose to participate in these institutions) to form nonterritorial minority self-governments with increased authority over their cultural affairs.[97] This policy proved to be ineffective as a model for policies of multilingualism in Romania or Slovakia, because majority political parties considered neither the formal recognition of group rights for minority cultures nor the notion of minority self-government to be acceptable solutions.

---

[96] After Prime Minister Antall's death in December 1993, Péter Boross became prime minister until July 1994. The conservative coalition was defeated in the 1994 parliamentary elections.
[97] "1993 Act on the Rights of Ethnic and National Minorities."

Another indirect effort that remained consistent despite government changes in Budapest was the attempt to "Europeanize" Hungarian minority issues. From the beginning of the 1990s, Hungarian parliamentary parties had agreed that future membership in the European Union for Hungary and its neighbors would be beneficial for Hungarian minorities.[98] Hungarian governments actively advocated the need for European institutions to intervene in the protection of minority rights in Romania and Slovakia. Arguing that minority rights constitute a common European value, consecutive Hungarian governments lobbied European institutions on behalf of Hungarian minority parties and pressed for the inclusion of a minority rights article in the European Union's constitution.[99] All Hungarian governments, regardless of their place on the political spectrum, have viewed minority efforts to create pluralist institutional structures in their states as legitimate and effective ways of dealing with issues of multilingualism.

The governments of Romania and Slovakia viewed this Hungarian position, which was in sync with the desires of Hungarian minority elites, with suspicion and countered it with the stance that Hungarian minorities were their internal minorities and that their issues should consequently remain in the domain of domestic affairs even in an integrated Europe. Romanian and Slovak officials also repeatedly argued that their treatment of the Hungarian minority was well within the spectrum of liberal democratic European norms.

European officials, for their part, were consistent in insisting that—whether minorities were internal or external—the governments involved in the dispute should conclude bilateral "friendship treaties" to settle their minority-related issues. As seven states neighboring Hungary included Hungarian minority groups and five of these were new states established after the collapse of the Communist federations, Western governments were especially eager to see Hungary and its neighbors commit themselves to good neighborly relations. Hungarian governments also realized the importance of such treaties, and by the time the EU made the bilateral resolution of minority issues a pre-accession criterion in 1994, Hungary had already signed bilateral treaties with neighboring Ukraine, Croatia, Slovenia, and Austria. Negotiations on bilateral treaties with Romania and Slovakia began as early as 1991.

---

[98] Csaba Tabajdi, head of the Office of Hungarians Abroad (HTMH), author interview, Budapest, Hungary, June 10, 1996.
[99] Ambassador András Simonyi, interview by the author and James M. Goldgeier, Washington, D.C., June 3, 2003; "EU Constitution a success," *BBC Monitoring European*, June 21, 2004; and "Hungarian Daily Urges Government to Bargain for EU Constitution Minority Rights," FBIS-EEU–2003–1126, November 28, 2004.

Hungary's treaties with Romania and Slovakia were the most difficult to conclude, as these two neighbors had the combination of large and politically highly organized Hungarian populations and governments that, in the first few years of the post-Communist era, were intent on a traditional (culturally homogenizing) nation-state strategy. Under these conditions, the EU played a significant role in facilitating the completion of Hungary's treaties with Romania and Slovakia. Before 1994, the insistence of the government of Hungarian prime minister Antall that basic treaties include guarantees for collective minority rights for Hungarians made agreement with these two neighbors an impossible task. The Hungarian-Ukrainian treaty that the Antall government had concluded in December 1991 contains recognition of both individual and collective cultural rights and guarantees for Hungarian minority administrative and cultural autonomy.[100] The terms that were acceptable in Ukraine in 1991 remained unimaginable in the Slovak and Romanian political contexts even at the end of the 1990s. It was the socialist-liberal government under Prime Minister Gyula Horn that concluded the bilateral treaties with Romania and Slovakia, and the process reflected a higher willingness on the part of this government to adapt its goals to regional conditions.

Responding to explicit signals from Western leaders that failure to sign the friendship treaties would slow down their accession to the EU and NATO, the Horn government concluded a Basic Treaty with Slovakia in March 1995 and a similar treaty with Romania in September 1996. In neither case did the Hungarian side achieve its goal of using bilateral treaties to negotiate with neighboring governments for the acceptance of minority self-government in exchange for Hungary's acceptance of the inviolability of frontiers. Although Hungary recognized the inviolability of frontiers, Romania and Slovakia ultimately refused to accept the legitimacy of institutions of national minority self-government. Equally noteworthy was the refusal of both states to allow the participation of Hungarian minority representatives at the talks, reinforcing the notion of Hungarians as an internal minority that could not participate as an autonomous third party in inter-state relations involving the kin-state. (Hungarian minority leaders relied on informal consultations with the government of Hungary.)[101]

---

[100] Margit Bessenyey Williams, "European Integration and Minority Rights," in *Norms and Nannies,* ed. Ronald Linden, 234–35.

[101] Following the 1994 parliamentary elections in Hungary, the Hungarian Socialist Party formed a new coalition government led by Prime Minister Gyula Horn. The new government invited the RMDSZ's parliamentary factions to Budapest for a two-day meeting from October 12 to 14, 1994. The participants agreed that increased consultations were needed between the Hungarian government and the RMDSZ. See Attila Sorbán, "Kis lépések, kis remények, kis csalódottság," *Erdélyi napló* 4, no. 162 (October 19, 1994): 9.

The Iliescu government in Romania was slower to conclude a basic treaty with Hungary than the Mečiar government in Slovakia and more successful in resisting Hungarian requests to accept the legitimacy of minority self-government. In the treaty with Slovakia, the Hungarian government agreed to the inviolability of frontiers, and the Slovak side agreed to include "as legal obligations" the norms of the UN Declaration on Human Rights No. 47/135, the Council of Europe Recommendation No. 1201, which would allow for various forms of territorial self-government for national minorities, and the minority-rights clauses of the 1990 Copenhagen session of the CSCE—all of which allowed for various forms of minority self-government. The ratification of the treaty in the Slovak parliament, however, showed that the inclusion of these international documents—so welcomed by the Hungarian Coalition—was unacceptable to the majority of the Slovak political actors. The government repeatedly postponed the date of ratification, until it finally succeeded in removing the main obstacles by giving assurances to the Slovak National Party that its demands for laws that would weaken the Hungarian community's potential for self-government would be fulfilled.[102] During the year between the signing and ratification of the treaty, the restrictive State Language Act was passed and the government drafted a plan on Slovakia's new administrative-territorial division to strengthen Slovak representation in all regions inhabited by ethnic Hungarians. The Hungarian deputies claimed that these legislative measures severely violated the spirit of the Slovak-Hungarian Basic Treaty. The parliamentary debate clearly indicated that Slovak and Hungarian deputies had contradictory understandings of the spirit of the treaty. The Hungarians regarded it as an international legitimization of their demands and made proposals for its implementation.[103] The Slovak parties, on the other hand, regarded the international documents to which the treaty referred as dangerous and had little desire to anchor Slovak minority policy in them.

The Slovak democratic opposition parties (and future governing partners of the Hungarian Coalition) were also critical of the international reference documents, because they created the potential for minority territorial autonomy. During the parliamentary debate over ratification, opposition deputies expressed support for a Basic Treaty with Hungary on the one hand, while rejecting the Council of Europe Recommendation No. 1201 on the other. KDH president Ján Čarnogurský said in this regard that "for the Christian

Democratic Movement, territorial autonomy is unacceptable on any territory of our country."[104] In March 1996, when the parliament ratified the Slovak-Hungarian Basic Treaty, the overwhelming majority of Slovak deputies voted in favor of a unilateral Slovak "interpretative" attachment declaring that Slovakia would not approve of collective rights or autonomous structures for national minorities.[105] Thus, the Slovak parliament was much slower to ratify the treaty than the Hungarian parliament, which ratified it in June 1995; by the end of the process the terms of the treaty meant something different to the two sides.

Although negotiations over the Hungarian-Romanian Basic Treaty also began in 1991, the burdensome progress in these negotiations bore little resemblance to Romania's speedy ratification of other European agreements. The key issues of contention were the same as those in the negotiations between Hungary and Slovakia. The Romanian demand that the treaty include a clause on the inviolability of existing borders was countered by the Hungarian government's condition that the treaty include Council of Europe Recommendation No. 1201. Romanian nationalists vehemently opposed this CE document, warning that its inclusion in the treaty would threaten the integrity of the Romanian state.[106] Against the backdrop of this "insurmountably divisive" issue, the conclusion of the Basic Treaty on September 16, 1996—just two months before general elections in Romania—was a sudden compromise that indicated the importance of the desire shared by both countries to join NATO and the European Union.[107] Euro-Atlantic membership became a central issue in the campaign preceding the November 1996 general elections in Romania, and the Hungarian government was also keen to demonstrate neighborly behavior to the West. Hungary accepted the inviolability of existing borders and Romania agreed to include Recommendation No. 1201, albeit with an attachment covering a joint interpretation that excluded "collective rights" and the establishment of autonomous territorial structures based on ethnic criteria.[108] (A year earlier, the Hungarian government had rejected a similar interpretation by the Slovak

---

[104] Quoted in *Figyelő*, Coexistence news analysis, December 1995–January 1996, 9–10.

[105] For reports on the ratification of the treaty, including the views of various Slovak deputies, see the newspapers *Republika; Sme; Pravda; Új Szó*, March 28, 30, 1996.

[106] Dan Ionescu, "Romania Complains about Treaty Talks with Hungary," *OMRI*, September 1, 1994; and "More Controversy in Romania over Treaty with Hungary," *RFE/RL Newsline*, September 16, 1996.

[107] Michael Shafir, "A Possible Light at the End of the Tunnel," 29–30.

[108] "Treaty between the Republic of Hungary and Romania on Understanding, Cooperation and Good Neighborhood," Article 4, September 16, 1996. Available at 193.6.118.39/dokumentumok/asz-ro-e.htm. Joel Blocker, "Romania/Hungary: Historic Basic Treaty Signed Today," *RFE/RL Newsline*, September 16, 1996; and Zsolt Mato, "Romanian Parliament Ratifies Treaties with Budapest, Belgrade," *RFE/RL Newsline*, October 4, 1996.

government.) The Romanian-Hungarian "friendship treaty" was a triumph for the Romanian government, which had succeeded, in the words of Romanian Foreign Minister Teodor Meleşcanu, in its efforts to "emasculate" Recommendation No. 1201 with the approval of the Hungarian government.[109] The RMDSZ leadership found the restrictive interpretation of the CE Recommendation No. 1201 unacceptable, especially as the Hungarian government had signed a joint declaration with the organizations of Hungarian minorities outside Hungary to support their pursuit of autonomy and self-government.[110] The RMDSZ also objected to the absence of any mention of either the government's commitment to restitution of Hungarian church property confiscated by the Communist regime or the right to use minority languages in public administration or in the courts.[111]

The signings of the Hungarian-Slovak and Hungarian-Romanian treaties, in both cases against strong domestic opposition and after intense negotiations involving numerous visits by Western officials, were applauded in the West as a major victory. Yet there is no evidence that these treaties advanced the cause of interethnic reconciliation. Having signed the treaty in September 1996, the Iliescu regime was ousted in the November 1996 elections, and subsequent changes in language policy were negotiated on the basis of the new government's cooperation agreement. In Slovakia, the Mečiar government designed its most exclusive language policies after the conclusion of the treaty with Hungary. In 1997, Mečiar proposed a "population exchange" to Hungarian Prime Minister Gyula Horn as a solution to bilateral issues.[112] It was only after the 1998 change in leadership that the Slovak government demonstrated a serious intention to change relations with Hungary and to cooperate in implementing the treaty.[113] Thus, the basic treaties had no measurable impact on policy change in either case, and the negotiating process itself, especially the controversy over the inclusion of the CE Recommendation No. 1201, did more to reinforce majority-minority division than to promote reconciliation.

By 1998, Hungarian minority parties in both Romania and Slovakia assumed governing partnership positions from which they could effectively negotiate for their demands. Nevertheless, the Hungarian government elected in 1998 under Prime Minister Viktor Orbán chose to intensify direct modes

[109] Quoted in Shafir, "A Possible Light at the End of the Tunnel," 30.
[110] Zsofia Szilagyi, "Hungarian Minority Summit Causes Uproar in Slovakia and Romania," *Transition* 2, no. 18 (September 6, 1996).
[111] Shafir, "A Possible Light at the End of the Tunnel," 32.
[112] Kelley, *Ethnic Politics in Europe,* 117.
[113] *RFE/RL Newsline,* November 16, 1998, February 9, 11, 1999.

of engagement in Hungarian minority cultural reproduction. The Orbán government decided to strengthen the complex network of trans-sovereign institutions that facilitated "Hungarian-Hungarian" relations in the Carpathian basin through a comprehensive kin-state law that the Hungarian parliament adopted in 2001.

Institutions that provide channels for relations between Hungarians across the border existed after the 1989 change of regime in Hungary, and these institutions continued their activities despite frequent shifts in government. The government of József Antall created the Governmental Office for Hungarians Abroad to coordinate interactions among the various institutions that provide financial and other kinds of support for Hungarians abroad in education, political organization, cultural activities, media, economic projects, health care, and science. A Hungarian Standing Conference (HSC) was also created to formalize the continuity of communication among Hungarian leaders in Hungary and in neighboring countries.[114] The HSC included representatives of all Hungarian parties and organizations of political significance and became a primary force behind the drive to create an integrated Hungarian institutional network in the Carpathian basin. The process of establishing this institutional network was intertwined with another important element of the trans-sovereign national strategy—support for the institutional autonomy demands of Hungarian minority political parties across the border. Throughout the 1990s, Hungarian government officials made statements of support for whatever autonomous structures the democratically elected representatives of Hungarian minorities in the various neighboring countries proposed, without specific institutional recommendations. At the same time, the activities of Hungarian politicians (visits, meetings, organized consultative sessions, conferences) indicated a preference for a united set of Hungarian minority aims in the neighboring countries. Hungarian officials frequently attended conferences and workshops focusing on ways of strengthening Hungarian institutions, and many of these meetings were organized or supported by the Governmental Office for Hungarian Minorities Abroad.[115]

[114] Government Decree 90/1992 "On the Governmental Office for Hungarian Minorities Abroad" went into force June 1, 1992. Available at www.htmh.hu/dokumentumok/kormang.htm, accessed June 1, 2004. The HSC was created in February 1999. Available at www.magyarorszag.hu, accessed June 1, 2004.
[115] Keynote speech by Csaba Tabajdi, head of the Governmental Office of Hungarians Abroad (HTMH), at the Conference on Minority Interest Representation, Self-Government, and Autonomy Forms, Budapest, Hungary, November 9–10, 1995, manuscript; Lecture by Tibor Szabó, head of the HTMH (Tabajdi's successor), Kossuth House, Washington, DC, August 11, 1999; Erika Törzsök, "The National Minorities and Stability," translation of article published in *Magyar Hirlap*, July 4, 1996.

From the early 1990s, direct forms of Hungarian state engagement in Hungarian minority affairs often generated tension in the Romanian and Slovak capitals.[116] Nevertheless, it was only after the Hungarian parliament adopted the "Law on Hungarians Living in Neighboring Countries"— commonly called the Status Law—in 2001 that the Romanian and Slovak governments expressed complaints internationally about the Hungarian state's trans-sovereign nation-building project.[117] The Status Law offered access privileges to cultural institutions (such as libraries and museums), free teacher training in Hungary for Hungarians living in neighboring countries, and an eighty-dollar annual allowance for Hungarian parents sending at least two children to a Hungarian-language school. The law also provided for socioeconomic benefits, such as public transportation, health care, and (limited) employment in Hungary.

The Hungarian government considered this legislation to be another expression of the Hungarian state's constitutional obligation to "care for Hungarians abroad." As the country was preparing to join the European Union, its leaders thought it necessary to address the issue of how cross-border interaction between Hungarian-speakers might deteriorate once the Schengen border (the EU's strict border-control policy) had taken effect between Hungary and those neighbors left outside of the EU with significant Hungarian minorities—such as Romania, Ukraine, Croatia, and Serbia. From the Hungarian perspective, the Status Law was a comprehensive answer to this question and to the broader issue of how to support Hungarian minorities' cultural reproduction without encouraging them to leave their homelands and move to Hungary, which would create a series of socioeconomic and political problems in Hungary. The Status Law articulated the position of the conservative Hungarian leadership under Prime Minister Viktor Orbán from 1998 to 2002, that Hungarians outside of Hungary are part of a unitary Hungarian cultural nation and thereby entitled to share certain benefits of common nationhood. Indeed, the preamble of the law, as initially adopted by the Hungarian parliament, declared the intent "to ensure that Hungarians living in neighboring countries form part of the Hungarian nation as a whole." Without issuing dual citizenship to Hungarian speakers abroad, the law offered eligible citizens of Romania, Slovakia, the Federal Republic of Yugoslavia, Croatia, Slovenia, and Ukraine "Hungarian identity" cards that looked like passports and entitled their bearers to benefits in

---

[116] "Nastase Says Hungarian Officials Cannot Act as Hosts in Romania," FBIS-EEU–2001–1005, October 5, 2001.

[117] See www.htmh.hu./torveny.htm for the law and related documents and other literature. Accessed August 25, 2003.

Hungary and outside Hungary, although they primarily served the purpose of helping to maintain a Hungarian culture in neighboring countries.

The Status Law became the center of vehement disputes both inside and outside of Hungary and thereby created the opportunity for participants in the debate to negotiate positions and attempt to shape European, regional, and domestic policies. In Hungary, socialist and liberal political parties (in opposition during the parliamentary debate of the law but in government after 2002) objected to the law both on the grounds of ideology and politics. The Alliance of Free Democrats (SZDSZ) was especially critical of the law's ethnocultural definition of a unitary Hungarian nation. Political opponents of Fidesz, the main governing party in 2001, also charged that the country's leadership was recklessly jeopardizing Hungary's improving relations with its neighbors and manipulated the popular theme of kinship ties for its own electoral benefits. There was evidence for an absence of strong support for the substance of the Status Law at both the elite and popular levels in Hungary.[118] Several leaders of the Hungarian minority expressed similar criticisms of the law. Yet its adoption with an overwhelming majority of the votes (93 percent) in the Hungarian parliament, the high number of applicants for Hungarian certificates in Romania and Slovakia, and the vehement reaction against the law on the part of majorities in these countries indicated that the legislation had addressed significant interests in the region. By mid-July 2003, an estimated 700,000 cards had been issued in Romania.[119]

Angered majority nationalists in both states began talking about the need for population exchange. Some were also afraid that Romanians or Slovaks might want to change their self-identification to take advantage of the benefits of the law.[120] The Hungarian state's offer to give financial support to parents who send at least two children to Hungarian school created especially heated controversy, as it provided a direct incentive for Hungarian cultural reproduction in neighboring countries. In both the Romanian and Slovak parliaments, measures were introduced to restrict the ability of their domestic institutions to comply with the Status Law.

[118] Zoltán Kántor, "Statue Law and 'Nation Policy,'" in *The Hungarian Status Law,* ed. Zoltán Kántor et al. (Sapporo, Japan: Slavic Research Center, Hokkaido University, 2004); see also Myra A. Waterbury, "Beyond Irredentism," paper presented at WPSA in 2004.

[119] Estimates for Slovakia vary widely. See Michael Stewart, "The Hungarian Status Law." Available at www.transcomm.ox.ac.uk, accessed May 27, 2004.

[120] "Jan Slota, chairman of the Real Slovak National Party [PSNS], yesterday confided [to journalists] his desire to dust off the so-called Benes Decrees and apply them to Slovakia's Hungarians. . . . Slota voiced his anger at the fact that some 25,000 of the half a million [ethnic] Hungarians [living in Slovakia] have applied to date for the so-called cards of foreign Hungarians." "Slovak Nationalist Head Wants to 'Dust Off' Benes Decrees, Deport Ethnic Magyars," FBIS-EEU–2002–0312, March 12, 2002.

The heated controversy over the Hungarian Status Law demonstrated the persistence of fundamental disagreements over sovereignty and cultural reproduction despite the resolution of specific points of disagreement on the various provisions of the law. The main points of Romanian and Slovak opposition were that the legislation had extraterritorial intent and that it discriminated against ethnic majority (Romanian and Slovak) citizens. The Hungarian government made certain bilateral efforts to persuade its Romanian and Slovak counterparts otherwise, and as a result in December 2001, Hungary and Romania signed a statement of cooperation in which Hungary extended the employment benefits of the law to all Romanian citizens and agreed to limit the extraterritorial aspects of the law. The Slovak government, by contrast, was less willing to accept a similar compromise.

Romania and Slovakia brought formal complaints against Hungary to the European Union and the Council of Europe. The Hungarian government countered that the Status Law was one of numerous examples of kin-state policy throughout Europe that together provided international legitimacy for a state's support for and preferential treatment of its kin abroad. As a response, the Council of Europe's Venice Commission compared a number of kin-state policies in various member states and concluded in the so-called Venice Report in October 2001 that kin-state laws are acceptable only if they do not violate territorial sovereignty.[121] The report found that states could issue legislation concerning citizens of other countries "inasmuch as the effects of these acts are to take place within its borders" and that a kin-state may grant preferential treatment to kin-minorities "insofar as it pursues the legitimate aim of fostering cultural links and is proportionate to that aim." The domain in which such kin-state legislation is acceptable, however, is limited to education and culture, "save in exceptional cases and if it is shown to pursue a legitimate aim and to be proportionate to that aim." The Venice Report can be interpreted as evidence for the European institutions' ambivalent stance on the question of whether minorities such as the Hungarians in Romania and Slovakia are external or internal minorities; indeed, both Hungary and its two neighbors claimed that the report legitimized their positions. The most important "ruling" of the Venice Report, however, was not about whether kin-state laws were acceptable in a democratic Europe. Rather, the Venice Report concluded that one state's extraterritorial provisions are only acceptable with the consent of the other state concerned. The same message

[121] European Commission for Democracy through Law (Venice Commission), Report on the Preferential Treatment of National Minorities by their Kin-State adopted by the Venice Commission at its 48th Plenary Meeting, Venice, Italy, October 19–20, 2001.

was evident in the report issued by Eric Jürgens, a rapporteur appointed by the European Parliament to evaluate the Status Law.[122]

The socialist-liberal coalition that came back to power after the May 2002 elections in Hungary, this time under Prime Minister Péter Medgyessy, promptly responded to this demand, changing the Status Law to eliminate the language that had raised questions about Hungarian irredentism as well as the articles that had raised questions about ethnic discrimination. Bilateral relations with Romania and Slovakia also improved significantly. Still, debate over the intent of this legislation continues, as home states and kin-states continue to manifest strong conflicting interests in influencing the language choices of minority (and majority) parents and students. Both sides continue to think their position represents, and the other side's position violates, "the spirit of European norms."

The tensions surrounding the Status Law cannot be properly understood in terms of a unique Hungarian effort to challenge the rules of Westphalian sovereignty. First, the states engaged in the EU integration process have already surrendered significant features of state sovereignty to the European level. Second, kin-state involvement in the cultural reproduction of external minorities is not a uniquely Hungarian phenomenon. Kin-state laws already constituted a feature of European politics when the Hungarian Status Law was adopted. While controversy over this law brought Hungary's relations with Romania and Slovakia to a post–Cold War low, other neighbors, such as Ukraine and Slovenia, expressed remarkably little anxiety over the law, and Croatian officials even expressed agreement with it.[123] The two states that most vehemently contested the Status Law also had kin-state laws in place at the time. Slovakia adopted a law in 1997 that included many of the same benefits for which Slovak officials so vehemently criticized the Hungarian law. A similar law was adopted in Romania in 1998.[124]

Although the standing consensus in the EU is that control over policies that guarantee the maintenance and reproduction of national cultures should stay at the state level—on this much, at least, titular interests in both East and West coincide—the reports of the Venice Commission and European Parliament rapporteur Jürgens restate the premise that kin-state laws are legitimate

---

[122] Eric Jürgens, "Preferential Treatment of National Minorities by Their Kin-States," Council of Europe, Parliamentary Assembly. Doc. 9744 rev., May 13, 2003. Available at assembly.coe.int, accessed July 7, 2004.

[123] Klara Kingston, "The Hungarian Status Law," *East European Perspectives* 3, no. 17 (October 2001), available at www.rferl.org/reports/eepreport/.

[124] Stephen Deets, "The Hungarian Status Law and the Specter of Neo-Medievalism in Europe," paper presented for the Annual Meeting of the International Studies Association, Montreal, Canada, March 17–20, 2004.

so long as they rest on bilateral consensus. Other European cases, such as agreements between Austria and Italy or between Sweden and Finland reflect the same principle.[125] What made the Hungarian law controversial was the scale of its regional impact and the unilateralism of its design.[126]

The story of the Hungarian Status Law highlights both the continued salience of kin-state politics in the region and the limits of this kind of nation-building in the context of EU integration. Hungary's kin-state activism also revealed divisions among Hungary's post-Communist political elites, demonstrating the influence of domestic electoral competition on nationalist strategies—the same factor that shaped majority-minority divisions and alliances in Romania and Slovakia. Nonetheless, Hungary as a kin-state shaped the dynamics of the debate in important ways: it reinforced the Hungarian minorities' continued interest in a separate national cultural reproduction, facilitated the articulation of Hungarian autonomy demands, and helped to "internationalize" Hungarian minority problems in the EU context. By refraining from irredentism, the Hungarian kin-state also reinforced the commitment of Hungarian minority elites to continue negotiating in their domestic parliaments.

Despite the difficulty of majority-minority consensus on language rights in the context of competitive nation-building, the examples of Romania and Slovakia demonstrate that even the most vehemently fought battles can reach language accommodation, if the constellation of domestic and international opportunities allows it. What these cases also demonstrate is that language accommodation is not achieved by direct Western influence. Western messages about minority language policy are always sifted through the lenses of domestic interest.

EU officials were consistently unsuccessful in achieving changes in minority language policy during the centralizing and authoritarian governments in Romania (until 1996) and Slovakia (until 1998). Western officials did succeed in pressuring these governments to sign bilateral friendship treaties with Hungary, but these treaties had no direct effect on language policy. The political elites willing to accept policy changes that EU officials supported were those that were more willing to compromise on minority language use in the first place. In both cases, government change was necessary for language policies to change.

---

[125] Liebich, "Ethnic Minorities," 117–36.
[126] Csergo and Goldgeier, "Virtual Nationalism in Comparative Context," paper prepared for the international conference on "The Status Law Syndrome: A Post-Communist Nation Building or Post-modern Citizenship?" at the Institute of Legal Studies, Budapest, Hungary, October 14–16, 2004.

Nonetheless, the promise of EU and NATO membership served as an important motivation for democratic majority-minority elites to join forces, oust nationalist governments, and form consensual cross-national alliances. Belonging to "Europe" and "the West" was an important part of the conceptions about nationhood in the region.[127] Western approval of accommodative policies also helped consensual majority parties in these states to legitimize their choice for allying with minority parties and negotiating with them over language liberalization. Once majority-minority alliances were formed, the Hungarian parties in both cases used the conditionality of co-operation agreements to negotiate their demands. The Hungarian minorities acted as "homeland communities," demanding language rights in the institutions they considered most important for cultural reproduction on the territory they inhabit: all levels of education, territory markings, and local government. They participated fully in the democratization process in their home states, negotiating for language liberalization in the Romanian and Slovak parliaments, while also appealing to the governments of Hungary and European institutions for support.

International conditionality was important in reinforcing commitments to democratic forms of competition, but the main vehicles for change in language rights were the *internal conditionality* that minority parties employed in their relations with consensual majority parties and the commitment by consensual majority elites to honor their cooperation agreements. Institutional guarantees for minority cultural reproduction through language use in local government, public places, and all levels of public education were central elements of coalition agreements and formal parliamentary cooperation protocols. In both cases, difficult negotiations continued after the signing of coalition or cooperation agreements. The Hungarian parties repeatedly threatened to leave the coalition if their requests were not satisfied, and they continued to negotiate within democratic channels even though their achievements were not always impressive. By the time the European Union admitted ten new members from CEE in 2004, the Hungarian minority parties had achieved their most important language policy demands in their own parliaments. It is important to note, however, that these achievements do not place Romania and Slovakia among the most friendly European countries on the issue of multilingualism and that majority-minority division continues in these countries over the question of substate minority self-government.

The dynamics of the relationship between these states and Hungary attests to the power of territoriality and the legacies of past relationships in the region. Even though Hungary agreed to the inviolability of borders in its basic

[127] Rawi Abdelal, *National Purpose in the World Economy.*

treaties with both states, Romanian and Slovak majority fears about losing territorial control over Hungarian-inhabited regions remain high. Although bilateralism was an important instrument in maintaining friendly terms between these countries, the bilateral friendship treaties that Western actors so actively promoted were of limited use in influencing policies of multilingualism. When bilateral treaties were concluded, each of the parties involved came away with a different interpretation of the outcome.

The home state (Romanian and Slovak) governments considered Hungarian groups internal minorities and sought to maintain control over language policy. The kin-state (Hungary) supported Hungarian minority demands, including the aim to Europeanize minority policy, that is, to create an enforceable European code on the equal rights of minority groups for cultural reproduction. The EU responded to these appeals with a flexible strategy: Western officials pressed Romanian and Slovak governments to adopt minority-friendly policies (rather than leaving the matter entirely at the domestic level) even in the absence of clear European standards on language protection. At the same time, these officials were wary of territorial fragmentation and therefore demonstrated reluctance in explicitly advocating institutional forms that would empower the minority. Instead of taking the matter to the European level, they insisted that these states sign friendship treaties to settle conflicting views over minority protection bilaterally.

This dual strategy toward Central and Eastern Europe reflects the influence of two mutually reinforcing conditions: (1) calls for uniform European policies of minority protection compete against demands for maintaining state sovereignty on this issue; and (2) the principal actors of European integration (that is, officials of titular majority governments in Western states) and their counterparts in the post-Communist region (that is, officials of titular majority governments in Central and Eastern states) share an interest in preserving majority ownership of the state's institutions of cultural reproduction. Under such conditions, as Liebich notes, "It is not practical to seek a unified strategy of coping with the minority issue, just as it is unrealistic to expect the peaceful assimilation of minorities along imagined Western patterns."[128]

Ultimately, the dynamics of the multilingualism debate reveals the extraordinary difficulties of creating European laws on multilingualism despite the normative recognition of the value of linguistic diversity and the need for language protection. The legacy of the Westphalian nation-state model remains powerful, as all participants of the debate attribute special significance to language and national cultural reproduction, even as they desire membership in an integrated Europe.

---

[128] Liebich, "Ethnic Minorities," 118.

Chapter 4

Language and the Official Domain

In states incorporating multiple language groups engaged in parallel processes of cultural reproduction, the issue of language use in the domains of government and public institutions goes to the heart of debates about the social contract. What language or languages can citizens use to interact with public officials in the state in which they live and with one another through public institutions? What language can they use to display public signs, such as names of settlements and institutions? These are questions that all states encompassing multilingual societies must address.

The ordering of languages in a multilingual society can be described as one of language dominance, language predominance, or language parity. Language dominance means that a single language becomes the exclusive official language in specific domains, usually including various levels of legislation, justice, public administration, the military, and education.[1] Language predominance emerges in a multilingual society when language policy allows the limited use of different languages in certain public places and institutions, but speakers of the one dominant language can function without restrictions in all public institutions and places in all localities of the state, while speakers of other languages are expected to learn the language of the

---

[1] Laitin called the establishment of language dominance "language rationalization." Laitin, *Language Repertoires,* ix. The term *language dominance* is used here in order to capture the hierarchy of power in the relationship and also to indicate that the ordering of languages evolves not simply by purposeful action, as "rationalization" suggests, but as a result of a complex process in which speakers (individuals and groups, elites and public) empower certain languages over others.

dominant group in order to function fully in the same settings.[2] Language parity means the coequal status of languages. In a situation of language parity, monolingual speakers of each of the languages concerned can function fully in the public sphere, including interactions in the official domain. Dominance, predominance, and parity may characterize relations among languages in an entire state territory, substate regions, or individual localities within a state.

Most contemporary democracies with multilingual composition accommodate linguistic diversity in their institutions in some form. Some states, such as Belgium, Canada, Finland, India, and Switzerland, have explicit policies that declare more than one language to be official. Others, such as the United States, rely on the norms of common practice to determine the conditions of multilingualism in public institutions and spaces. To describe the difference between explicit and implicit rules, scholars distinguish between "official language" and "norm-and-accommodation" approaches.[3] Regardless of which approach a state takes, however, the policies that establish the rules of linguistic exchange are key components of the social contract. Even where these rules are not openly contested and negotiated, political elites make choices about language policy, and language policy has far-reaching consequences for fundamental principles of equality, rights and responsibilities, and inclusion.[4]

When national majorities and minorities are renegotiating the social contract after a major regime shift, the significance of establishing a broadly acceptable relationship among languages in the public domain becomes particularly apparent. Post-Communist Romania and Slovakia represent such processes of re-negotiation; from the beginning of the 1990s, fierce legislative battles developed in these countries over the ordering of languages in the official domain. As the Hungarian minority viewed itself as a homeland community, the debate in both states centered on the question of whether minority languages can or should be included in the following settings: the marking of territory and public places (especially place names) and government (including official publications and documents, sessions of government at various levels, and communication between citizens and public officials). The battles over language use in these settings demonstrated that both majority and minority viewed language as a marker of

[2] This definition adopts Karklins's notion of language predominance as "the ability of a monolingual person to function fully in a multilingual environment." Karklins, *Ethnopolitics and Transition,* 144.
[3] Patten and Kymlicka, "Language Rights and Political Theory," 33.
[4] Barry, *Culture and Equality,* 107; David D. Laitin and Rob Reich, "A Liberal Democratic Approach to Language Justice," 80, Kymlicka and Patten, "Language Rights and Political Theory," 3, and Ruth-Mario Marin, "Language Rights: Exploring the Competing Rationales," 55, all in *Language Rights and Political Theory,* ed. Kymlicka and Patten.

legitimate authority over a "national space," including the territory they considered their "homeland" and the institutions of government in the democratizing state.

The significance of language as a marker of "homeland" rights was most apparent in the battles over the display of Hungarian language place names in both states. Throughout the first years after Communism, the language of territory markers remained a forcefully contested issue in the Romanian and Slovak parliaments. From the majority perspective, the underlying question was whether the display of minority language place names threatened the state's territorial integrity. Majority nationalists and moderates in both cases gave different answers to this question. Majority nationalists preferred to exclude minority language place names. The moderates were willing to allow the use of these place names where minorities lived in significant numbers, but they were disinclined to also recognize them as coequal "official" territory markers. From the perspective of the Hungarian minority, the question was whether the legitimate presence of the Hungarian community in the state could gain full recognition unless the places where Hungarians lived could also be posted in the Hungarian language. The Hungarian minority parties in Romania and Slovakia argued that in a legitimate democratic state, minority communities should have the right to officially recognized territory markers in their language. Clearly, participants in this contestation viewed place names as markers of rightful ownership over domains that each considered their national space. The use of Hungarian place names was a vital issue for both majority and Hungarian minority political actors because these names signified the presence of Hungarian communities in the territory. Perhaps even more importantly, historical Hungarian place names were politically salient: they preserved a Hungarian link with the history of these spaces. Consequently, the placement and removal of bilingual signs became a continuing source of conflict in the Hungarian-inhabited regions of Transylvania and southern Slovakia.

The question of whether government could or should "speak" in a minority language was similarly divisive. From the perspective of the majority, the underlying question was whether national sovereignty suffered if government spoke in a minority language. In both Romania and Slovakia, nationalists and moderates disagreed on this question. Committed to a unitary nation-state, Slovak and Romanian nationalists opted for language *dominance,* aiming to establish their language as the exclusive marker of the official domain. Moderate majority elites were willing to allow limited use of Hungarian in official interactions. Because they did not accept a pluralist (multinational) state model, however, moderates were unwilling to recognize language parity under any circumstances. Instead, they sought to maintain a clear *predominance* of the majority language across the entire territory of the state. From the perspective of the Hungarian minority, the question was whether members of the Hungarian minority would receive their share of popular sovereignty if their language was not recognized as a legitimate language of government. The Hungarian minority elites in Romania and Slovakia favored a multinational pluralist state and demanded a share of the official domain for their language, arguing for institutional bilingualism in areas where the minority represented a significant percentage of the population and for language *parity* in the territorial units where they comprised a local majority.

The Nationalist Majority and the Pursuit of Language Dominance

For the better part of the 1990s, political elites in charge of post-Communist institutionalization in both Romania and Slovakia committed themselves to a "nation-state" project, declared the majority language as the only official language, and endeavored to mark the territory of the state exclusively in the majority language. Together, these policies reflected a desire to establish "titular" ownership over the state, in both the spatial projection of authority and control over institutions of self-government. There were, however, differences in the degrees to which Romanian and Slovak nationalists sought to exclude minority languages. In Slovakia, the goal to establish an independent nation-state heightened the nationalists' desire to exclude minority languages from public spaces and all forms of official interaction. Romanian nationalists sought to consolidate a national state within already established boundaries and pursued a somewhat less exclusionary policy of language dominance, allowing limited use of minority languages in selected areas of the official sphere of interaction.

The Slovak nationalists articulated a direct link between the exclusive use of Slovak literary language in the official domain and Slovak territorial sovereignty. Prominent linguists introduced the concept of "linguistic sovereignty" to the debate about statehood in early 1990. Linguistic sovereignty, in the definition of linguist Ján Kačala, meant the establishment of the proper use of the Slovak language and the dominant status of this language in relation to other languages.[5] Accordingly, the goal was both to enforce a unitary Slovak literary standard ("corpus planning") and to establish the

---

[5] Ján Kačala, "Naša jazyková suverenita," *Slovenský národ,* June 14, 1990. See also Kačala, "Co je to jazyková suverenita," in *Slovenčina—vec politická?* (Martin, Slovakia: Matica slovenská, 1994), 162–69.

dominance of this language in the name of national sovereignty ("status planning").[6]

Nationalist linguists gained a prominent role in advancing the idea that national sovereignty required language dominance. Kačala, for instance, took part in drafting the first language law proposal (the so-called Matica bill discussed in chapter 2), which restricted the use of minority languages to private interaction.[7] A revised version of this bill submitted by the Slovak National Party (SNS) permitted minority speakers to use their languages in certain public spheres (such as culture, information, art, and religious services) but excluded non-Slovak languages from official communications altogether.[8] In 1990, liberal and moderate politicians in the Slovak government prevented the Matica bill from passing and adopted a less exclusive law. By 1995, however, as power relations changed dramatically in newly independent Slovakia, the alliance between SNS and the governing HZDS secured the success of the nationalist project of language dominance. Anna Maliková, then the vice president of the SNS, explained in 1996 that her party already "supported the Matica slovenská proposal . . . in 1990, because we hold that language defines a people and the state, in other words, the Slovak state equals the Slovak people, which equals the Slovak language."[9]

The 1995 State Language Act was a clear expression of the dominant Slovak elite's desire to mark the state domain exclusively in the majority language, rejecting the idea of Slovakia as a multinational state. This law contained no specific references to minority language use in government. It did, however, establish the hegemony of Slovak by stating: "The state language (i.e. the standard Slovak language, codified by the Ministry of Culture) is an expression of the sovereignty of the Slovak Republic. . . . The Slovak language is the national language of the Slovaks, who comprise the only state-forming element of the Slovak Republic. . . . The state language enjoys priority over all languages used on the territory of the Slovak Republic."[10] The arguments that HZDS and SNS deputies presented in the parliamentary debate demonstrated that language and territory were closely linked in the nationalist perspective.[11]

---

[6] For definitions of these terms, see chapter 2, page 51.

[7] This proposal was published in June 1990 in *Slovenské národné noviny.* The original Slovak text of the proposal was reprinted in Berényi, *Nyelvországlás,* Appendix 1.

[8] Berényi, *Nyelvországlás,* Appendix 2.

[9] Maliková, author interview, Bratislava, Slovakia, April 24, 1996.

[10] "Law on the State Language of the Slovak Republic" ("Zákon Národnej Rady Slovenskej Republiky o štátnom jazyku Slovenskej Republiky"), no. 270, 1995, in *Zbierka zákonov Slovenskej republiky,* preamble, Paragraph 1, p. 1.

[11] Excerpts from the parliamentary debate published in the Coexistence newsletter *Figyelő* (November 1995), 6–7.

The 1995 language law contained no specific provisions on minority language use, and Hungarian minority politicians pointed out that this law left a gap in minority language legislation by canceling the 1990 language bill—which had allowed at least limited use of minority languages in official contact. They also charged that nationalist government officials had taken advantage of this legislative hiatus to limit the use of minority languages.[12] The Slovak nationalists had no intention of updating the provisions for minority language use in the 1990 law; during its tenure, the Mečiar government also refused Hungarian requests to adopt an equitable law.[13]

The Slovak nationalists were so resolute in their effort to establish Slovak language dominance that they restricted even the use of minority language personal names in official communications. Consequently, the form in which personal names were recorded in the birth register and used in official documents became a hotly contested political issue. In the absence of newer legislation on the issue, officials of the Mečiar government defended their positions by referring to the 1990 language law, according to which all official documents had to be completed in Slovak, and to a 1977 law that stipulated that parents choose a name from an official name list to record their newborn children in the birth register. For Hungarian parents, this list provided eighty-three names, all of which were either commonly used Hungarian names or Christian names with both Slovak and Hungarian equivalents. If they had questions about the adequacy of a particular name, parents were required to consult with the Linguistics Institute of the Slovak Academy of Sciences, though the recommendation of the institute was not legally binding. Local registrars made the final decision about the registering of individuals. Before 1989, the use of the official name list was mandatory, but in practice birth registrars were very liberal.[14] After the adoption of the 1990 language law, however, many registrars refused to register Hungarian names. As nationalists gained power, government officials declared that the use of personal names in Slovakia had to comply with the laws of the Slovak language. One law of Slovak grammar that the Hungarians vehemently fought was the mandatory use in official documents of the Slovak-language feminine name suffix "–ová" at the end of family names for all women.[15] Slovak linguists in favor of nationalist language policies

---

[12] József Berényi, Hungarian Civic Party education and language policy specialist, author interview, April 25, 1996; see also MK criticism in "Position of the Hungarian Coalition in Slovakia on the Minority Rights in the Slovak Republic Under the Third Government of Prime Minister Mečiar (1994–1996)," undated MK document, 2.

[13] Dostál, "Minorities," 40.

[14] Gizella Szabómihály, linguist, author interview, Bratislava, Slovakia, April 20, 1996.

[15] Zalabai, *Mit ér a nyelvünk, ha magyar?* 194–99, 294, 298–99.

argued that a non-Slovak personal name placed in a Slovak sentence had to assume a form acceptable in Slovak grammar.[16]

Nationalist politicians were eager to embrace this argument in the language debate. Interior Minister Ladislav Pittner declared in April 1992 that the registration of a personal name was legal only if it adhered to the grammatical rules of the Slovak language.[17] Minister of Culture Dušan Slobodník, a linguist by training, articulated the same position in his succinct statement that "language is the law above any other law."[18] National Letters Ministry Director Milan Ferko called the writing of "foreign women's surnames" without the suffix "–ová" a "conflictual interference with the rules of literary Slovak."[19]

In Romania, the Hungarian claim that the official use of minority language personal names was a fundamental right triggered no conflict. The Romanian nationalists designed legislation that established Romanian language dominance in the official domain without the complete exclusion of minority languages. Although this language policy was less exclusive than the one pursued by the Slovak nationalists, it also represented a step back from the Romanian constitution of the Ceaușescu period, which had entitled minorities to use their language in public administration and required public officials in minority-inhabited localities to be competent in the minority language.[20] The 1991 law mandated minority language use in only one type of official contact: dissemination of local council decisions where national minorities were represented in "significant numbers," the definition of which was never specified.[21] While a completed version of the law published in April 1996 (under the Iliescu regime) added a new provision allowing minority citizens to be informed of the local council agenda in their language,[22] the Romanian

[16] Ján Dorula, linguist, author interview, Bratislava, Slovakia, June 5, 1996.

[17] Pittner's letter is quoted in Zalabai, *Mit ér a nyelvünk, ha magyar?* 249–51.

[18] "Jazyk je zákon nad zákonom." Quoted in ibid., 282.

[19] Ferko, "Zásady zákona Národnej Rady Slovenskej Republiky o štátnom jazyku Slovenskej Republiky," *Slovenská Republika,* August 26, 1995, 10.

[20] József Somai, "A 69–es Közigazgatási Törvény és a Helyi Önkormányzatok Európai Chartája," in *Valóság és lehetőség* (Csíkszereda: Pro Print, 1995), 25.

[21] Law on local public administration No. 69/1991, Article 30. "Legea administrației publice locale," published in *Monitorul Oficial al României,* part I, no. 238, November 28, 1991, was completed by the Law No. 24/1996, published in *Monitorul Oficial,* part I, no. 76, April 13, 1996, and republished in *Monitorul Oficial,* part I, No.79, April 18, 1996. (Throughout the analysis, where the 1996 version includes no additions to the original text, I will refer to the text of Law No. 69/1991.) The territorial units specified are communes (larger villages; in Romanian the word is *comune*), towns, and counties (Article 2). Hungarian critics have pointed out that smaller villages ("*sate*") were excluded. See Somai, "A 69-es helyi Közigazgatási Törvény és a Helyi Önkormányzatok Európai Chartája," 25.

[22] Law on local public administration No. 69/1991 as completed by the Law No. 24/1996, republished in *Monitorul Oficial* Part I, No. 79, April 18, 1996. See Article 23, paragraph 6.

law on local public administration at the same time prohibited the use of minority languages among elected councilors during their sessions.[23] Minority citizens were allowed to address officials in their own language, but local governments were not required to employ officials who could respond in the minority language. Officials could respond in the minority language or use an interpreter. If citizens wrote to officials using the minority language, they were required to attach a notarized Romanian translation.[24] As both Hungarian and Romanian critics have pointed out, these restrictions indicated that the Iliescu regime had no intention of facilitating the use of minority languages in official communication. While it did not completely exclude the use of minority languages, the law rendered these languages subordinate in the official domain.[25] (See table 4.1 on majority nationalist positions.)

In parliamentary opposition after 1998, the Slovak nationalists continued to regard the adoption of a minority language law as a threat to Slovak statehood. HZDS leader Vladimír Mečiar declared that "a state divided in its language will disintegrate otherwise as well."[26] SNS leader Ján Slota stated that "the minority language law will become the first nail in the coffin

TABLE 4.1
Majority nationalist positions on the inclusion of minority languages in government

	Publications, documents	Sessions of government	Communication between officials and citizens
Slovakia	Excluded Use of minority personal names must comply with Slovak grammar	Excluded	Excluded
Romania	Local councils may publish agendas and decisions in the minority language	Excluded	Citizens may use minority language Public officials not re- quired to respond (may use interpreter) In written petitions, notarized Romanian translation required

Note: Required minority threshold in Romania unspecified ("significant numbers")

[23] Law on local public administration No. 69/1991, Article 26.
[24] Law on local public administration No. 69/1991, Article 54.
[25] For analyses of these provisions, see Andreescu and Weber, *Evolutions in the D.A.H.R. Conception,* 38; Andreescu, Stan, and Weber, "Două proiecte de lege privind drepturile minorităţile naţionale," 86; and Somai, "Az 69-es Helyi Közigazgatási Törvény és a Helyi Önkormányzatok Európai Chartája," 24–25.
[26] Mečiar made this statement in an answer to a journalist of the Hungarian daily *Új Szó,* May 11, 1999.

of independent Slovakia."[27] HZDS and SNS fought against the adoption of such a law inside and outside of parliament. They organized public demonstrations and gathered signatures for a referendum in which they hoped to demonstrate that Slovak society rejected institutionalized minority language use in official communications.[28]

Like their Slovak counterparts, Romanian nationalists fought vigorously against the new government's effort to liberalize minority language use after the November 1996 regime change. In the parliamentary debates between mid-1997 and mid-1999, they called the government's emergency decree unconstitutional and warned that allowing the use of Hungarian in local government threatened the integrity of the Romanian state. They claimed that the true intention behind Hungarian language claims was federalization and the eventual detachment of Transylvania from Romania.[29] After another reversal of fortunes in 2000, the returning Iliescu government assumed a moderate approach to nation-building and completed the parliamentary process of adopting the liberalizing legislation its predecessors had introduced in 1997. Meanwhile, the Greater Romanian Party in opposition remained consistent in its fight for complete minority language exclusion.

The significance of territoriality in the contestation over language use was most visible in the battles over the display of Hungarian language place names in both states. Territory markings became a domain in which majority nationalists in both Romania and Slovakia sought complete exclusion of minority languages, triggering vehement contestations by Hungarian minority parties. As historic Hungarian place names began appearing in southern Slovakia after the fall of the Communist regime, Slovak nationalists warned that the Hungarians were aiming at recreating the map of "Greater Hungary."[30] In the view of this group of Slovak elites, national sovereignty required the exclusive use of Slovak names for towns and cities, streets and squares, and geographic places of all kinds in all public displays and publications—even in the media.[31] The furthest that Slovak nationalists intended to go in allowing the display of minority language names was to

---

[27] Slota quoted in *Új Szó,* June 8, 1999.

[28] *Forum News,* June 7, 14, 15, 1999; *Új Szó,* June 1, 19.

[29] An especially interesting article by former Reform Minister Ilie Şerbănescu in *Adevărul,* October 8, 1998. See also *Népújság,* December 12, 1998; *Szabadság,* December 16, 1998; *RMDSZ Tájékoztató,* April 27, 28, 1999; *Transilvania Jurnal,* June 24, 1999; and *HHRF Monitor,* December 8, 1999.

[30] See Štefan Hrčka commentary in *Pravda,* September 6, 1993. Relevant statements of SNS deputies are cited in *Új Szó,* January 29, 1994.

[31] See quote from Law No. 517/1990 on territorial and administrative districts in Berényi (1994), 118. See also Milan Ferko, "Zásady zákona Národnej Rady Slovenskej Republiky o štátnom jazyku Slovenskej Republiky," 10.

permit bilingual signs for minority cultural and social organizations.[32] After the adoption of the 1990 language law, nationalist government officials issued orders for the forcible removal of bilingual place names.[33] The minister of transportation fired the presidents of four road maintenance offices in counties that were slow to comply with the ministerial orders.[34] By the end of December 1992, the removal of Hungarian signs was complete.

During the period of nationalist coalition governments in Slovakia, efforts to suppress Hungarian place names from public sight went to considerable lengths. At Slovak state television, Hungarian editors were instructed not to use Hungarian place names—even in the Hungarian language program.[35] The Hungarian language newspaper *Komáromi Lapok* was fined for using the city's Hungarian name, *Komárom,* in its title instead of the Slovak *Komárno.*[36] After considerable European pressure, the Slovak government approved a draft law in November 1993 on non-Slovak place names. Instead of legalizing the use of Hungarian place names, however, this law provided only for the use of names translated or transcribed from Slovak into Hungarian. The Hungarian parties and the Slovak moderates in parliamentary opposition considered this restriction excessive; with only HZDS and SNS deputies voting for it, the parliament rejected this bill at the end of January 1994. The nationalists strongly opposed the "road sign law" accepted by the moderates later in 1994, which liberalized (unofficial) bilingual designation of localities with more than 20 percent minority population, and fought consistently for its reversal.

As had their Slovak counterparts, the Romanian nationalizing elite refused to allow the display of Hungarian place names (see table 4.2). Although the law on local public administration adopted in Romania in 1991 was more liberal than Slovak nationalist legislation on language use in local government, it failed to legalize the display of minority language place names. Despite strong domestic and international pressure, this policy remained unchanged until the end of the Iliescu regime in November 1996. After this regime changed, the former ruling parties remained consistent in their advocacy of their earlier stance and fought against the new government's effort to amend the restrictive 1991 law. After the moderate Romanian government issued Emergency Decree No. 22 in 1997 that provided for the placement of bilingual signs in localities where the minority comprised at least 20 percent of the population, nationalist political leaders in opposition called on local

---

[32] See "Matica law" in Berényi, *Nyelvországlás,* Appendix 2.
[33] Zalabai, *Mit ér a nyelvünk, ha magyar?* 20–34.
[34] Ibid., 85–86, 94–95.
[35] See letter in *Új szó,* December 3, 1992.
[36] *Új szó,* January 18, 1993.

TABLE 4.2
Positions on minority language territory markers in Romania and Slovakia

Majority nationalist positions	
Slovak	Excluded
Romanian	Excluded
Hungarian minority positions*	
Hungarian in Slovakia	Bilingual signs
	Use of historical Hungarian names in all localities***
Hungarian in Romania	Bilingual signs
Majority moderate positions **	
Slovak	1990: Excluded
	1994: Informative signs only
	Excluded: localities named after Slovak historical figures
	1999: Bilingual signs within city boundaries
Romanian	Bilingual signs

*Required minority threshold is 10%
**Required minority threshold is 20%
***Historical Hungarian place names contested only in Slovakia

officials to disregard the decree as unconstitutional and encouraged the public to remove Hungarian language sign boards.[37] Nationalist local authorities and other political activists vehemently fought against the posting of bilingual signs in localities eligible under the new regulation. Some mayors used financial means to block the placement of bilingual signs.[38] Public acts of vandalism against Hungarian place markers occurred in several localities in Transylvania. In Cluj county, according to local newspaper reports, by March 1998 only thirteen out of the eighty-six eligible localities had placed bilingual sign boards.[39] In Cluj, the city that both Hungarians and Romanians in Transylvania regarded as their cultural center, ultra-nationalist mayor Gheorghe Funar refused to allow the placement of Hungarian language markers altogether and encouraged public acts of vandalism against them.[40] He was unwilling to tolerate Hungarian language signs even at the city's Hungarian-language high schools.[41]

Similar conflicts occurred in other Transylvanian localities. In many places, nationalist-dominated city councils replaced Hungarian street names.[42] Opposition to Hungarian place markers turned particularly uncivil in the

---

[37] *RMDSZ Sajtófigyelő,* April 3, 1998; and *Romániai Magyar Szó,* February 27, 1999.
[38] *Szabadság,* October 18, 1997, November 15, 1997; and *Romániai Magyar Szó,* May 11, 1999.
[39] *Actualitatea Clujeană,* March 20, 1998.
[40] The leading Hungarian daily in Cluj, *Szabadság,* regularly covered Funar's actions between August–November 1997 and January–February 1998. The Romanian newspapers *Ştirea* and *Adevărul de Cluj* voiced arguments opposing bilingual signs.
[41] RMDSZ vice president József Kötő, author interview, Cluj, Romania, May 10, 1996.
[42] *Romániai Magyar Szó,* October 9, 1998, April 1, 1999.

city of Tîrgu-Mureş, where the ethnic Romanian population had increased dramatically during the decades of Communist rule to approximately 50 percent.[43] In counties where the nationalists had less political influence, the placement of bilingual signs was more successful. There were few instances of opposition, for instance, in the two counties with overwhelmingly Hungarian populations, Harghita and Covasna, as well as in Satu-Mare county where the government-appointed prefect was a member of the RMDSZ.[44] Even in these counties, there were occasional incidents of vandalism, and the perpetrators were rarely brought to justice.[45]

The nationalists in both Romania and Slovakia were committed to maintaining language dominance in places where both the majority and the minority perceived strong historical significance. Slovak nationalists fiercely opposed the use of historical Hungarian place names, which the Czechoslovak government had replaced with the names of Slovak historical figures in 1948.[46] In Romania, the contestation of historical names was particularly heated in Cluj. After the 1997 amendment transferred authority for the naming and renaming of places to local councils, ethnic Hungarians fought to regain some of the historical Hungarian street names in the city, with little success. The Romanian nationalists, however, showed no intention of compromising on this issue.[47]

As the Hungarian minority parties in both Romania and Slovakia linked their language claims to their respective demographic compositions, nationalists in both countries tried to alter the ethnic composition of mixed towns and regions to limit the number of territorial units where minority languages could be used under such conditions. For the Slovak nationalists, administrative redistricting appeared to be the most effective method. The Hungarian minority, constituting approximately 10 percent of the population, lives mostly in southern Slovakia, on land that stretches from east to west along the Hungarian border.[48] A new administrative structure adopted in 1996 by the Mečiar government created regions that stretched

---

[43] *Szabadság,* October 4, 1997; *News Mirror-DAHR MTI Press Service,* January 7, 1998; *Népújság,* March 24, 1998; *Evenimentul zilei,* February 23, 1998; and *Adevărul,* February 9, 1998.

[44] *Szabadság,* September 20, 1997, January 15, 1998.

[45] *Erdélyi napló,* February 3, 1998. In one reported case in Tîrgu-Mureş, one perpetrator was identified and charged in court. *Népújság,* March 24, 1998.

[46] In an interpellation in the Slovak parliament on November 15, 1999, Coexistence deputy Edit Bauer gave a history of legislation on the "forcible" renaming of Hungarian settlements. See *Új szó,* November 16, 1991.

[47] *Szabadság,* March 14, 22, 1997, September 19, 1997, March 28, 1998, April 27, 1998, November 13, 1998, March 17, 1999.

[48] For comprehensive statistics on demographic changes in the Hungarian community, see László Gyurgyík, *A szlovákiai magyarság a népszámlálási és a népmozgalmi adatok tükrében* (Bratislava: Kalligram, 1994).

from north to south, instantly making the Hungarians a minority in each new region. Under the new territorial design, Hungarians would be able to use their language in regional government in only two of eight regions even if the Slovak political elites agreed to the Hungarian demand for language use in regional government with a 20 percent minority threshold. If these elites had accepted language use in regional government with a 10 percent minimum, Hungarian could have been used in only four of eight regions. The new territorial design also ensured that Slovaks would become a majority in all but two of the seventy-nine new districts.[49]

Although no redistricting took place in Romania after the fall of the Ceauşescu regime, a series of territorial changes had occurred during the previous period. First, the 1952 constitution created a Hungarian Autonomous Region in Transylvania. In 1968, this region was eliminated when the current administrative map of forty counties was drawn. The 1968 territorial restructuring, however, left two counties in the middle of Romania with overwhelmingly Hungarian populations (Harghita and Covasna).[50] Since then, Romanian governments have concentrated considerable resources on strengthening the Romanian presence in these counties. The Ceauşescu regime facilitated the movement of ethnic Romanians into Harghita and Covasna. The Iliescu regime continued the effort to strengthen the status of the Romanian language in this region. Notwithstanding Hungarian demands, this government refused to appoint ethnic Hungarian prefects in these counties. In May 1996, Harghita prefect Doru Voşloban spoke emphatically about the necessity and difficulty of attracting new settlers, primarily professionals, from other parts of the country. He also articulated the view that Romanian language and literature should receive greater respect in this overwhelmingly Hungarian-inhabited county.[51] As part of the PDSR electoral campaign before the 1996 local elections, visiting members of the Iliescu government promised ethnic Romanian residents of the county that they would increase the number of Romanian language publications in libraries and bookstores.[52] These promises also reflected nationalist majority desires to establish language dominance in all regions of the country.

[49] These districts were majority-Hungarian under the old administrative system. The 1996 restructuring, however, increased the number of districts from thirty-eight to seventy-nine in such a way that only these two districts retained a majority of Hungarian citizens. Krivý, "Slovakia and Its Regions," 55–56; and Dostál, "Minorities," 41.
[50] Gábor Hunya, Tamás Réti, Andrea R. Süle, László Tóth, *Románia 1944–1990* (Budapest: Atlantisz, 1990), 161–64.
[51] Doru Voşloban, Miercurea-Ciuc (Harghita County) prefectorate, author interview, Miercurea-Ciuc, Romania, May 28, 1996.
[52] PDSR campaign meeting, recorded by the author, Miercurea-Ciuc, May 24, 1996.

The Minority: Bilingualism to Language Parity

Hungarian parties in Romania and Slovakia articulated a consistent position of institutionalized bilingualism in areas where Hungarians comprised a sizeable percentage of the population. Institutional bilingualism means that two languages are recognized in governmental institutions.[53] Where Hungarians constituted a local or regional majority, the Hungarian parties claimed the right to language parity. All Hungarian minority proposals for language policy argued for language rights on the basis of the principle of territoriality rather than that of personality. According to the principle of personality, "language rights follow *persons* wherever in the state they may choose to live," whereas the territoriality principle accords language rights depending on the part of the territory of the state in which speakers reside.[54] Hungarians claimed rights to a "native land" in specific parts of their states and argued that in these territories the official use of the community's language in territory markings and government was a necessary part of popular sovereignty.[55]

The importance of the homeland community concept from the Hungarian perspective was particularly evident in demands for the right to preserve and display their historical place names (see table 4.2). Hungarian parties included this demand in their legislative proposals and argued for it at home and at various international fora.[56] In both cases, Hungarian minority politicians looked for ways to reinterpret restrictive legislation favorably and called on their constituencies to display Hungarian space markers despite the difficulties they faced in some settlements. In their efforts to circumvent the limitations of the 1990 language law in Slovakia, for instance, Hungarian leaders referred to bilingual signs as "information boards" and issued

[53] Government institutions are considered bilingual if they recognize two languages. See Alan Patten, "What Kind of Bilingualism?" in *Language Rights and Political Theory,* ed. Will Kymlicka and Alan Patten, 296.

[54] Ibid., 297.

[55] The right to the "native land" was expressed in the MKDM-Coexistence "Draft of Fundamental Principles of a Constitutional Law" (July 1993), 2. A Coexistence analysis of the situation of Hungarians charged that the policies of consecutive Slovak governments threatened the existence of Hungarians in their historical settlements. See "Hungarians in the Second Slovak Republic (1993–1995–?)," Coexistence document, Bratislava, Slovakia, June 28, 1995. RMDSZ President Béla Markó expressed the view that the language rights of historical national communities were a necessary part of democratic government. Author interview, Tîrgu-Mureş, Romania, June 26, 1996. This concept of language rights was developed in the legislative proposals of the Hungarians in Romania and Slovakia.

[56] See 1990 Coexistence-MKDM proposal in Berényi, *Nyelvországlás,* Appendix 5; "Law on the Use of the Languages of National Minorities and Ethnic Groups: Draft Law of the Hungarian Coalition, Slovakia," MK, 1996; and "Draft Bill of a Group of MP's of the National Council of the Slovak Republic on the Use of the Languages of the National Minorities," RMDSZ draft, 44.

statements of support for local governments in the Hungarian settlements that refused to comply with governmental orders to remove these signs.[57] They encouraged local councils to organize referenda to demonstrate public support for the return to historical Hungarian names. Indeed, public referenda were held in several localities of southern Slovakia, indicating overwhelming support among Hungarians for the old place names.[58] Similarly, RMDSZ leaders in Romania called on local officials to implement the 1997 emergency decree that allowed the display of bilingual place names immediately after its publication, regardless of the long delay in parliamentary ratification and the constitutional court's unfavorable ruling about this decree.[59] Hungarian minority politicians also called on their Romanian governing partners to take a stand against organized acts of vandalism against Hungarian place signs.[60]

Hungarians in both Romania and Slovakia demanded protection against what they perceived as deliberate, systematic modifications of the demographic composition of traditionally Hungarian-inhabited regions. The RMDSZ minority law proposal submitted to the Romanian parliament in November 1993 declared that national minorities "shall have the right to live freely and without interference in their homeland" and "to maintain the historically developed patterns of their settlements."[61] In Slovakia, a joint Coexistence and MKDM draft national minority bill submitted to the Slovak parliament in July 1993 expressed the same claim in unambiguous terms when it called for the right of minority national communities "to have a native land . . . as well as the right for protection against the deliberate transformation of the demographic structure of the regions inhabited mostly by the minority communities."[62] The MKP's 1999 minority language proposal also aimed to outlaw "any administrative measures" that would alter existing demographic conditions.[63] From the beginning of the debate over administrative restructuring, the Hungarian parties argued intensely against the Mečiar government's plan for redistricting and for preserving the territorial sub-units in southern Slovakia where the Hungarians continued to comprise

---

[57] "Nem tiltja egyetlen törvény sem!" *Új Szó,* November 12, 1992.
[58] Zalabai, *Mit ér a nyelvünk, ha magyar?* 46–65.
[59] *Szabadság,* September 20, 1997, May 25, 1998.
[60] *Szabadság,* February 9, 11, 1998.
[61] Democratic Alliance of Hungarians in Romania, *Documents,* no. 1, pp. 38–39.
[62] "Draft of Fundamental Principles of a Constitutional Law of the National Council (Parliament) of the Slovak Republic about the Legal Status of National and Ethnic Minority Communities in the Slovak Republic," Hungarian Christian Democratic Movement—Coexistence, undated, 2.
[63] "Draft Bill of a Group of MP's of the National Council of the Slovak Republic on the Use of the Languages of the National Minorities." MKP document, paragraph 2, Article 5.

a regional majority.[64] The Hungarian proposals would have achieved a notion of "almost parity" in the ethnic composition of the southern Slovakian
region. According to Coexistence calculations, 7 percent of the ethnic Slovak
population would have lived within Hungarian-dominated administrative
units and 10 percent of the ethnic Hungarian population within Slovak-
dominated units.[65]

Hungarian parties in Romania and Slovakia articulated virtually identical
positions on language use in the official domain. Conversations with Hungarian minority leaders as well as articles published in the leading Hungarian
language periodicals in the two countries indicated that each group of Hungarian minority elites followed the other's activities and studied the other's
legislative proposals closely. Their communication was also facilitated by
the Hungarian government's Office for Hungarians Living Abroad, which
maintained relations with Hungarian parties outside Hungary and organized regular meetings among minority leaders from neighboring states.[66]
(See chapter 3 for a discussion of the Hungarian state's role in the language
debate.)

A commonly shared view among Hungarian minority elites in Romania
and Slovakia was that members of the Hungarian minority would become
equal citizens only if their language was recognized in government at the
local, regional, and, to a limited degree, central levels of government. In
Romania, the RMDSZ language bill provided minority deputies with the
right to speak in the parliament on special occasions in their own language.[67]
In Slovakia, the Hungarian Coalition listed among the "serious negative im-
pacts" of the 1995 state language act the law's failure to grant minority citizens the right to use their language in the Slovak Parliament.[68] Similarly, in
the parliamentary debate of the 1999 minority language law, the Hungarian
Coalition Party proposed an amendment that would entitle minority speakers to communicate in their language with the office of the Slovak president,
the parliament, and other offices of the central government.[69]

---

[64] These proposals were included in the Komarno declaration, which became part of the Hungarian
Coalition agreement of 1994; "Szerződés a Magyar Kereszténydemokrata Mozgalom, az Együttélés
és a Magyar Polgári Párt sokoldalú együttműködéséről és koalíciójáról," in *Közösségünk szolgálatában*
(Bratislava: MKDM, 1990–1995), 131.
[65] See Kevin Krause, "Slovak-Hungarian Issues in the Political Party System of Slovakia," paper
presented at the Association for the Study of Nationalities, Columbia University, New York, 1996.
[66] Csaba Tabajdi, head of the Governmental Office for Hungarians Living Abroad (HTMH),
author interview, Budapest, Hungary, June 10, 1996.
[67] "Law on National Minorities and Autonomous Communities (Draft)," *Documents* (Cluj:
Democratic Alliance of Hungarians in Romania, 1994), no. 1, Article 37.
[68] "Position of the Hungarian Coalition in Slovakia on the Minority Rights in the Slovak
Republic," 1.
[69] For the amendments proposed by the MKP, see *Új Szó,* July 8, 1999.

Demands to include the Hungarian language at the regional and local levels of government focused on two kinds of territorial units. Where Hungarians represented a regional or local majority (over 50 percent of the population), the Hungarian elites envisioned equal "official status" for the Hungarian language. In territories where the minority composed at least 10 percent of the population, they asked for institutionalized bilingualism— without formally declared official status for the minority language.

In Romania, the Hungarian party conceived of regions where Hungarians composed over 50 percent of the population as "regional autonomies." The RMDSZ's draft minority law defined these territorial units as regional self-governments "of special status," where the Hungarian language would enjoy equal official status, meaning that the use of Hungarian would be mandatory along with Romanian in all workings of the public administration.[70] In practice, this provision affected only the two counties in the middle of Romania, Harghita and Covasna. In Slovakia, the first draft minority law prepared by the three-party Hungarian Coalition in 1996 envisioned "equal official language" status for the language of any national minority or ethnic group that constituted the majority in a territorial unit (including local as well as regional levels). According to this bill, "every action taken" by authorities in these territories would have to be bilingual.[71]

In territorial units where the Hungarians composed a minority, the Hungarian parties in both countries asked for the use of their language in official contacts without demanding language parity in such settings. In Romania, the RMDSZ bill defined towns and villages where the minorities composed at least 10 percent of the population as "bilingual or multilingual local units of public administration" and provided for full inclusion of the minority language in all government settings. The draft also required governmental offices to publish official publications and documents in the minority language, to allow minority officials to use their language at sessions of government (if they attached a Romanian translation to the minutes), and to enable minority citizens to use their language in oral and written communication. To this end, these offices were to include among their employees competent users of the minority language.

In Slovakia, the Hungarian parties asked for language inclusion in the same domains and under the same conditions of proportionality. (See table 4.3 on Hungarian minority positions.) Facing more vehement opposition from the majority than their counterparts in Romania, however, the Hungarian parties in Slovakia often moderated either the terms in which they presented their

---

[70] "Law on National Minorities and Autonomous Communities (Draft)," Article 41.
[71] "Law on the Use of the Languages of National Minorities and Ethnic Groups: Draft Law of the Hungarian Coalition, Slovakia" MK document, April 1996, Paragraph 3, Article 1.

demands or the specific provisions of their policy proposals. During the 1990 language debate, the Hungarian Coalition asked for "official bilingualism" in territories where minorities constituted at least 10 percent of the population.[72] In these settings, the offices of regional and local government would be required to guarantee minority language use in the same spheres as those specified in RMDSZ proposals in Romania. The 1996 minority language bill of the three-party Hungarian Coalition provided for the use of minority languages in official contact under the same conditions of proportionality. This draft, however, asked for a more limited space in official settings. Council sessions, for instance, could no longer be held in the minority language. The minority language bill that the Hungarian Coalition Party proposed in 1999 contained the full spectrum of language rights that the 1990 Hungarian Coalition proposal had envisioned—but without the divisive term "official bilingualism." In Slovakia, the Hungarian minority fought an additional battle over one language right that their counterparts in Romania gained without opposition: the official use of minority language personal names. Hungarian parties in Slovakia vehemently opposed restrictions on the use of personal names.[73] In October 1991, Coexistence and MKDM deputies proposed an amendment to the constitution to declare that "citizens belonging to national and ethnic minorities are entitled . . . to have their family and Christian names registered in the birth registry in their mother tongue and to use their names freely and without restrictions also in official contact."[74]

TABLE 4.3
Hungarian minority positions on the inclusion of minority languages in government

	Publications, documents	Sessions of government	Communication between officials and citizens
Hungarians in Slovakia	Forms, decrees, public information Equal official use of Hungarian personal names	(No provision in 1996 proposal) In 1999 proposal: Elected officials entitled; bilingual documentation required	Two-way communication guaranteed
Hungarians in Romania	Forms, decrees, agendas of council meetings, public information	Elected officials entitled; bilingual documentation required	Two-way communication guaranteed

Notes: Required minority threshold is 10%. Where the minority represents a local or regional majority, the minority language should enjoy equal official language status, therefore the spheres of language use need no specification.

[72] The 1990 Coexistence-MKDM proposal published in Berényi, *Nyelvországlás,* Appendix 5.
[73] Zalabai, *Mit ér a nyelvünk, ha magyar?* 254–55.
[74] Ibid., 242–46.

The Slovak parliament did not accept this amendment, but the moderate Moravčik government later liberalized the use of minority personal names in legislation adopted in 1994.[75]

The Moderate Majority and Bilingualism with Language Predominance

Majority moderates did not support the nationalist quest for complete language dominance; rather, they were willing to allow minority citizens to use their language in certain official settings. In the ordering of languages, however, moderates sought to maintain the predominance and, in some settings, dominance of the majority language at all levels of the official domain throughout the entire territory of the state. Because they were in opposition during the significant first years after Communism, the moderates had limited influence on the design of the post-Communist constitutional and legislative framework. After the shift of power in Romania (in November 1996) and Slovakia (September 1998), however, they introduced substantive changes to restrictive language legislation. Although the terms under which minority languages might be included in the official domain remained a matter of continued debate between the moderates and their Hungarian coalition partners, their negotiations resulted in significantly greater language inclusion in both states by the end of the 1990s.

Throughout the language debate, Hungarian demands for language parity remained a significant fault line between the majority moderate and Hungarian minority positions. Both Romanian and Slovak moderates ruled out the idea of language parity at any level, arguing that the state could not recognize the minority language as equally "official." The notion that the "titular" and minority relationship might change from hierarchy to equivalence in any region of the state was unimaginable. Even the minority law proposal of the liberal Romanian circle at the Center for Human Rights stopped short of granting official status to minority languages.[76] The image of "regional autonomies" that the RMDSZ envisioned for territories in Romania where Hungarians represented a majority evoked fears that Petre Lițiu, moderate mayoral candidate in Cluj in 1996, articulated concisely: "Romanians would be strangers in their own country."[77] In Slovakia, Minister of Culture Milan

---

[75] Ibid., 261.
[76] See Andreescu, Stan, and Weber, "Un proiect de lege privind minoritățile naționale elaborat de Centrul pentru drepturile omului."
[77] Lițiu, author interview, PL'3 office, Cluj, Romania, May 9, 1996. Lițiu was PL'3 party candidate for mayor of Cluj in the 1996 local elections.

Kňažko expressed the same perspective when he called the Hungarian effort to introduce official bilingualism in southern Slovakia "extreme."[78] In this spirit, the 1999 minority language bill restated the language hierarchies already established in the 1995 language law: "The Slovak language is the state language of the Slovak Republic."[79]

Another question on which majority moderates in Romania and Slovakia were unwilling to compromise concerned the minimum proportion of minority population that would be required in order to allow space for the minority language in official settings. The Hungarian parties in both countries argued for a 10 percent threshold. In Romania, a Hungarian liberal alternative to the official RMDSZ minority statute required an even lower minimum, 8 percent.[80] In Slovakia, the Hungarian elite maintained in 1999 (as they had in 1990) that a threshold higher than 10 percent would exclude smaller language communities—such as the Ukrainian, Ruthenian, Polish, and German minorities in Slovakia—from exercising their language rights.[81] Both Romanian and Slovak moderates, however, refused to go below a 20 percent threshold. The liberalizing amendments to the local administration law that the Romanian moderates approved in 1997 (and ratified in 2001) established a 20 percent minimum. The minority law proposal of the liberal circle at the Center for Human Rights adopted the same minimum percentage.[82] The amendments to the constitution that the Romanian parliament adopted in 2003 that granted minority language use in courts and public administration also institutionalized the 20 percent threshold.[83] The Slovak moderates were similarly unwilling to go below the 20 percent minimum. They established this threshold in the 1990 language law, argued for the same during their 1994 negotiations with the Hungarian Coalition, and again rejected the Hungarian demand for a 10 percent minimum in 1999.[84]

[78] *Új Szó,* June 24, 1999.
[79] "Zákon z 10. júla 1999 o používaní jazykov národnostných menšín" (Law on the Use of National Minority Languages) *Zbierka zákonov* No. 184, 1999, Preamble, 1. Compare with "Law on the State Language of the Slovak Republic," No. 270, 1995, Preamble, 1.
[80] Sándor N. Szilágyi, "Tervezet."
[81] See "Standpoint of the Political Movement Coexistence on the Law on Language Use," undated document. See also amendments proposed by the Hungarian Coalition to the government's bill, published in *Új Szó,* July 8, 1999; "A Short Analysis of the Law on the Use of the Languages of National Minorities," MK document, July 23, 1999.
[82] See Andreescu, Stan, Weber, "Un proiect de lege privind minorităţile naţionale elaborat de Centrul pentru drepturile omului," 102–12. Although not broadly debated in the Romanian political arena, this proposal was nevertheless significant in expressing the Romanian liberal approach represented by a small group of individuals who were influential in Romanian liberal intellectual circles.
[83] "Romanian Public Administration Is Difficult To Implement," FBIS-EEU–2001–0523, May 23, 2001.
[84] Berényi, *Nyelvországlás.* See "Együttműködés a Szlovák Köztársaság Kormánya és a szlovákiai magyar parlamenti pártok (Együttélés, MKDM) között 1994–ben" (Coexistence analysis), Bratislava, Slovakia, March 9, 1995; *MKP Közlöny,* March 24, 1999; and *Új Szó,* June 5, 1999.

Beyond significant similarities, there were equally important differences in the degrees of flexibility that Romanian and Slovak moderates showed during the language debate. Participating in the establishment of a new state, the Slovak moderates were consistently less willing than their Romanian counterparts to include minority languages in both territory markings and government communications. The debate over independence heightened "titular" majority desires to mark their ownership of the state in the national language. As a consequence, the 1990 language law that the Slovak moderate elite designed failed to affirm the rights of minority communities to display place names in their language. Later, in their 1994 negotiations with the Hungarian parties, Slovak moderate leaders agreed only to bilingual signs that would clearly indicate the difference between *official* Slovak place names and merely informative Hungarian names.[85] The more liberal 1999 minority language law permitted the display of minority language names of streets and other local geographic names, but it underscored the fact that the use of these signs was legal only within the boundaries of a locality.[86]

The Hungarian demand to use historical place names was also more divisive in the newly established Slovakia than in Romania. Slovak moderates were hesitant to accept the use of historical (pre-1945) Hungarian names of towns and villages that had been renamed by the Czechoslovak Communist government after 1945. The 1994 road sign law, for instance, excluded thirteen communities from reclaiming historical Hungarian place names.[87] In 1999, these same settlements were again missing from the government's initial list of localities that satisfied the 20 percent requirement for minority language use. Later, the list was revised to include them.[88]

The Romanian moderates did not contest the use of historical Hungarian place names. The liberalizing amendments that the moderate government designed in 1997 not only allowed the posting of bilingual place names and public information in localities and counties where the minority comprised over 20 percent of the population, they also transferred authority over the

---

[85] "Zákon Národnej rady Slovenskej republiky zo 7. júla 1994 o označovaní obcí v jazyku národnostných menšín," Articles 1 and 2. Full text of the law published in Zalabai, *Mit ér a nyelvünk, ha magyar?* 341–42. On the 1994 bargaining among the Hungarian parties and the Slovak democratic opposition, see "Együttműködés a Szlovák Köztársaság Kormánya és a szlovákiai magyar parlamenti pártok (Együttélés, MKDM) között 1994-ben."

[86] "Zákon z 10. júla 1999 o používaní jazykov národnostných menšín," Article 4, paragraph 1.

[87] "Zákon Národnej rady Slovenskej republiky zo 7. júla 1994 o označovaní obcí v jazyku národnostných menšín," Article 3. On the 1994 negotiations between the Hungarian party leaders and the Slovak democratic opposition leaders, see "Együttműködés a Szlovák Köztársaság Kormánya és a szlovákiai magyar parlamenti pártok (Együttélés, MKDM) között 1994-ben." See also "Position of the Hungarian Coalition in Slovakia on the Minority Rights in the Slovak Republic . . . (1994–1996)."

[88] *Új Szó,* July 22, 1999.

naming and renaming of places to local councils. RMDSZ leaders found this legislation satisfactory. The difficulty of securing the support of moderate parliamentarians for bilingual place signs indicated that a significant number of Romanian moderates were just as reluctant to accept the display of Hungarian place markers as their Slovak counterparts. During the debate, some moderate politicians explained that bilingualism was not appropriate for Romania either because Romanian society was not yet ready to accept it or because bilingualism was inconsistent with the unitary structure of the Romanian state.[89] In several Transylvanian counties, prefects appointed by the moderate government refused to comply with the government's 1997 emergency decree, arguing that the decree was unconstitutional without its ratification by Parliament. In the summer of 1999, the moderate leadership succeeded in gaining the necessary support to begin adopting the liberalizing amendments. After a moderate shift in its nation-building strategy, the post-2000 Iliescu government finally put this legislation into force in May 2001. (See table 4.2 for positions on territory markers.)

The distance between the language policy preferences of the majority moderates and the Hungarian minority was also greater in Slovakia than Romania in the sphere of government. The Slovak moderates were responsible for adopting the first post-Communist language law in 1990, which instituted Slovak language dominance in all forms of official interaction. All official publications had to be issued in Slovak, and minority languages were prohibited from use by public officials during their sessions. In relations between officials and citizens, the law only provided for informal, nonmandatory use of a minority language in local administration in cities and villages, but not at any higher level. Minority citizens were permitted to address public officials in their own language, but officials were not required to respond in the minority language or to use an interpreter. The law specifically prohibited ethnic Slovak citizens from addressing officials in a minority language and authorized public officials to judge "the possibility, appropriateness, and means of language use in official contact."[90] In fact, this legislation—although in 1990 it represented the Slovak moderate approach when compared to the "Matica law" that the majority nationalists supported—allowed less space for minority language use in official contact than the local administration law that the Romanian nationalist government had designed in 1991. The 1991 Romanian law mandated

[89] Minister of the Interior Gabriel Dejeu was reported in the Hungarian press as expressing the former view on a Transylvanian tour aimed at "smoothing the tensions" triggered by the placement of Hungarian language signs. "Az eltévedt politika," *Magyar Közélet,* August 1997. The latter was the opinion of a DP deputy in Cluj, cited in *Szabadság,* October 1, 1997.
[90] "Law on Language Use in the Slovak Republic" No. 428/1990, paragraphs 6 and 7.

the dissemination of decisions and regulations in the minority language in mixed communities where the minority composed unspecified "significant numbers." By contrast, the 1990 Slovak language law provided no room for government publications in the minority language. (Compare tables 4.1 and 4.4.)

When compared to the 1995 state language act later adopted by the Mečiar government, the 1990 law was moderate in the Slovak context. Commenting on the 1995 law, then vice president of the MPP Kálmán Petőcz noted that the 1990 bill, "though in somewhat controversial form, still allowed the persons belonging to national minorities to use their mother tongue in official business."[91] The Slovak moderate position changed significantly between 1990 and 1999. The 1999 minority language law allowed considerably more space for minority language use than the language law approved by the moderates in 1990. Nevertheless, the Slovak moderates were less willing than their Romanian counterparts to share certain spheres of the official domain with minority languages.

In Slovakia, the difference between the nationalist desire for total exclusion and the moderate approach of limited inclusion was most evident in the debate over the use of Hungarian personal names in official documents. On this issue, the Slovak moderates consistently supported the Hungarian claims.[92] When the position of the nationalist parties was temporarily weakened in the legislature in the summer of 1993, the moderates succeeded in passing a law that legalized the registration of minority language names in the birth register and the use of minority language names in official documents.[93] During negotiations between the leaders of the Slovak opposition and the Hungarian Coalition in 1994, KDH leader Čarnogurský agreed to lift legal restrictions on the official use of personal names in exchange for Hungarian support for the ousting of Prime Minister Mečiar. Eventually, the Slovak moderates resolved the conflict over personal names under the Moravčik government in 1994. The law on registration adopted in May 1994 legalized the official recording, upon request, of minority language personal names and female surnames without the Slovak suffix "–ová"[94]

Nevertheless, Romanian moderates exhibited higher degrees of flexibility on language inclusion in most spheres of the official domain. After their

---

[91] Petőcz, "The Slovak Law on the State Language," 1.
[92] Challenging the approach of Slovak nationalist linguists, sociolinguist Slavo Ondrejovičclaimed that the use of non-Slovak personal names in Slovak sentences did not violate Slovak grammar in any important way. Author interview, Bratislava, Slovakia, April 26, 1996.
[93] Zalabai, *Mit ér a nyelvünk, ha magyar?* 277–78.
[94] "Zákon Národnej rady Slovenskej republiky z 27. mája 1994 o matrikách," Article 16, in Zalabai, *Mit ér a nyelvünk, ha magyar?* 336.

electoral victory in 1996, the Romanian moderate leadership, in governing coalition with the Hungarian party, agreed to reverse the restrictive leg-
islations that the Iliescu regime had adopted. In summer 1997, the new
government issued Emergency Decree No. 22, which liberalized language
use in government to a degree acceptable to the Hungarian coalition partners.[95] Thereafter, the only remaining task in achieving the resolution of
the language conflict was passing these liberalizing amendments through
parliament. When the Romanian Senate finally adopted the amendments
in virtually unchanged form in May 1999, the RMDSZ celebrated the vote
as a significant victory. In Slovakia, by contrast, the majority moderate and
Hungarian minority leaders who shared power after the September 1998
elections could not agree on mutually acceptable language legislation in
1999. The Slovak moderates rejected their Hungarian coalition partners' demand for a comprehensive reversal of the 1995 language law. Although the
final bill became more inclusive than the initial drafts, MKP leaders continued
to express dissatisfaction with the 1999 minority language law in Slovakia and
abroad.[96] Romanian moderates accepted the inclusion of minority languages
in the activity of government at local and county levels, reserving only the
central government exclusively for the majority language.[97] The Slovak moderates, on the other hand, agreed to include minority languages only at the
local level.[98] Even there, they were less willing to allow room for minority
language use in the activity of local offices of the state administration than
in the offices of elected self-governments.[99]

In both states, majority moderates preferred informal and *voluntary* inclusion of the minority language to a *requirement* that local governments
communicate with minority citizens in their language. Although the publication of all documents in the majority language was mandatory, local
governmental offices were required to issue documents in the minority
language only upon request. Still, the specific categories of governmental
publications that were publishable in the minority language remained more

[95] Béla Markó, RMDSZ president, author interview, Bucharest, Romania, June 10, 1997.
[96] "A Short Analysis of the Law on the Use of the Language of National Minorities." See also *Új
Szó,* July 12, 1999.
[97] According to the RMDSZ interpretation, the amendments include county-level government.
See "A helyi közigazgatási törvényt módosító 22–es számú sürgösségi kormányrendeletről,"
Magyar Közélet 1, no. 4 (September 1997). Emergency decree No. 22 does not specifically
say that minority languages may be used at the county level. It defines local government as
government in territorial units, which can be communes, towns, or counties. The articles on
minority language use, however, are included only in the chapter about commune and town
councils.
[98] Hamžík stated this view in an interview in *Új Szó,* June 9, 1999. Concerning the rejection of
Hungarian requests that minority citizens be allowed to address the offices of the President and the
central government in their language, see *Új Szó,* June 10, 1999, July 8, 1999.
[99] *MKP Közlöny,* March 2, 1999; *Új Szó,* June 5, 1999, July 14, 1999.

limited in Slovakia. For example, Romanian moderates agreed to require local councils to publish their agenda in the minority language prior to a meeting.[100] The minority language law in Slovakia made no provision for the publication of the local council agenda in minority languages.[101] Even though the idea that government should speak in a minority language was a matter of controversy among majority moderate parliamentarians in both countries, Romanian moderates were more open-minded than their Slovak counterparts in this regard.

The difference between Romanian and Slovak moderate positions was most apparent in the sphere of interactions between citizens and government. The key question was whether government should be *required* to respond to citizens in the minority language. In Romania, the liberalizing amendments entitled minority citizens to use their language in official communication and required the local government to employ the necessary number of public officials who could speak the minority language. If public officials were not competent in the minority language, the mayor's office had to provide a professional interpreter.[102] In Slovakia, the 1999 minority language bill allowed minority citizens in mixed communities to address local officials in their own language but did not require any number of officials to speak the minority language. Bilingual reply was mandated only in written communication.[103] Although the vehement parliamentary debates in Romania about the subject made clear that many majority moderates in Romania were just as reluctant as their Slovak counterparts to require government officials to speak the minority language, in the end the Romanian parliament approved a bill that required civil servants directly dealing with the public in communities that were at least 20 percent minority-inhabited either to hire employees who speak the minority language or to provide an interpreter.[104] The Slovak moderates, by contrast, refused to require public officials to use a minority language under any circumstances.[105] (See table 4.4 on moderate positions.)

For both majorities and minorities who conceived of the democratic state as government over "national" spaces, the mapping of these spaces with the national language became a political imperative. Therefore, language use in the domains most directly linked to government and territoriality (the

---

[100] "Emergency Ordinance No. 22/1997 for the Modification and Completion of the Law on Local Public Administration No. 69/1991" ("Ordonanţă de urgenţă pentru modificarea şi completarea Legii administraţiei publice locale No. 69/1991, republicată"), republished in *Monitorul oficial al României,* part I, no. 105, May 29, 1997, Articles 25 and 32.

[101] "Law on the use of National Minority Languages," No. 184/1999, Article 2, paragraph 4.

[102] Emergency Decree No. 22, Articles 58 and 61.

[103] "Law on the use of National Minority Languages," No. 184/1999, Article 2, paragraph 2.

[104] See the description of the December 8, 1999, bill in *HHRF Monitor,* December 8, 1999.

[105] See Pavel Hamžík's statement, quoted in *Új Szó,* June 23, 1999.

TABLE 4.4
Majority moderate positions on the inclusion of minority languages in government

	Publications, documents	Sessions of government	Communication between officials and citizens
Slovak	1990 law: Excluded	1990 law: Excluded	1990 law: Minority citizens allowed to use it; ethnic Slovak citizens prohibited; officials not required to respond
	Official use of minority personal names allowed (law No.300/1993)		
	1999 law: Local council decisions upon request; forms and public information upon request; village chronicle	1999 law: Sessions in minority language if all participants agree; individual minority council members may use it; local government provides interpreter	1999 law: Minority citizens may address officials in minority language; in written communication, they are entitled to bilingual response; in oral communication, officials not required to respond in the minority language
Romanian	Local government decisions; agenda of council meetings upon request	Council members entitled to use it, where a third of councilors agree; official documentation of meeting in Romanian	Two-way communication guaranteed

Note: Required minority threshold is 20%

official domain of government as well as territory markers) became strongly contested in post-Communist Romania and Slovakia. The same pattern of similarities and differences emerged in the debate in the positions of nationalist and moderate majorities and of Hungarian minority political actors.

Committed to a traditional nation-state model, majority nationalists in both states were keenly interested in mapping the territory and governing institutions of the state with the language of the titular nation. Working from a dominant position during the formative first years after Communism in both Romania and Slovakia, these political actors pursued complete language dominance in these spheres. In response to the majority pursuit of language dominance, the Hungarian minority parties in both states articulated a similarly consistent demand for pluralist democracy in which national communities (majorities as well as minorities) should be entitled to map their spaces of popular sovereignty in their language. The recognition of Hungarian as a legitimate language of government was central to the minority conception of sovereignty. The Hungarian minority conception of equal citizenship also included an expectation that historical Hungarian place names be officially recognized and displayed alongside the Romanian or Slovak place names, respectively, in areas where the Hungarian culture had a historical presence and Hungarians continued to represent a sizeable population. In both cases, Hungarian parties argued for language parity, asking that the Hungarian language be included as a coequal language of government in areas where Hungarians made up the majority of the population. They also asked that Hungarian be recognized as a language of official contact in localities where Hungarians made up more than 10 percent of the population.

Majority moderates in both states were willing to negotiate the inclusion of minority languages in the official domain. At the same time, they remained suspicious of Hungarian demands for language parity and, due to their concerns about consolidating majority control over the institutions of government, majority moderates did not articulate a fundamentally different alternative to the nationalist conception of popular sovereignty. The moderates pursued a language hierarchy where their language remained superior to other languages in every setting. In the moderate view, language parity—that is, coequal status for minority languages—in any community in the territory of the state was inconceivable. To institutionalize majority language predominance, the moderates expressed a strong preference throughout the debate for maintaining a distance between the mandatory use of the majority language and the informal, nonmandatory use of minority languages.

The questions that remained divisive in both states between majority moderates and the Hungarian minority in this debate highlighted the challenges of harmonizing the territorial national state model with the democratic regime in societies in which multiple cultural groups define themselves in national terms and view language as a marker of "ownership" over culturally significant spaces. What should be the minimum percentage of minority presence required for the exercise of language rights? Was language parity acceptable under any circumstances, or should the use of minority languages in territory marking and government always reflect majority language supremacy? (For instance, should a place name in the "titular" language and its minority language equivalent be displayed differently? In Slovakia, another question was whether the use of historical Hungarian names could be allowed, or only Hungarian translations of the Slovak place name.) Should government be *required* to speak in a minority language where minorities constitute a significant percentage of the population? Should the minority language be included in *all* spheres of government? The answers that majority moderate and Hungarian minority parties gave to these questions demonstrated that the continuing influence of the traditional nation-state model, of past relations between the groups, and of the historical Hungarian state in the region had a pronounced tendency to lock majority and minority national groups into conflict with each other.

Majority moderates in both Romania and Slovakia were unwilling to compromise on the 20 percent threshold condition and accept the 10 percent minimum for the exercise of minority language rights in the official domain. They also consistently opposed the Hungarian pursuit of official bilingualism, rejecting the notion of language parity in any substate administrative unit—regardless of the historical presence of the Hungarian culture or its current ethnic composition. Slovak moderates were more committed than their Romanian counterparts to the necessity of marking their ownership over the territory and institutions of the new state. In the matter of bilingual signs, they accepted only signs that unequivocally indicated a difference between the official Slovak name and a merely "informative" name in the minority language. They also contested the use of historical Hungarian place names—a Hungarian demand that faced no particular opposition among majority moderates in Romania. Similarly, they were willing to allow the use of the Hungarian language in government, but only at the local level and without requiring public officials to respond in the minority language. The Romanian moderate position eventually accepted the notion that local and regional government in minority-inhabited areas should speak in the minority language.

Although majority political elites in both states were wary of the legacies of past Hungarian statehood in territories that both majority and minority national groups claimed as their homeland, the process of establishing a new state increased majority suspicions of Hungarian language claims. The pursuit of an independent national state rendered Slovak political actors across the board more likely than their Romanian counterparts to opt for marking the official domain exclusively in their language. Indeed, in some respects the position of Slovak nationalists concerning language exclusion was more ambitious than that of the Romanian nationalists. Furthermore, in the first years of state construction, when independent statehood was intensely debated in Slovakia, Slovak moderates showed less willingness to share the official domain with minority languages than Romanian elites, a statement that applies to both moderates and nationalists. Later in the decade, the inclination of Slovak moderates to include minority languages in official contact increased. In 1999, the moderate leadership articulated a position similar to that of the Romanian moderates, although they remained more reluctant than their Romanian counterparts to allow room for minority language use in certain settings.

Equally important, however, the compromises that majority moderate and Hungarian minority parties were able to reach in both countries by the end of the decade demonstrated that the democratic process offered the potential for peacefully negotiated language policy even in societies where multiple national groups claimed rights for cultural reproduction. In the course of more than a decade's worth of debates that involved heated arguments and negotiations around parliamentary elections and coalition-building, moderate majority and minority parties in both Romania and Slovakia were unable to agree fully on the principles of language inclusion. Nonetheless, they were able to negotiate peacefully and design policies that, while preserving the predominance of the majority language throughout the country, gradually included the minority language in ways that satisfied the main aspirations that minorities had articulated from the beginning of the 1990s. The dynamic of power relations between majority and minority parties evolved differently in the two countries toward the end of the following decade. As Romania prepared to join the European Union in 2007, the Hungarian party continued to participate in a coalition government, and began difficult negotiations over the terms of a comprehensive law on national minorities. The 2006 parliamentary elections in Slovakia, however, brought to power a majority nationalist governing coalition that threatened to reverse the consensual approach to minority policy that had characterized the period after 1998. Yet the achievements of consensual politics in the domain of language rights remained in place in both states.

Chapter 5

Contesting Cultural Reproduction

The Language of Education

In societies where multiple groups aim to reproduce their culture, the public education system becomes an institution of primary political significance. Will Kymlicka, a prominent theorist of "multinationalism," explains that "having publicly-funded education in one's mother tongue is crucial, since it guarantees the passing on of the language and its associated traditions to the next generation."[1] From this perspective, the key question that political elites in multilingual societies around the world must address is not simply whether public education should allow the teaching of multiple languages but also whether (or how) this institution should enable the reproduction of multiple "national" cultures. Despite increased recognition of the importance of this question, however, relatively few comparative studies systematically explore majority-minority debates about language use in education. This chapter offers a comparative exploration of the positions that majority and minority political actors in Romania and Slovakia formulated on this issue, the key factors that influenced their choices, and the dynamics of conflict and cooperation that emerged among them in the process.

Majority and minority political actors in Romania and Slovakia shared the view that the public education system was the most important institution for maintaining and reproducing a national language and, through this language, a national culture and community. Because they held competing notions about state and popular sovereignty—minority concepts of "homeland

---

[1] Kymlicka, "Introduction," *Can Liberal Pluralism be Exported?* 17.

community" rights challenged majority ideas of "titular" rights—majority and minority political actors developed different approaches to the questions of language use in education.

Nationalist majorities in both cases consistently pursued education policies that would compel the minority to shift gradually to the majority language and culture. To assure a unitary system of socialization, these majorities also opted for centralized control over all educational institutions—including the administration of schools and the content of education, especially in the domain of the national canon (the national literature, including classical and modern authors who wrote in the national language, the historiography that narrates the story of the nation, and the geography that maps the connection between the nation and the national territory).

A substantial body of literature on multilingual societies confirms that language planning in education is indeed a powerful tool that states can use to achieve language shift among minority language speakers. Language minorities living in prolonged contact with a majority language under a majority government in a modern territorial state usually shift to the language of the dominant group.[2] Some language minorities, however, especially those incorporated in the state through border change or colonization—and with their social institutions (marriage and kinship) and religious and other traditions largely intact—are more likely to resist policies of language shift and to make efforts to maintain their language.[3] Language maintenance is easier to achieve in larger groups that draw self-imposed boundaries between their language and the language of the dominant group. In this dynamic, as Woolard argues, "language choice does not simply follow from ethnic identity, but may actually constitute it."[4] The Hungarians in Romania and Slovakia represent such language minorities, and from the beginning of democratization they manifested a consistent desire not only to use Hungarian as the language of instruction at all levels of the educational system but also to maintain separate schools to assure community authority over public education—including its content and administration.

In both states, the moderate majority actors, who expressed less interest than their nationalist counterparts in language dominance, also understood that an education policy that challenges strongly held public interests is not likely to succeed in a democratic state.[5] Moderates also shared minority

---

[2] See especially Christina Bratt Paulston, *Linguistic Minorities in Multilingual Settings* (Philadelphia, PA: John Benjamins, 1993), 9–20. See also Kathryn A. Woolard, *Double Talk* (Stanford, CA: Stanford University Press, 1989), 3–9.

[3] Paulston, Linguistic Minorities in Multilingual Settings.

[4] Woolard, *Double Talk,* 63.

[5] Paulston, "Linguistic Minorities and Language Policies," 394.

interest in decentralization and greater local authority in the public education system. Nonetheless, they emphasized the need for public education to prepare minority students for an integrated society in which majority language predominance should prevail. Consequently, majority moderates in both cases favored bilingual education that placed certain limitations on the use of the minority language, on the content of education, and on the autonomy of minority educational institutions. Moderates were also reluctant to allow higher educational institutions that would reproduce a minority national elite and a complex minority society.

Thus, the key issues of contestation in the decade-long educational debate in both states were the language of instruction in minority schools, the language of admission tests to higher levels in the education system, the language and content of the national canon, the scope of higher education in the Hungarian language, and authority over Hungarian educational institutions.

Majority Pursuit of Minority Language Shift

The nationalist majority elites in both Romania and Slovakia envisioned an educational system that would create constraints and opportunities to compel all minority students to shift gradually from the minority language to the majority language. The main elements of this strategy in both cases were the gradual introduction of instruction in the majority language in minority schools, the exclusion or strict limitation of minority language instruction in secondary-level vocational and professional schools, and the exclusion of minority language instruction from higher education—with the exception of teacher training. From the majority perspective, another important role of an educational system (gradually consolidated under majority control) was to socialize minority students into thinking about their place in the world in terms of the words, ideas, and values provided by the majority culture. For this reason, the content of education also gained significance. Majority nationalist elites placed special emphasis on the teaching of a unitary national canon in history, geography, and literature.

Nationalist elites in both states sought language dominance in all schools, but the Slovak elites created a constitutional framework less favorable to minority language use in education than the constitution drafted by the state-consolidating Romanian elites. The Slovak constitution established no guarantees for education in minority languages at any level of the educational system. Instead, it granted members of national minorities the right to "cultivate their minds to a degree necessary for their development" in their native language, as well as in Slovak, in elementary and secondary schools.[6] By contrast, the constitution that the Romanian elite designed in the same period included a more generous provision guaranteeing the right of national minorities "to learn their mother tongue and their right to be educated in this language." The institutional ways in which this right could be exercised remained open to further legislation, however, and the legislative battles of the 1990s left no doubt that the Romanian nationalists also had little intention of facilitating the establishment of a comprehensive system of education in Hungarian.[7]

The educational policies of the coalition government in Slovakia led by the Movement for a Democratic Slovakia (HZDS) were explicitly designed to promote Slovak language dominance in the newly established state. The Mečiar government's 1994 program declared its commitment to protect the majority language and culture, especially in minority-inhabited regions. In these regions, declared the program, the school system had to "safeguard Slovak language rights."[8] The 1995 State Language Act reiterated that "the state language is the language of instruction and examination in the territory of the Slovak Republic" and offered no specifics on minority education.[9] A justification of the law published at the time of its enactment confirmed that the lack of detail was intended to limit minority language use in this domain.

Although bilingual education was the dominant form of education for smaller minority groups in both states, most Hungarian students learned in Hungarian either in separate Hungarian schools or in mixed schools that included both majority-language and Hungarian sections or classes. In both states, approximately 20 to 32 percent of Hungarian students attended schools with majority-language instruction.[10]

In post-Communist Czechoslovakia, Hungarian was the language of instruction in Hungarian schools, except for the teaching of Slovak language and literature. To achieve language shift, the government of newly

---

[6] See excerpts from the constitution in *Dokumenty zborník medzinárodných menšín,* part I (Bratislava: Danubiaprint, 1995), 123.

[7] Constitution of Romania, Article 32, paragraph 3. See excerpts in *Învăţămîntul cu predarea în limbile minorităţilor naţionale din România. Anul şcolar 1995–1996* (Bucharest: Romanian Ministry of Education, 1996), 4.

[8] *Dokumenty zborník medzinárodných menšín,* 133.

[9] "Zákon Národnej Rady Slovenskej Republiky o štátnom jazyku Slovenskej Republiky" ["Law on the state language of the Slovak Republic"], 270/1995, in *Zbierka zákonov Slovenskej Republiky* [Collection of Laws of the Slovak Republic], Preamble; Article 4, paragraph 1.

[10] For Slovakia, see Zoltán Sidó, "Magyar nyelvű oktatás Szlovákiában," manuscript, April 1999, appendix 6; and Erzsébet Dolník, "A szlovákiai magyar oktatásügy helyzete," *Regio* 5, no. 3 (1994), p. 29. For Romania, András Gábos, "Adatok a romániai tanügyi törvényhez," *Regio* 5, no. 3 (1994), p. 50.

independent Slovakia developed an ambitious new plan to establish a system of "alternative" schools that Hungarian parents could voluntarily choose over Hungarian schools. These schools would immerse Hungarian children into the Slovak language in preschool and teach a gradually increasing number of subjects in Slovak through higher grades.[11] Advocates of the "alternative education" plan argued that Hungarian schools in southern Slovakia were unable to teach satisfactory Slovak language skills and found the practice of teaching Slovak as a second language offensive to Slovaks.[12] Hungarians countered that the aim of an alternative education was gradually to weaken the system of Hungarian schools.[13] Most Hungarian educators agreed that the Slovak language competence of Hungarian students needed improvement and proposed more effective methods of teaching Slovak as a second language—rather than teaching subjects *in* Slovak.[14] Despite Hungarian opposition, the government was determined to introduce bilingual education in Hungarian schools. Education Ministry officials ordered school principals to advertise the alternative school plan to Hungarian parents and dismissed principals who resisted the orders.[15]

Hungarian minority efforts to establish schools that would guarantee language maintenance at all levels and thereby reproduce a complex Hungarian minority society also became a deeply divisive issue in Romania. Soon after the fall of the Ceauşescu dictatorship in December 1989, the only violent Romanian-Hungarian conflict broke out in May 1990 over Hungarian attempts to regain a historically Hungarian high school in the Tîrgu-Mureş. This incident exposed a fault line that remained a source of bitter controversy between the Romanian nationalists and the Hungarian minority and that later found expression in the battle over the law on education adopted in 1995.[16] Through this legislation, the Romanian elite in power drew distinct limits to

---

[11] Original Slovak text in Dolník, "Az egyes tantárgyak alternatív oktatásának koncepció–javaslata a nemzetiségileg vegyes területek iskoláiban (Elemzés)," undated document.

[12] Ferko, "Zásady zákona Národnej Rady Slovenskej Republiky o státnom jazyku Slovenskej Republiky" 10; and comment by Vice-Premier Katarina Tothova in "Tothova: Education Ministry Measure 'Not Fortunate,'" FBIS-EEU–97–107, April 17, 1997; Slovak linguist Ján Dorula, author interview, Bratislava, Slovakia, June 5, 1996.

[13] See Sidó, "Magyar nyelvű oktatás Szlovákiában," 4.

[14] Dostál, "Minorities," 65. See also "Position of the Hungarian Coalition in Slovakia on the Minority Rights in the Slovak Republic Under the 3rd Government of Prime Minister Meciar (1994–1996)," undated MK document.

[15] See Dostál, "Minorities," 66.

[16] Law on education No. 84/1995 ("Legea învăţămîntului") published in *Monitorul Oficial* [Official Gazette of Romania], part I, No. 167, July 31, 1995. The law was modified and completed by the Law No.131/December 29, 1995, published in *Monitorul Oficial,* Part I, No. 301/December 29, 1995 and republished in *Monitorul Oficial,* Part I, No. 1/January 5, 1996.

minority-language education. After declaring that national minorities had the right to "study and receive instruction in their mother tongue at all levels and forms of education," the law did little to accommodate Hungarian demands for such rights and in some ways even constituted a setback from legislation enacted under the Ceaușescu dictatorship.[17]

The 1995 education law allowed instruction in minority languages only to the extent that it "did not impair" learning in the Romanian language.[18] The establishment of classes with Romanian language instruction was mandatory in every settlement in the country regardless of ethnic composition or demand, yet the creation of minority classes was permitted only "in function of local necessities."[19] Although "acquiring" the Romanian language became an unconditional requirement in all public schools, the study of minority languages was made possible only upon request and "under the conditions of the law."[20] The teaching of the Romanian language and literature was mandatory in all schools. The teaching of minority languages and literatures in schools with Romanian as the language of instruction, however, was made possible only to students belonging to national minorities and "upon their request and within the conditions of the law."[21] The study of certain subjects in Romanian was mandatory in all schools, and high school graduation examinations in these subjects required that minority students master the Romanian language at the same level as their counterparts who had studied in Romanian schools.[22]

In contrast to the mandatory inclusion of Romanian instruction in certain subjects in Hungarian schools in Romania, the Slovak "alternative education" plan was voluntary. At the same time, the Slovak project included more subjects in the majority language, even within its moderate variants. Had it been successfully implemented, the law would have imposed more dramatic limitations on Hungarian-language education in

---

[17] Law on education 1995, Article 118. On the legislative setback, see Weber, "Legea învățământului: între contestare și supra-apreciere," 21.

[18] Law on education 1995, Article 119, paragraph 2.

[19] Law on education 1995, Article 8, paragraph 1; Article 119, paragraph 1.

[20] Law on education 1995, Article 8, paragraph 3; Article 119, paragraph 1; and Article 121. The restrictive clause "under the conditions of the law" is one of the most frequently used phrases in the section on minority language education. See analysis by Weber, "Legea învățământului: între contestare și supra-apreciere," 22. RMDSZ critics argued that the state could legitimately require the study of the official language of the country, but mandating and enforcing the obligation of an individual to "acquire" language proficiency in any language was a violation of fundamental rights. See "The Romanian Law on Education in the Context of the Framework Convention for the Protection of National Minorities of the Council of Europe," RMDSZ document, August 2, 1995, 2.

[21] Law on education 1995, Articles 120 and 121.

[22] Law on education 1995, Article 22.

Slovakia than had the Romanian education policy. Three years before the change in government in Slovakia in September 1998, however, were insufficient for the nationalist coalition to establish the desired alternative classes in Hungarian schools, and the post-1998 government abandoned the project.[23]

Besides limiting the use of the minority language as a language of instruction, the education policy that nationalist majorities designed in both states excluded minority languages from the entrance exams necessary for successful advancement to higher levels in the education system. This policy served as one of the most powerful tools to bring about language shift among minority students in both states. Ruling policymakers defended this policy as common sense.[24] Critics claimed, however, that the intent was to apply socioeconomic pressure on Hungarian parents to opt for majority language education. Communist-era legislation in Romania had permitted university entrance exams in minority languages, although ministerial orders severely limited this right beginning in the late 1980s. The post-Communist government reinstituted this right in 1989 but revoked it in the education law of 1995.[25] Responding to strong domestic and international pressure, the Ministry of Education soon felt compelled to suspend the majority-language requirement, and later the moderate government eliminated it through the 1997 amendments to the education law.

In Czechoslovakia, Communist-era education policy had already limited university admissions exams to the two state-forming majority languages. Studies showed that the percentage of Hungarian students who chose Slovak over Hungarian grammar schools (high schools that traditionally best prepared students for university admission) increased significantly under those conditions.[26] Slovak-only university admissions continued after the establishment of independent Slovakia, and ministerial decrees in 1996 ordered that

[23] Dostál, "Minorities," 66. See also Rosa, "Education and Science," 182.
[24] Iliescu's comments at press conference on July 24, 1995, quoted in "Legea învăţămîntului: opinii pro şi contra," 80. Gheorghe Dumitraşcu, Senate Education Committee chairman, voiced the same opinion. Author interview, Bucharest, Romania, May 21, 1996.
[25] Education State Secretary András Béres talked about this practice during the Ceauşescu period in author interview, Bucharest, Romania, June 11, 1997. For legal provisions on minority language examinations between 1989 and 1995, see "Decision of the Government on the Organization and Functioning of Education in Romania" in *The Education System of Romania. Tuition in the Languages of National Minorities. The 1994/1995 School Year* (Bucharest: Ministry of Education [undated]), 32. The respective article in the 1995 education law is Article 123.
[26] See Soňa Gabzdilová, "Schools in the Slovak Republik with Instruction in the Hungarian language: Present Status," in *Minorities in Politics,* ed. Jana Plichtová (Bratislava: 1992), 169.

admission tests to secondary schools should also be administered exclusively in Slovak.[27]

The education strategy aimed at achieving minority language shift by the end of secondary school also targeted minority students in both countries who wanted to apply to secondary vocational and technical schools. From the majority perspective, the school had to socialize minority students who chose professional or vocational secondary education to think about their profession in the majority language. In Slovakia, at the beginning of Slovak statehood, the opportunities for professional secondary education in Hungarian were limited to five separate Hungarian schools and seventeen mixed schools. In vocational programs for skilled labor, more than half of the Hungarian students received Slovak language instruction.[28] After Slovak independence, the government expressed a desire to increase Slovak language dominance in this area.[29] In a similar vein, the Romanian government issued a decree in 1990 to mandate the teaching of vocational subjects exclusively in Romanian and sanctioned this requirement in the 1995 education law, which required Romanian-only secondary and postsecondary school training in the "professional, technical, economic, administrative, agricultural, forestry, and mountain-agricultural fields." Minority language terminology could only be taught in these fields "depending on the circumstances."[30]

A Unitary National Canon

Majority elites in both states followed a traditional nationalist strategy when they emphasized the teaching of a national canon that would develop loyal citizenship.[31] In Romania, central control over the language and content of literature, history, and geography in minority schools increased dramatically in the later Ceauşescu years.[32] After the fall of his regime, the post-Communist nationalizing government maintained this control, as ministerial orders emphasized the need for minority education to correspond to a unitary national canon.[33] The 1995 law on education formalized control over the content and

---

[27] József Berényi, MPP education specialist, author interview, Bratislava, Slovakia, April 25, 1996.
[28] Dolník, "A szlovákiai magyar oktatásügy helyzete," 30.
[29] Dolník, "Az egyes tantárgyak alternatív oktatásának koncepció–javaslata a nemzetiségileg vegyes területek iskoláiban (Elemzés)."
[30] Law on education 1995, Article 122, paragraph 1. On decree No. 521/1990, see "Memorandum by the Democratic Alliance of Hungarians in Romania on Romania's Admission to the Council of Europe," 19.
[31] Anderson, *Imagined Communities;* Gellner, *Nations and Nationalism.*
[32] László Murvai, author interview, Bucharest, Romania, June 19, 1997.
[33] See "Atribuţiile Direcţiei Învăţătmântul Pentru Minorităţi naţionale," *Învăţământul cu Predarea în limbile minorităţilor naţionale din România* (Bucharest: Guvernul României, Consiliul Pentru Minorităţile Naţionale, 1995), 7.

language of history and geography courses taught to minority students. According to the law, Romanian history—"History of Romanians," as it was titled—and the geography of Romania had to be taught in Romanian from textbooks used in classes with Romanian language instruction, beginning in middle school.[34] Non-Romanian cultural groups living in Romania received a marginal place in this curriculum.[35]

Slovak nationalists also looked for ways to affirm majority control over the content of Slovak language and literature, history, and geography instruction in Hungarian schools. The Mečiar government emphasized the need for all schools to follow the same curriculum and use the same textbooks. In its 1994 program, the government pledged to help develop "basic textbooks and instructional materials that strengthen national pride and awareness of Slovak statehood."[36] Textbooks used in Hungarian schools were designed or approved by the Education Ministry. (Government officials were especially concerned about alternative history and geography textbooks published in Hungary.)[37] The Slovak Ministry of Education decreed in 1995 that only ethnic Slovaks could teach Slovak language, history, and geography. Another ministerial order in the same year offered financial incentives to ethnic Slovak teachers working in regions where the percentage of Hungarians was greater than 40 percent.[38] The governing coalition during the Mečiar period was not united on the adoption of legislation to mandate the ethnicity requirement, and after the change in government in 1998, the new leadership dropped this initiative entirely.

Educating Majority-Language Elites

From the perspective of majorities working to create a unitary national culture, the notion that minorities should maintain higher educational institutions and train their elites in the minority language, especially in separate institutions, was inconceivable. Nevertheless, in the two states the question of Hungarian higher education presented different challenges to these political actors.

Although they constituted a smaller proportion of the country's population, the Hungarians in Romania represented a larger community in

---

[34] Law on Education, Article 120, paragraphs 1 and 2; Articles 15, 127, 128, 142, 143, 144.
[35] Law on Education, Article 120, paragraph 4. Weber, "Legea învăţământului: între contestare şi supra-apreciere," 22. See also Iliescu's comments at press conference on July 24, 1995, quoted in "Legea învăţămîntului: opinii pro şi contra," 79.
[36] *Dokumenty zborník*, 35.
[37] Ferko, "Zásady zákona Národnej Rady Slovenskej Republiky o štátnom jazyku Slovenskej Republiky," 10.
[38] Dostál, "Minorities," 40.

absolute numbers than did the Hungarians in Slovakia. The legacies of the Communist period also differed significantly in this respect. In Romania, the Hungarians enjoyed relative freedom to maintain public educational institutions in the first two decades after the Communist takeover. The systematic weakening of the Hungarian educational system began in earnest only during Ceauşescu's dictatorship. Beginning in the 1960s, the policies of the dictatorship were highly successful in eliminating higher educational opportunities in Hungarian and weakening the socioeconomic position of the Hungarians in Romania. Yet relatively strong Hungarian cultural and academic elites remained in Romania that began to reestablish Hungarian higher education after the fall of the dictatorship. (See tables 5.1 and 5.2 on the ethnic composition of Romania and the educational structure of the population by ethnicity.)

In Czechoslovakia, by contrast, the Hungarian community lost a large percentage of its educated class—first in 1920, when most educated Hungarians

TABLE 5.1
The ethnic composition of Romania, 1956, 1992, and 2002

Nationality	1956	1992	2002
Romanian	85.7%	89.5%	89.5%
Hungarian	9.1	7.1	6.6
Roma	0.6	1.8	2.5
German	2.2	0.5	0.3
Ukrainian	0.3	0.3	0.3
Russian	0.2	0.2	0.2
Turkish	0.1	0.1	0.2
Jewish	0.8	0.1	
Other	1.0	0.4	0.4

Source: Vladimir Trebici, "Commentaria in Demographiam," *Revista de cercetări sociale* 3 (1995), 121–22. Data for 2002 from the *CIA World Factbook*, www.cia.gov/cia/publications/factbook/geos/ro.html, accessed February 4, 2005.

TABLE 5.2
The educational structure of the population by ethnicity in Romania

Highest educational level completed	Nationality			
	Romanian	Hungarian	Roma	German
Eighth grade or lower	28.2%	21.8%	64.3%	18.9%
Secondary school	66.5	74.6	35.6	74.3
Higher education	5.3	3.6	0.1	6.8
Total	100.0	100.0	100.0	100.0

Source: Compiled from Vladimir Trebici, "Commentaria in Demographiam," *Revista de cerceîri sociale* 3 (1995), 127; based on the 1992 census.

were forced to leave after the creation of the new state, and again in 1945, when ethnic Hungarians were deprived of citizenship rights in the reestablished Czechoslovakia and almost a third of the Hungarian population was forced to leave the southern Slovak region. The size and social structure of the Hungarian population changed dramatically between 1945 and 1948 as well. After the Communist accession to power in Czechoslovakia in 1948, Hungarians were granted citizenship rights, and the prohibitions on language use were gradually lifted. Hungarian schools and cultural organizations were again permitted.[39] The Communist Czechoslovak government, however, made no efforts to recreate a Hungarian educated class. Teacher training remained the only area where higher education in Hungarian was allowed, and even this field was severely restricted after 1970. In the College of Pedagogy in Nitra, the number of graduating Hungarian elementary school teachers decreased from a yearly average of ninety-three between 1963 and 1980 to eleven between 1981 and 1995.[40] Although the first government of post-Communist Czechoslovakia liberalized Hungarian teacher training, the Hungarian minority in Slovakia still remained an overwhelmingly rural community with a disproportionately small educated class.[41] (See tables 5.3, 5.4, and 5.5 on the ethnic composition of Slovakia, the educational structure of the Slovak population, and the ethnic composition of university students in Slovakia.) After the establishment of independent Slovakia, the ruling elites refused to expand opportunities for higher education in Hungarian and consistently opposed the demand for a separate Hungarian-language department of teacher training in the Nitra College of Pedagogy.[42]

The Romanian nationalizing parties also aimed to restrict higher education in Hungarian to the training of teachers and artists. According to the 1995 education law, higher education had to be conducted in Romanian in all other professions. The only exceptions to this requirement were the existing sections in one medical school, which were allowed to continue training in Hungarian.[43] President Iliescu claimed that Hungarian demands for a comprehensive educational system were "based on an incorrect interpretation that would lead to exaggerated separatism."[44] Hungarian

---

[39] Magocsi, "Magyars and Carpatho-Rusyns," 117.
[40] See Zoltán Sidó, *A magyar anyanyelvért folytatott küzdelem Szlovákiában* (Bratislava: Szent László Akadémia, 1999), 3.
[41] Gabzdilová, "Schools in the Slovak Republik with Instruction in the Hungarian Language: Present Status"; *A magyar anyanyelvért folytatott küzdelem Szlovákiában*, 2–3.
[42] See Soňa Gabzdilová and Mária Homošinová, "Az iskolaügy a szlovákiai magyar politikai pártok és mozgalmak tevékenységében," *Regio* 5, no.3 (1994), p. 25; see also *HHRF Monitor*, August 17, 1999.
[43] Law on education 1995, Article 122, paragraph 2; and Article 123.
[44] Quoted in "Legea învăţămîntului: opinii pro şi contra," 78.

TABLE 5.3
The ethnic composition of Slovakia, 1991 and 2001

Nationality	1991	2001
Slovak	85.7%	85.8%
Hungarian	10.8	9.7
Roma	1.4	1.7
Czech	1.0	0.8
Ruthenian	0.3	0.4
Ukrainian	0.3	0.2
Other	0.6	1.4

Source: Peter Mach, "Structure by Nationality of Population in the Slovak Republic." Available online at www.czso.cz,
accessed September 3, 2006.

TABLE 5.4
The educational structure of the population by ethnicity in Slovakia

Highest educational level completed	Nationality		
	Slovak	Hungarian	Ukrainian
1980			
Middle school	50.41%	63.55%	54.05%
Secondary school	20.87	13.49	21.90
Higher education	5.50	2.22	9.35
1991			
Middle school	36.45%	49.66%	37.90%
Secondary school	28.14	21.21	30.19
Higher education	8.16	3.63	13.31

Source: Soňa Gabzdilová and Mária Homošinová, "Az iskolaügy a szlovákiai magyar
politikai pártok és mozgalmak tevékénységében," *Regio* 3 (1994), 24.
Note: In each category, some percentage never completed middle school, so columns do
not add up to 100%.

minority elites countered that these limitations continued the familiar poli-
cies of the Ceauşescu dictatorship of "state-sponsored assimilation" of the
Hungarian minority.[45] Statistics compiled by education specialists from the
Democratic Alliance of Hungarians in Romania (RMDSZ) indicated that
the percentage of ethnic Hungarian students in Romanian higher education
had decreased from 5.4 percent in 1970 to 3.7 percent in 1994, while the
Hungarians made up approximately 7 percent of the country's population.
They also showed that the percentage of Hungarian students preparing for

[45] "Analiza şi consecinţele articolelor legii învăţământului referitoare la minorităţile naţionale,"
[RMDSZ document], July 17, 1995, 3. "The Romanian Law on Education in the Context of
the Framework Convention for the Protection of National Minorities of the Council of Europe,"
[RMDSZ document], August 2, 1995, 2. See also Weber, "Legea învăţământului: între contestare
şi supra-apreciere," 25–26.

TABLE 5.5

The ethnic composition of university students in Slovakia compared to the ethnic composition of Slovakia's population (main ethnic groups)

	Slovak		Hungarian		Ukrainian	
	Students	Population	Students	Population	Students	Population
1970–71	87.7%	85.3%	3.8%	12.2%	1.0%	0.9%
1975–76	88.8		4.3		0.9	
1980–81	88.9	86.5	4.6	11.2	1.1	
1985–86	87.8		4.7		1.1	
1989–90	88.1		4.9		0.8	
1990–91	88.5	85.6	4.9	10.8	0.5	0.5
1992–93	90.9		4.6		0.5	
1994–96	91.3		4.5		0.4	

Source: Data on the ethnic composition of university students compiled from Soňa Gabzdilová, "Schools in the Slovak Republik with instruction in the Hungarian language—present status," p. 172 for 1970–91; Soňa Gabzdilová and Mária Homošinová, "Az iskolaügy a szlovákiai magyar politikai pártok és mozgalmak tevékénységében," Regio 3 (1994), p. 23 for 1992–93; Vladislav Rosa, "Education and Science," *Slovakia 1996–1997: A Global Report on the State of Society*, p. 181 for 1994–96. Data on the ethnic composition of Slovakia's population between 1970 and 1990 from Štefan Šutaj, "Changes of National Identity in Historical Development," *Minorities in Politics*, 182.

socioeconomically more empowering professions, such as law and economics, at the Babeş-Bolyai University (BBU) in Cluj, the university that traditionally attracted the largest number of ethnic Hungarian students, continued to decrease dramatically after the fall of the dictatorship.[46]

Control over Schools

Both Slovak and Romanian nationalists argued that continued state control over education served fundamental national interests. Romanian Senator Gheorghe Dumitraşcu, chairman of the Senate's Education Committee in 1995, explained that the public educational system was the institution that had to remain the most centralized, because the future of the state rested on it.[47] Slovak nationalist elites also justified state control over schools as a condition for the success of Slovak state-building. SNS vice president Anna Maliková suggested that the government might increase local authority over schools in some distant future, but only after Slovakia was fully consolidated as a nation-state.[48]

[46] "Analiza şi consecinţele articolelor legii învăţământului referitoare la minorităţile naţionale," tables 5 and 6.

[47] Gheorghe Dumitraşcu, author interview, Bucharest, Romania, May 21, 1996.

[48] Anna Maliková, author interview, Bratislava, Slovakia, April 24, 1996. Ľubomir Hud'o, Slovak journalist at the HZDS daily *Slovenská republika,* articulated the same argument in an author interview, Bratislava, Slovakia, April 18, 1996.

The Iliescu government in Romania preserved the centralized structure they had inherited from the Ceauşescu period. The Ministry of Education continued to control Romania's schools through a system of inspectorates responsible for complete educational planning and oversight. In Slovakia, where the federalist government had introduced a degree of decentralization between 1990 and 1992, nationalist political elites took steps to re-centralize education after the establishment of the independent state. One of the most controversial of these steps was the Mečiar government's legislation that revoked the right of local school boards to appoint and dismiss school principals.[49] The new law enabled the Education Ministry to use the dismissal of principals as an instrument of power over Hungarian schools. Unsurprisingly, such dismissals triggered massive civil disobedience, as the Hungarian community considered the ministry's actions to symbolize illegitimate domination; the dismissed principals soon became symbols of integrity and courage.[50]

In both Romania and Slovakia, Hungarian schools constituted the overwhelming majority of minority schools. In the 1994–1995 school year, separate Hungarian schools composed 86 percent of all minority schools and minority sections in mixed schools in Romania and 90 percent in Slovakia.[51] Yet Romanian nationalists were more inclined than their Slovak counterparts to recognize the relatively large size of the Hungarian minority by creating separate offices for Hungarian education within the centralized educational structure. The Romanian government's Directorate for the Education of National Minorities included a special Hungarian department.[52] In Slovakia, although Hungarians constituted a larger segment of the population (11 percent, compared to 7 percent in Romania), the nationalist government rejected Hungarian requests to establish a similar office in the educational ministry.[53]

To buttress their argument that minority schools belonged to a state in which the majority language was the exclusive language of official interaction,

---

[49] Dostál, "Minorities," 66.

[50] In April 1995, for instance, 5,000 to 7,000 Hungarian teachers and parents participated in a conference in Komárno to protest these measures. Reacting to another round of dismissals in June, the Association of Hungarian Teachers in Slovakia organized a general boycott of the first day of school in September 1995. Approximately 70 percent of Hungarian students participated. See Sidó, "Magyar nyelvűoktatás Szlovákiában," 4; and Dostál, "Minorities," 66. See also *Forum News,* November 7, 1997.

[51] For Romania, see *Învăţământul cu predarea în limbile minorităţilor naţionale din România: Anul şcolar 1995/1996* (Bucharest: Guvernul României, Consiliul Pentru Minorităţile naţionale, 1996), 8. For Slovakia, see Rosa, "Education and Science," 181.

[52] *Învăţământul cu predarea în limbile minorităţilor naţionale din România: Anul şcolar 1995/ 1996,* 7.

[53] The equal treatment of all minority ethnic groups was articulated in the Mečiar government's 1994 program; see *Dokumenty zborník,* 133.

nationalist political elites in both states sought to exclude the use of minority languages from official school documents.[54] Although Hungarian parties in both states opposed this limitation, the issue became much more controversial in Slovakia, where the government used this requirement in January 1997 to end a seventy-five–year practice of issuing bilingual school reports in Hungarian schools. The Slovak Ministry of Education remained determined to enforce the new restriction despite massive demonstrations of opposition from the Hungarian community and pressure from European institutions.[55]

The nationalist governments did allow ethnic Hungarians to hold high administrative positions in separate Hungarian schools. In Romania, 64 percent of separate Hungarian schools had ethnic Hungarian principals in the 1994–1995 school year.[56] In the administration of mixed language schools, the 1995 education law guaranteed "proportional representation" for minority educators.[57] The ratio of separate to mixed schools, however, decreased considerably in both states, as education in Hungarian proceeded from lower to higher levels. (See tables 5.6 and 5.7 on schools in Romania and Slovakia.)

In both cases, Communist-era educational policies had significantly reduced the number of separate Hungarian schools. The government of

TABLE 5.6
Schools in the Slovak public school system with instruction in Hungarian, 1994–1995

	Kindergarten	Primary		Secondary	Vocational[1]
		Grades 1–4	Grades 1–9		
Total country	3,333	2,394		150	719
Total minority	451	312		21	89
Hungarian					
Total	403	164	135	19	81
Separate	297	151	117	11	31
Mixed	106	13	18	8	50
% separate	73.7	92.0	86.7	57.9	38.2

Source: Vladislav Rosa, "Education and Science," *in Global Report on Slovakia: Comprehensive Analysis from 1995 and Trends from 1996*, ed. Martin Bútora and Péter Hunčík, 180–81.

[1] Includes also healthcare schools and apprenticeships.

[54] Law on Education 1995, Article 8, paragraph 4; "Zákon Národnej Rady Slovenskej Republiky o štátnom jazyku Slovenskej Republiky" [Law on the State Language of the Slovak Republic No. 270/1995] in *Zbierka zákonov Slovenskej republiky,* Article 4, paragraph 3.

[55] Dostal, "Minorities," 40. This new restriction on language use was one of the reasons for the formation of the Association of Hungarian Parents in Slovakia. This organization, along with the association of teachers, organized protests against the new policy. See Sidó, *A magyar anyanyelvért folytatott küzdelem Szlovákiában,* 8–9; "Education Minister Insists on Slovak-Only School Reports," FBIS-EEU-97–318, November 14, 1997; "Education Official Defends 'Monolingual' Certificates," FBIS-EEU-97–178, June 27, 1997; *Forum News,* November 13, 1997, January 21, 1998, January 22 1998, January 30 1998. On European pressure, see *Forum News,* October 18, 30, 1997.

[56] László Murvai, *Fekete fehér könyv* (Cluj: Studium, 1996), 86.

[57] Law on Education 1995, Article 126.

TABLE 5.7
Schools in the Romanian public school system with instruction in Hungarian
1993–1994

	Kindergarten	Elementary grades 1–4	Middle grades 5–8	Secondary	Vocational
Total country					
Total minority					
Hungarian					
Total	1,077		692	141	
Separate	603		241	39	
Mixed	474		451	102	
% separate	56.0		34.8	27.7	

1994–1995

	Kindergarten	Elementary grades 1–4	Middle grades 5–8	Secondary	Vocational
Total country	12,665	6,162	7,154	1,276	1,309
Total minority	1,338	594	675	151	55
Hungarian					
Total	1,127	471	612	131	53
Separate	659	272	272	42	4
Mixed	468	199	340	89	49
% separate	58.5	57.7	44.4	32.0	7.5

1995–1996

	Kindergarten	Elementary grades 1–4	Middle grades 5–8	Secondary	Vocational
Total country	12,772	6,180	7,637	1,284	1,400
Total minority	1,325	531	768	148	48
Hungarian					
Total	1,121	456	686	128	46
Separate	719	321	277	49	2
Mixed	402	135	409	79	44
% separate	64.1	70.4	40.4	38.3	4.3

Source: Data for 1993–94 compiled from László Murvai, *Fekete fehér köny,* 95, 107. Data on elementary schools in the 1993–94 school year is inconclusive: see Murvai, *Fekete fehér köny,* 100; for 1994–1996, data is compiled from Education Ministry, *The Education System in Romania: Tuition in the Languages of National Minorities,* 1994/95, 21–22; 1995–96, 43–44.

Czechoslovakia launched an intensive project of school consolidation in the 1970s.[58] As part of this process, elementary schools in smaller villages were closed, and students and teachers were moved to larger schools in bigger settlements.[59] The policy of school consolidation in this period affected minority schools disproportionately.[60] Under the first democratizing government

[58] Gabzdilová and Homosinová, "Az iskolaügy a szlovákiai magyar politikai pártok és mozgalmak tevékénységében;" see also Sidó, "Magyar nyelvű oktatás Szlovákiában."
[59] See Gabzdilová and Homošinová, "Az iskolaügy a szlovákiai magyar politikai pártok és mozgalmak tevékénységében," 22.
[60] Ibid., 21.

TABLE 5.8
Elementary schools in the public school system in Slovakia by language
of instruction

	Slovak	Hungarian	Ukrainian
1970–71	3,299	490	43
1988–89	2,035	243	17
1990–91	2,082	257	17
1992–93	2,116	268	13

Source: Compiled from Soňa Gabzdilová and Mária Homošinová, "Az iskolaügy
a szlovákiai magyar politikai pártok és mozgalmak tevékénységében," *Regio* 3 (1994),
21–22.

of Czechoslovakia after 1989, the number of Hungarian schools increased
significantly.[61] (See table 5.8 for information on elementary schools in the
public school system in Slovakia by language of instruction.) After the establishment of independent Slovakia, however, the nationalist government
proposed bilingual schools for Hungarians. In Romania, the Communist
government in the 1970s had also introduced a policy of gradually eliminating separate minority language schools and creating mixed language schools
in which the percentage of Hungarian classes decreased over time. Although
Hungarians regained some of their historically separate schools after 1989,
the post-Communist nationalizing elites in Romania maintained a preference for mixed-language schools, as their Slovak counterparts had.[62]

Minority Pursuit of Language Maintenance

Within the pluralist state that Hungarian minority political elites in both
Romania and Slovakia envisioned, an educational system in the minority
language represented the institutional guarantee for the reproduction of a
complex minority culture. From this perspective, the independent Hungarian
school became the touchstone of community sovereignty.[63] The various
articulations of self-government by Hungarian political parties in Romania
and Slovakia came together in agreement on the need for a comprehensive
system of Hungarian schools in which all ethnic Hungarian students could
study all subjects in Hungarian (except for the majority language and literature), at all levels of education from preschool to university, in a manner

[61] Ibid., 22.
[62] See Murvai, *Fekete fehér könyv,* 49. For an account of educational policies in the Communist
period, see also Gábos, "Adatok a romániai tanügyi törvényhez," 46–68. Education State Secretary
Béres, author interview, Bucharest, Romania, Ministry of Education, June 11, 1997.
[63] Education State Secretary Béres articulated this argument in author interview, Bucharest,
Romania, June 11, 1997.

acceptable from the perspective of a Hungarian national canon.[64] These political elites sought to create a system of schools that, notwithstanding the dominance of the majority language, would help create parity between the languages in a largely bilingual Hungarian community.

In a jointly prepared proposal for an amendment to the Slovak constitution in July 1993, Coexistence and MKDM deputies granted national minorities "the right to education in the native language and to their own minority school system" as well as to "self-government in the sphere of culture and education."[65] In its 1994 electoral program, MPP declared as its "primary goal the establishment of cultural and educational self-government," arguing that the community "must take charge of issues concerning our culture, education, and traditions."[66] In the course of a decade-long language debate, the term *autonomy* gradually faded from Hungarian proposals. Yet the Hungarian Coalition, whether in parliamentary opposition or (after 1998) in the coalition government, preserved the goal of establishing an institutional framework favorable for education in Hungarian. The draft minority language law submitted by the MKP during the 1999 parliamentary debate left the door wide open for comprehensive Hungarian education, stating simply that "members of the national minorities shall have the right to be educated in their own mother tongue."[67]

Hungarian political elites in Romania were committed to an independent system of Hungarian educational institutions. The 1991 program of the Democratic Alliance of Hungarians in Romania (RMDSZ) called for an "autonomous institutional network" to serve the Hungarian community's educational needs.[68] The organization sustained a consistent effort to build such a network, both in opposition under the Iliescu regime and in the coalition government after November 1996. The Hungarians argued that, to preserve itself, a minority community must exercise "cultural autonomy" primarily in education, where "decision-making and executive authority must lie in the hands of those who represent the minority."[69]

---

[64] The "Hungarian canon" refers to Hungarian literature that includes classical and modern Hungarian writers who lived and wrote in Hungarian (in Hungary and outside) and a historiography that includes the major landmarks of Hungarian history.

[65] "Draft of Fundamental Principles of a Constitutional Law," 3.

[66] *A Magyar Polgári Párt választási programja 1994,* 4.

[67] "Draft Bill of a Group of MPs of the National Council of the Slovak Republic on the Use of the Languages of the National Minorities," Article 1, paragraph 11.

[68] For the 1991 RMDSZ program, see István Schlett, *Kisebbségnézőben: Beszélgetések és dokumentumok* (Kossuth Könyvkiadó, 1993), 177. See the same idea in the first RMDSZ "Declaration" in 1989, published in *Magyar Kisebbség* 1, no. 1 (May 1995): 16.

[69] See József Kötő "Önrendelkezés—az identitás megőrzésének garanciája," *Magyar Közélet* 1, no. 8 (January 1998). (Kötő became state secretary for education after June 1998.) For the RMDSZ commitment to the goal of Hungarian education at all levels, see *RMDSZ Tájékoztató,* June 28, 1998.

Hungarian minority politicians, educational elites, and linguists in both states argued tirelessly that learning all subjects in Hungarian constituted the only way that Hungarians could achieve complete competence in their native language. "All communities are loyal to their language," explained MKDM education specialist László Szigeti, "but minorities develop a conscious attachment," because for them the preservation of the language in its complexity becomes a specialized task, as the spheres in which minority languages are used are already limited in the larger society.[70] For language minorities, argued these elites, the school remained the only public site of socialization where thinking in the native language could develop fully. Children deprived of this possibility and compelled to shift to the majority language were likely to assimilate into the majority culture.[71] Therefore, the minority school needed to "counteract" the intrusion of the majority language in order to achieve true bilingualism or—in the words of linguist István Lanstyák—serve as a "strong castle" capable of "withstanding the siege from the outside."[72]

Hungarian linguists in both Slovakia and Romania participated actively in the political debate about bilingual schools. Linguists at the Hungarian philology department at the Comenius University in Bratislava called for a "depoliticized" look at the question of bilingual education and a better understanding of the way bilingualism "worked" in society. They argued that Slovak linguists in the structuralist tradition were more interested in language purity and standardization than in language use as an aspect of social relations.[73] They charged that Slovak nationalists misused the term *bilingualism* to describe an imaginary situation in which all members of a language group have high language competence in two languages. Hungarian linguists claimed that no such bilingualism could be achieved, because individuals had different

[70] László Szigeti, *Oktatásügyünk helyzete* (Pozsony: Magyar Kereszténydemokrata Mozgalom, 1995), 11.
[71] "Position of the Hungarian Coalition in Slovakia on the Minority Rights in The Slovak Republic Under the Third Government of Prime Minister Mečiar (1994–1996)," 4; Erzsébet Dolník, Coexistence deputy and education specialist, author interview, Bratislava, Slovakia, April 9, 1996. See also István Lanstyák and Gizella Szabómihály, *Magyar Nyelvhasználat—iskola—kétnyelvűség* (Bratislava: Kalligram Könyvkiadó, 1997); and "A teljeskörű anyanyelvű oktatásról," *Magyar Kozélet* 1, no. 7 (December 1997).
[72] István Lanstyák, "Az anyanyelv és a többségi nyelv oktatása a kisebbségi kétnyelvűség körülményei között," *Regio* 5, no. 4 (1994), p. 90. A study conducted in Slovakia that compared degrees of competence in the Hungarian literary standard among Hungarian students who were educated in Hungarian with those who are educated in Slovak and reached the conclusion that students who went to Hungarian schools had a higher level of competence in the standard. Lanstyák and Szabómihály, *Magyar nyelvhasználat—Iskola—Kétnyelvűség.*
[73] Gizella Szabómihály, linguist, author interview, Bratislava, Slovakia, April 18, 1996. Slovak linguist Slavo Ondrejovič drew the same distinction between Slovak linguists in interview conducted by the author, Bratislava, Slovakia, April 26, 1996.

abilities and, while some could develop high levels of competence in two or more languages, an entire community could not. Most members of bilingual societies—according to this argument—had a dominant and a second language, and the purpose of bilingual institutions in democratic societies was to create parity for the two languages concerned, so that speakers of both languages could function fully in their everyday life. By contrast, bilingual schools that restricted learning in the native language promoted language shift.[74]

Hungarian linguists in Romania formulated similar calls for a systematic study of social bilingualism before any state implementation of majority language planning in minority schools. They also argued for bilingual institutions that served language parity rather than language dominance.[75] All of these linguists argued for teaching the majority language as a second language, with specially developed methods, instead of full-scale experimentation with the "immersion" of all Hungarian children in a majority language environment at school. Hungarian linguists and education specialists in Slovakia were especially concerned about language immersion for children at an early age in Hungarian preschools.[76]

Hungarian minority politicians in Romania and Slovakia embraced these arguments and used them in the political debate over education policy.[77] They advocated the teaching of all subjects in Hungarian schools in the Hungarian language and the gradual introduction of the teaching of the majority language as a second language.[78] Consequently, these elites campaigned to persuade Hungarian parents to send their children to Hungarian

---

[74] For an elaboration of this argument, see István Lanstyák and László Szigeti, *Identitásunk alapja az anyanyelvű oktatás: Érveink az ún. alternatív—kétnyelvű oktatással szemben* (Bratislava: Mécs László Alapítvány, 1995); and Lanstyák, "Az anyanyelv és a többségi nyelv oktatása a kisebbségi kétnyelvűség körülményei között," 100.

[75] Author's conversations with Hungarian linguists Sándor Szilágyi and János Péntek at the National Conference on Bilingualism, University of Bucharest, Faculty of Foreign Languages and Literatures, June 16–17, 1997. See also the discussion of the "asymmetric bilingualism" characteristic in Romania in János Péntek, "Factori de asimetrie în bilingvismul social," paper presented at the same bilingualism conference. Sándor Szilágyi articulated his vision of institutions that allow for equal bilingualism in his minority statute proposal in "Tervezet. Törvény a nemzeti identitással kapcsolatos jogokról és a nemzeti közösségek méltányos és harmonikus együtteléséről."

[76] Szigeti, *Oktatásügyünk helyzete,* 19.

[77] For example, "Position of the Hungarian Coalition in Slovakia on the Minority Rights in the Slovak Republic Under the Third Government of Prime Minister Mečiar (1994–1996)," 4; Erzsébet Dolník, Coexistence deputy and education specialist, author interview, Bratislava, Slovakia, April 9, 1996.

[78] "Position of the Hungarian Coalition in Slovakia on the Minority Rights in The Slovak Republic Under the Third Government of Prime Minister Mečiar (1994–1996)," 5; and RMDSZ, "A teljeskörű anyanyelvű oktatásról." András Béres, state secretary of education, author interview, Bucharest, Romania, June 11, 1997.

schools.[79] The loss of Hungarian students to majority schools was a major concern of Hungarian minority parties in both states. In Romania, Hungarian teachers conducted a public debate about the ways of preventing Hungarian parents from sending their children to Romanian schools.[80] In their view, the most endangered members of the community were the so-called diaspora, by which they meant domestic diaspora, that is Hungarians who lived in regions where they represented less than 15 percent of the local population. The RMDSZ and the Association of Hungarian Educators in Romania placed particular emphasis on providing access to education in Hungarian for Hungarian students in these regions.[81] In both Romania and Slovakia, Hungarian elites asked to be able to create Hungarian classes even for small numbers of Hungarian children in localities lightly populated by Hungarians. In Slovakia, Coexistence called for Hungarian classes for as few as six Hungarian students. To support such demands, the Hungarian Coalition pointed to statistical data indicating that Hungarian pupils had less access than Slovak students to native language schools.[82] In Romania, the RMDSZ challenged the government's policy that only allowed the formation of minority language classes for a minimum of ten pupils, while mandating establishment of a Romanian-language class for a single ethnic Romanian pupil in a mixed settlement.[83]

In pursuit of language maintenance, these elites conceptualized every level of public school as equally important. MKDM educational expert László Szigeti explained that preschool and elementary school were critical in helping children acquire knowledge about themselves and the world through the mother tongue. During secondary school, students were formed into young adults by developing a strong foundation in "general culture," again obtained primarily by way of the mother tongue. Hungarian language education in high schools was crucial as well, because high schools

---

[79] "Position of the Hungarian Coalition in Slovakia on the Minority Rights in The Slovak Republic Under the Third Government of Prime Minister Mečiar (1994–1996)," 4. See also the Union of Hungarian Educators on the need for Hungarian children to attend Hungarian schools, *Új Szó,* October 28, 1999.

[80] *Szabadság,* September 24, 1997, April 28, May 9, 1998.

[81] "Cselekvési irányelvek a romániai magyar nyelvű oktatás fejlesztésére," RMDSZ document, December 30, 1994, 5; and *Szabadság,* September 13, 1997.

[82] "Position of the Hungarian Coalition in Slovakia on the Minority Rights in The Slovak Republic Under the 3rd Government of Prime Minister Mečiar (1994–1996)," 4. Coexistence education specialist Erzsébet Dolník made the same argument, author interview, Bratislava, Slovakia, April 9, 1996.

[83] See *Az Együttélés politikai mozgalom választási programja* (Bratislava: Coexistence, 1994), *27; for the same idea, see also Az Együttélés IV. Országos Kongresszusának programértékűdokumentumai* [undated], 66. For Romania, see "Memorandum by the Democratic Alliance of Hungarians in Romania on Romania's Admission to the Council of Europe," 19.

began preparing Hungarian intellectuals for careers in the humanities and sciences.[84] In both Romania and Slovakia, Hungarian elites emphasized the need to learn professional terminology in the majority language, but they called for a network of Hungarian vocational schools to train technical professionals and middle-level Hungarian professionals in health, administration, and other spheres.[85]

In the chain of subsequent levels of education, examinations constituted an important link. Hungarian politicians and educators charged that language restrictions in this sphere hindered Hungarian children from demonstrating their talent and knowledge, damaged their self-esteem, and limited their access to higher education.[86] In both states, Hungarian parties proposed legislation that guaranteed examinations and competitions in the minority language.[87]

A Minority National Canon

Socializing Hungarian students to the idea of belonging to a Hungarian national community was an important element of the Hungarian educational project, so learning about Hungarian history and traditions and teaching history and geography in the Hungarian language gained central significance.[88] During the educational debate in Romania, the RMDSZ consistently demanded the right to teach history and geography in Hungarian.[89] Similarly, the Hungarian parties in Slovakia fought SNS attempts to introduce Slovak-language instruction of these subjects in Hungarian schools.

[84] Szigeti, *Oktatásügyünk helyzete,* 22–28; *RMDSZ Tájékoztató,* December 12, 1997.
[85] Education State Secretary Béres emphasized the salience of recreating Hungarian vocational education after decades of "atrophy" under the Ceauşescu dictatorship; author interview, Bucharest, Romania, June 11, 1997. Szigeti, *Oktatásügyünk helyzete,* 28; *RMDSZ Tájékoztató,* December 12, 1997; and *Szabadság,* May 9, 1998.
[86] József Berényi, MPP education specialist, author interview, Bratislava, Slovakia, April 25, 1996; Erzsébet Dolník, Coexistence education specialist, author interview, Bratislava, Slovakia, April 9, 1996.
[87] 1996 minority language law, Article 5, paragraph 2; 1999 MKP minority language law, article 6, paragraph 11. See "Analiza şi consecinţele articolelor legii învăţămîntului referitoare la minorităţile naţionale," RMDSZ document, July 17, 1995. State Secretary of Education András Béres as well as his successor József Kötő emphasized the key significance of the language of university admissions in an author interview. András Béres, author interview, Bucharest, Romania, June 11, 1997. József Kötő, author interview, Cluj, Romania, June 25, 1997.
[88] "Az MKDM-Együttélés Koalíció javaslata önálló fejezet beiktatására a Szlovák Köztársaság készülő alkotmányába," *Dokumentumok* 1, no. 2 (Bratislava: MKDM, 1995), 17; *Szabadság,* October 20, 1998; and "Javaslat új történelemtankönyvekre. Helyükre kerülnek a nemzeti közösségek?" *Magyar Kisebbség* 2, no. 5 (May 1998).
[89] "A teljeskörü" anyanyelvü" oktatásról"; see also *Szabadság,* October 20, 1998, February 25, 1998.

In both cases, Hungarian elites demanded the right to use alternative text-books published in Hungary in order to preserve a "universal" Hungarian national canon. The expression "universal Hungarian literature" appeared often in Hungarian discussions, meaning Hungarian literary works written by Hungarian authors in Hungary and abroad.[90] In both cases, educators and politicians emphasized the importance of teaching Hungarian students about their nation's past in order to nurture self-respect.[91] They also called for the teaching of Hungarian traditions to majority children, to foster mutual understanding and respect.[92]

Educating a Strong Minority Elite

In both Romania and Slovakia, Hungarian political elites conceived of public education as the institution that would reproduce the Hungarian community as an entity with its own complete socioeconomic structure, including a strong Hungarian cultural, political, and economic elite.[93] To promote the concept of a "national community" as a complete social entity, these elites introduced the expressions "Hungarian society in Romania" and "Hungarian society in Slovakia."[94]

To maintain such a complete social structure, Hungarian political elites in both Romania and Slovakia shared a desire for higher education in the Hungarian language and advocated separate higher educational institutions. Yet significant differences in circumstances led these elites to articulate substantively divergent positions on the question of higher education. The Hungarian minority in Slovakia advanced more moderate claims. For

---

[90] The minority language laws drafted by the Hungarian Coalition in 1996 and 1999 guaranteed the right to use textbooks published abroad. See "Law on the Use of the Languages of National Minorities and Ethnic Groups: Draft Law of the Hungarian Coalition, Slovakia" and "Draft Bill of a Group of MP's of the National Council of the Slovak Republic on the Use of the Languages of the National Minorities." See also "Position of the Hungarian Coalition in Slovakia on the Minority Rights in The Slovak Republic Under the Third Government of Prime Minister Mečiar (1994–1996)," for criticism of restrictions on the use of alternative textbooks. See also *Szabadság*, May 9, 1998.

[91] Lanstyák, "Az anyanyelv és a többségi nyelv oktatása a kisebbségi kétnyelvűség körülményei között," 90.

[92] In Slovakia, leaders of the Hungarian Civic Party also advocated extracurricular programs that would provide children who grew up in mixed (Slovak-Hungarian) families with the opportunity to study about both languages and cultures. Kálmán Petőcz, MPP vice president, author interview, Bratislava, Slovakia, April 16, 1996.

[93] Éva Gyimesi, author interview, Cluj, Romania, May 13, 1996; and László Szigeti, *Oktatásügyünk helyzete.*

[94] In Romania, a debate emerged about the concept of "Hungarian society in Romania" during summer 1996. For an example of the use of the expression in the Slovak context, see Szigeti, *Oktatásügyünk helyzete,* 29.

them, the creation of a separate Hungarian university comprising all academic disciplines was not a priority or even a matter of consensus in the debate.[95] Regarding the forced "exodus" of Hungarian intellectuals twice in recent history as the main cause of an "unbalanced" social structure in the Hungarian community, these minority leaders viewed the emergence of a strong educated class as a very difficult and lengthy process. They described the Hungarians after 1948 as primarily a rural community that lived in small villages with poor access to secondary schools that would have prepared students for university admission.[96] Educating a Hungarian minority elite in all professions remained an important goal, however, and Hungarian politicians called on secondary school teachers in Hungarian schools to encourage students to pursue higher education in Slovak universities.[97] They also spoke for a better distribution of professions among Hungarians with higher education, describing the current situation as "skewed" in favor of teachers (as teaching was the only profession for which training in Hungarian was available).[98]

At the same time, these elites shared an overwhelming concern about the shortage of Hungarian teachers and religious leaders in Slovakia. (The shortage of priests was a result of the expulsion of Hungarian priests in 1920 and 1945 and the lack of training for Hungarian priests in post-1945 Czechoslovakia.)[99] This concern was reflected in proposals that Hungarian parties formulated for higher education in Hungarian. The solution that both politicians and educators preferred was to create a separate Hungarian department at the College of Pedagogy in Nitra that would train teachers

---

[95] A joint Coexistence-MKDM proposal submitted to parliament in 1990 called for a Hungarian university in Komarno. The scope of this university (the "Jókai Mór University") would have been limited mainly to the training of teachers and priests. The Independent Hungarian Initiative (FMK), a member of the first coalition government of post-Communist Czechoslovakia, preferred a multicultural Central European University over a separate Hungarian university. Gabzdilová and Homošinová, "Az iskolaügy a szlovákiai magyar politikai pártok és mozgalmak tevékénységében," 25.

[96] Author interviews: Gizella Szabómihály, Hungarian linguist, Bratislava, Slovakia, April 18, 1996; Erzsébet Dolník, Bratislava, Slovakia, April 9, 1996; and Kálmán Petőcz, MPP vice president, Bratislava, Slovakia, April 16, 1996.

[97] Szigeti, *Oktatásügyünk helyzete,* 31.

[98] The head of the Hungarian section of the Nationalities Department of the university in Nitra reported in June 1999, for example, that over 100 applications arrived to the department for 30 places in Hungarian-language studies. See *Új Szó,* June 4, 1999. At the same time, statistics showed that Hungarians applied in disproportionately low numbers to Slovak universities. Szigeti, *Oktatásügyünk helyzete,* 31. Szabómihály, author interview, Bratislava, Slovakia, April 18, 1996; Dolník interview.

[99] Hunčík and Gál, "The Historical Background to the formation of Slovak-Hungarian Relations," 22–28; and Sidó, "Magyar nyelvű oktatás Szlovákiában," 3. On the teacher shortage, see "Position of the Hungarian Coalition in Slovakia on the Minority Rights in The Slovak Republic under the Third Government of Prime Minister Mečiar (1994–1996)," 5.

in Hungarian for all subjects.[100] Advocates of this solution claimed that Hungarians deserved at least a separate department for the education of their teachers, because they constituted a historical national community that made up 11 percent of Slovakia's population. From this perspective, the initiative that the Slovak parliament had approved in 1992, to allow a "Department of Nationality Cultures" in Nitra for all of Slovakia's minorities, was unacceptable to the Hungarians.[101] Whether in opposition or in government, the Hungarians continued to demand a separate department as a necessity for continued education in Hungarian in all types of schools and "a potential foundation for a future independent Hungarian higher educational institution."[102]

In Romania, a consensus emerged within the RMDSZ that an independent public university was necessary to serve the educational and cultural needs of the Hungarian community.[103] Unlike Hungarians in southern Slovakia, the Transylvanian Hungarians claimed cultural and institutional traditions that were independent from institutional centers in Hungary, and the RMDSZ articulated the goal of reviving these traditions.[104] The political battle for a Hungarian university, however, began in earnest only after the adoption of the 1995 law on education and gained particular intensity during the debate about the liberalizing amendments to this law. In this debate, the RMDSZ leadership demanded that its ruling coalition partners reopen the historical Bolyai University in Cluj.

The Bolyai University was founded in the Austro-Hungarian monarchy at the end of the nineteenth century and functioned as a Hungarian university until the creation of Greater Romania in 1919. From that time onward, the university had been a central arena of Romanian-Hungarian contestation for

---

[100] This was the preference of Hungarian parliamentary deputies as well as of the Association of Hungarian Students in Slovakia (founded in November 1989) and of the Association of Hungarian Educators in Slovakia (founded in December 1989). See Gabzdilová and Homošinová, "Az iskolaügy a szlovákiai magyar politikai pártok és mozgalmak tevékénységében," 25.

[101] "Position of the Hungarian Coalition in Slovakia on the Minority Rights in The Slovak Republic under the Third Government of Prime Minister Mečiar (1994–1996)," 5.

[102] The call issued by Hungarian party leaders together with the leaders of other Hungarian organizations was published in *Közösségünk szolgálatában,* 159. See also *Új Szó,* August 17, 1999, November 6, 1999, December 6, 1999.

[103] Education State Secretary Béres talked about the process of systematically restricting the reproduction of the Hungarian elite since the beginning of the 1970s and emphasized the necessity of a complex institutional framework, including not only a university, but also publishing houses, bookstores, theaters, and other sites of intellectual life, for the survival of a Hungarian elite. Author interview, Bucharest, Romania, June 11, 1997.

[104] On the "Transylvanist" institutional culture, see József Kötő, *Szabadság,* March 28, 1998; József Kötő, "Kiművelt fők közössége," manuscript. The Hungarians in Slovakia were more severely affected by losing the ties with institutional centers in Hungary. Szabómihaly, author interview.

cultural space. In the interwar period, the government of Greater Romania established Romanian hegemony over the university, and the Hungarian faculty "emigrated" to Szeged, Hungary. In 1940, after the return of northern Transylvania to Hungary, the Hungarian university returned to Cluj and the Romanian faculty was exiled to Sibiu and Timişoara. In 1944, northern Transylvania returned to Romania and the Romanian faculty reestablished its dominance at the university until 1949, when the two universities (Hungarian and Romanian) were merged into a new entity called "Babeş-Bolyai University."[105] During the Ceauşescu dictatorship, the Hungarian side of the university decreased dramatically.[106] After the collapse of the dictatorship in 1989, the Hungarian demand for the reopening of the Hungarian university revived the contestation over institutional space in Cluj, which by that time had become a city with an overwhelmingly Romanian population and a democratically elected extreme nationalist Romanian mayor.

Under these conditions, the Hungarian struggle to regain the Bolyai University became a highly charged contestation of institutional space. In the course of this contestation, the independent university became such a cause célèbre that influential Hungarian minority elites came to view it as "the touchstone of Romanian democracy."[107] They claimed that "the re-establishment of the independent Hungarian university in Cluj [was] a matter of life or death for the Transylvanian Hungarians."[108] They asserted that only in an independent university would the Hungarian community have real authority over the reproduction of its educated class.[109] The question, they argued, was not what the majority saw as the best solution for the minority. Instead, the test of the democratic potential of Romanian society was whether the majority was capable of granting the minority's request.[110]

---

[105] Gábor Vincze and János Lázok, *Erdély magyar egyeteme 1944–49*. Vol. I (Marosvásárhely: Custos, 1995) and vol. II (Marosvásárhely: Mentor, 1998).

[106] For an excellent account of the interwar process of establishing Romanian dominance, see Irina Livezeanu, *Cultural Politics in Greater Romania* (Ithaca: Cornell University Press, 1995). For a brief history of Romanian-Hungarian contestations of the university after this period, see Enikő Magyari-Vincze, "Analiza antropologică a naţionalismelor Est-Europene," Ph.D. dissertation, Babeş-Bolyai University, June 1997, 219–20. For an account of the contemporary Hungarian perspective on the reversal of political power in Transylvania during the interwar period, see Imre Mikó, *Huszonkét év* (Budapest: Studium, 1941).

[107] See article by the president of the Bolyai Society, Ágnes Neményi, "Az önálló magyar egyetem időszerűségéről," *Szabadság*, August 5, 1998. About the debate among Romanian and Hungarian faculty within the university, see Magyari-Vincze, *Analiza antropologică a naţionalismelor Est-Europene*, 224–27.

[108] Mária Kincses-Ajtay, "A kolozsvári magyar egyetem ügye," *Szabadság*, March 19, 1998.

[109] Kötő, "Kiművelt fők közössége."

[110] János Kiss, "Ultikultúra," *Szabadság*, August 4, 1998; RMDSZ executive chairman Csaba Takács expressed the same view; see *RMDSZ Sajtófigyelő*, July 31, 1998.

Minister for Minority Affairs György Tokay declared that the creation of a Hungarian university presented a chance for Romanian-Hungarian reconciliation.[111]

These minority elites overwhelmingly rejected the "multicultural" solution that their Romanian coalition partners proposed. They considered multiculturalism to be another way of expressing Romanian dominance over Hungarian higher education.[112] Only a minority among the Hungarian elites found multiculturalism acceptable, and even they defined the concept differently from the multiculturalism that was practiced at Babeş-Bolyai University. Hungarian proponents of the principle argued for equal relations between the Romanian and Hungarian parts of the university, to be reflected in the language of instruction as well as in the distribution of authority in university management.[113] Hungarian faculty and students pressed for increased Hungarian representation in the university governing body and proportional representation of ethnic Hungarian professors at the top level of each department. At the beginning of 2000 they also asked for the establishment of five new independent Hungarian-language departments.[114]

The RMDSZ accepted its coalition partner's proposal to establish a bilingual Hungarian-German university (the Petőfi-Schiller University). This possibility, however, did not decrease the party's interest in establishing an independent university in Cluj.[115] The primary justification for this demand was that the Hungarian community in Transylvania was the rightful heir to the Bolyai University.[116] Another argument was that an independent Hungarian university could be successful only if it built on the Hungarian institutional and cultural traditions of Cluj, meaning that any colleges or departments formed elsewhere should function as the "satellites of this university."[117] Paralleling their historical case, Hungarian elites supported

---

[111] *RMDSZ Sajtófigyelő,* December 19, 1997.

[112] Júlia Németh, "Multimaszlag," *Szabadság,* September 4, 1998. The same view was expressed at EME (128) congress, *Szabadság,* April 27, 1998. Éva Gyimesi, letter to Education Minister Andrei Marga in *Szabadság,* December 12, 1997.

[113] The deputy dean of the Department of Religious Studies at Babes-Bolyai University, István Szamoskozy, argued for this concept of multicultural university, see *RMDSZ Sajtófigyelő,* July 14, 1998. See also Magyari-Vincze, *Analiza antropologică a naţionalismelor Est-Europene,* 232–34.

[114] *Szabadság,* January 8, 2000, February 1, 2000).

[115] For statement by RMDSZ President Markó, see *Szabadság,* March 5, 1999.

[116] This argument was emphasized especially by members of the Bolyai Society and other historical Hungarian societies, such as the Erdélyi Múzeum Egyesület (EME). For the EME congress, see *Szabadság,* April 27, 1998.

[117] This argument was presented forcefully by Hungarian university professors and other Hungarian elites in Cluj. Miklós Gáspár Tamás, a Hungarian intellectual who moved to Hungary from Cluj, articulated the same argument in "A Bolyai Egyetem ügyéről," *Élet és Irodalom,* December

their demand with another argument. They claimed that the Hungarian community in Transylvania, comprising almost 1.7 million people and more than 7 percent of Romania's population, was large enough that it deserved its own separate public university. Advocates of this position pointed out that numerous smaller minorities in European countries had their own native language public universities.[118] Based on the principle of democratic plurality, RMDSZ leaders argued that the Hungarians were entitled to establish a Hungarian university in any Transylvanian city.[119]

Unsuccessful in their efforts to form a separate public university, the Hungarian political elites in both Romania and Slovakia turned to private education as an alternative domain for educational autonomy. In the first years after Communism, private education did not emerge as a site of real power in these societies. Majority political elites in both states were wary of the establishment of Hungarian private schools and colleges, and they were especially reluctant to reinstate private (mostly denominational) Hungarian institutions appropriated after 1945. Still, in both cases Hungarians were able to found private schools and colleges, and the greater acceptance of these institutions by majority (especially moderate majority) elites demonstrated that the debate over language dominance concerned primarily, if not exclusively, the institutional spaces of the state. In 2002, fifty-four private higher education institutions with approximately 130,000 pupils were active in Romania, while Slovakia had only two such institutions enrolling only 2,000 students.[120]

12, 1997, 3–4. Education State Secretary Béres discussed differences among Hungarian approaches, author interview, Bucharest, Romania, June 11, 1997. See also "Az RMDSZ felsőoktatási koncepciójában Kolozsváron kell működnie az önálló magyar egyetemnek," *Szabadság,* May 8, 1998; statement by RMDSZ president Markó, *RMDSZ Tájékoztató,* June 4, 1998; RMDSZ demand for a specific law for the establishment of an independent Hungarian university in Cluj, *RMDSZ Tájékoztató,* June 1, 1998. Éva Gyimesi, head of Hungarian literature department at Babeş-Bolyai, author interview, Cluj, Romania, May 13, 1996. Gyimesi also served as RMDSZ vice president for education during 1993 and authored "Cselekvési irányelvek a romániai magyar nyelvű oktatás fejlesztésére," esp. 5. Her proposal for a Cluj-centered Hungarian higher education network was published in "Kolozsvár-központû erdélyi magyar felsőoktatási hálózat," *Romániai magyar szó,* February 11, 1998.

[118] An RMDSZ document, for example, refers to minority communities in Finland, Germany, Denmark, Italy, Spain, Belgium, the Netherlands, and England. See "Memorandum on the Objections and Requirements of the Democratic Alliance of Hungarians in Romania on Minority-Language Education in Romania, with Emphasis on the Hungarian Community," *Documents* (Cluj, Romania: Democratic Alliance of Hungarians in Romania, 1994), vol. 2, p. 20.

[119] "A teljeskörű anyanyelvű oktatásról."

[120] "Private Education in Central Europe: Less of the State, Please" *The Economist,* January 3, 2002, available at www.economist.com/displayStory.cfm?story_id=922868, accessed July 18, 2004.

An Independent System of Minority Schools

Although they articulated different approaches to an independent university, Hungarian minority elites in the two states shared an overwhelming interest in a large degree of autonomy for Hungarian schools. They envisioned a school environment capable of "counteracting" the dominance of the majority language.[121] Whether in opposition or in government, Hungarian minority parties in Romania and Slovakia pressed for the devolution of authority over schools to self-governments.[122] Notwithstanding this fundamental agreement, Hungarian elites in the two states emphasized different aspects of community authority over schools. In Slovakia, where the first democratically elected Czechoslovak government had placed school boards in charge of appointing principals and where the Mečiar government later revoked this power and dismissed a number of Hungarian principals, Hungarian parties placed most of their emphasis on reinstating the decision-making power of local school boards and the right of communities to participate in selecting school principals.[123] The 1999 minority language law drafted by the MKP also required that principals of minority schools communicate in the language of the minority.[124]

The language of school administration was also more salient in the educational debate in Slovakia than in Romania. The Mečiar government invalidated the earlier practice in Hungarian schools of issuing bilingual certificates with bilingual seals. Hungarian educators and politicians considered the loss of this right as another decline in Hungarian authority over the schools.[125] The minority language law proposals drafted by the Hungarian Coalition in 1996 and 1999 included special paragraphs to allow the use of

---

[121] On consensus among Hungarian minority parties in Slovakia, see Gabzdilová and Homošinová, "Az iskolaügy a szlovákiai magyar politikai pártok és mozgalmak tevékénységében," 21. See also the 1996 MK minority language law, Article 5, paragraph 1; 1999 MKP minority language law, paragraph 12; Shafir, "Controversy Over Romanian Education Law," 34; and "Cselekvési irányelvek a romániai magyar nyelvű oktatás fejlesztésére," 3.

[122] See *Az Együttélés IV. Országos Kongresszusának programértékű dokumentumai*, 63; Miklós Duray, Coexistence president, author interview, Bratislava, Slovakia, April 18, 1996; Dolník interview. For Romania, see "Memorandum on the Objections and Requirements of the Democratic Alliance of Hungarians in Romania on Minority-Language Education in Romania, with Emphasis on the Hungarian Community," 20; Szilágyi, "Tervezet. Törvény a nemzeti identitással kapcsolatos jogokról és a nemzeti közösségek méltányos és harmonikus együttéléséről," Article 78.

[123] Pál Csáky, deputy prime minister in charge of minorities and regional development, even proposed that his government apologize for the previous government's mistreatment of Hungarian principals; *HHRF Monitor*, January 25, 1999. Csáky's office also called for reinstating the authority of school boards. See *Új Szó*, April 14, 1999, August 12, 1999.

[124] 1999 MKP minority language law, Article 6, paragraph 12.

[125] József Berényi, MPP education specialist, author interview, Bratislava, Slovakia, April 25, 1996.

bilingual certificates and seals as well as bilingual documentation of educational activities.[126] Eventually, the Slovak parliament approved amendments to the education law to restore the right to issue bilingual certificates and to record school documents in the language of instruction.[127]

No significant devolution of state power was introduced in the Romanian educational system after 1989. The RMDSZ therefore concentrated primarily on the separate Hungarian department within the Education Ministry as a potential resource for establishing community authority over Hungarian schools.[128] With the appointment of a Hungarian state secretary of education after the regime change in 1996, the RMDSZ increased its control over educational policy concerning Hungarian schools.[129] The desire for a separate government office to coordinate minority schools was also expressed in the various Hungarian proposals in Slovakia, but these attempts were unsuccessful.[130]

The common preference of Hungarian minority parties in both states was a system of separate Hungarian schools under the authority of community self-governments and overseen by a Hungarian "peak" organization that would coordinate its activity with a special Hungarian department in the Ministry of Education. In Slovakia, the Hungarian parties separately proposed general outlines for the structure of such an organization.[131] In Romania, the RMDSZ developed a unified strategy for building an independent system of Hungarian schools under the organization's oversight. The RMDSZ strategy called for a "complete and dynamic system from pre-school to university" that at the same time would be "integrated in the state educational system."[132] Concerning the role of the state in public education, Hungarian minority elites in both states also demanded a proportional share of the state funding for Hungarian schools. They emphasized

---

[126] See 1996 minority language law, Article 5, paragraph 3; 1999 Hungarian minority language law proposal, Articles 3, 4, and 5, paragraph 12.
[127] *Új Szó,* January 15, 1999.
[128] "Cselekvési irányelvek a romániai magyar nyelvű oktatás fejlesztésére," 3.
[129] András Béres, education state secretary, author interview, Bucharest, Romania, June 11, 1997. József Kötő, RMDSZ vice president, author interview, Cluj, Romania, June 25, 1997. Kötő became State Secretary of Education after Béres's resignation.
[130] Coexistence asked for a separate department for nationality education; *Az Együttélés IV. Országos Kongresszusának programértékű dokumentumai,* 66. The MK requested such a department again in the 1994 negotiations with the Slovak opposition. See Coexistence account of negotiations, "Együttműködés a Szlovák Köztársaság kormánya és a szlovákiai magyar parlamenti pártok (Együttélés, MKDM) között 1994–ben," March 9, 1995. In 1999, the Union of Hungarian Educators asked for a network of independent Hungarian school superintendents. See *Új Szó,* January 22, 1999.
[131] For the February 1993 MKDM nationality statute proposal, see *Közösségünk szolgálatában,* 78; Coexistence's 1994 program: *Az Együttélés politikai mozgalom választási programja,* 27.
[132] "Cselekvési irányelvek a romániai magyar nyelvű oktatás fejlesztésére," 4.

that Hungarians were tax-paying citizens entitled to equal rights and a fair share of state support for education and culture.[133]

Moderate Pursuit of Integration with Majority Predominance

Moderate majority political parties in both countries sought to develop an educational strategy that would reconcile "titular" majority interest in national integration with minority rights. In pursuit of an acceptable equilibrium, these elites on the one hand were willing to allow a relatively large degree of freedom in the language of instruction in minority schools while, on the other, maintaining control over the content of education in these schools as well as over the degree to which public universities would be able to provide higher education in minority languages. These elites agreed that national minorities had a right to education in their own language. At the same time, they were reluctant to allow an independent minority public educational system from preschool to university. Instead, they opted for an integrated education system within which minorities could maintain their language and still develop native level proficiency in the majority language by the time they graduated from secondary school. They expected public schools to prepare minority students for the larger society in which majority language predominance, rather than language parity, would remain the rule.

During the first part of the decade, when moderate elites found themselves in parliamentary opposition, they could do little more than criticize the nationalists in power for preserving a high degree of centralization in the education system. Later in the decade, however, when moderate leaders formed coalition governments in both states, they began to look for consensual ways of responding to Hungarian educational demands. Romanian and Slovak moderates faced different challenges in the decade-long debates about policies of language shift in Hungarian schools. In Slovakia, where the nationalist government developed its strategy without adopting a specific education law, Slovak moderates were able to maintain a noncommittal position in parliament.[134] Joining a government with the Hungarian Coalition Party after September 1998, the same parties were also able to abandon

[133] For Slovakia, *Az Együttélés IV. Országos Kongresszusának programértékű dokumentumai,* 65; Béla Bugár, MKDM president, author interview, Bratislava, Slovakia, April 25, 1996; Duray interview; Dolnik interview. For Romania, Tibor Coltea "Mire alapozhat egy kisebbség, ha önálló intézményrendszert kíván kiépíteni," *Magyar Kisebbség* 4, no. 18 (1999). Available at www.hhrf.org/magyarkisebbseg/m990402.html; Kötő, "Önrendelkezés—az identitás megőrzésének garanciája."
[134] "Együttműködés a Szlovák Köztársaság kormánya és a szlovákiai magyar parlamenti pártok (Együttélés, MKDM) között 1994-ben," Coexistence analysis, March 9, 1995.

the previous government's "alternative instruction" plan without having to adopt new legislation. In Romania, by contrast, the post-Iliescu Romanian government had to lift previously adopted restrictions on minority language education. Consequently, the language of education remained a continuing matter of legislative debate, and in the process coalition leaders concluded a slightly less generous compromise (regarding the teaching of the national canon) than the agreement they had reached in 1997.[135]

The 1997 emergency decree declared "the right of national minorities to education in their native language at all types, levels, and forms of education, under the conditions of the law."[136] To assure such comprehensive native language education, the government also lifted restrictions on secondary and postsecondary vocational and professional training and allowed for the organization "upon request and under the conditions of the law, of groups, sections, colleges, faculties, and institutions" of higher education with instruction in minority languages.[137] The requirement of the law that professional education at secondary and university levels include the teaching of Romanian terminology was acceptable to RMDSZ leaders.[138] To assure equal chances for minority students throughout the education system, the government's decree also restored the right to take graduation and admission examinations at all levels in the languages in which students had studied the subjects in which they were examined.[139]

In the early months of the consensual period, it appeared that the agreement among coalition leaders could easily resolve the fierce controversy that the 1995 law had triggered over minority education. Yet instead of reaching such closure, the education debate continued with renewed force after the publication of the liberalizing decree, lasting two more years before the Romanian parliament adopted the amendments in July 1999. The strongest challenge to the coalition leaders' agreement emerged from the ranks of the largest coalition partner, the National Christian–Democratic Peasant Party (PNȚCD).[140] Nevertheless, the leaders of the power-sharing

---

[135] Education State Secretary Béres expressed the view that coalition leaders gradually altered their initial agreement to lift all restrictions of the 1995 law. Author interview, Bucharest, Romania, June 11, 1997.

[136] "Proiectul legii pentru modificarea legii învățământului," Article 29. State Secretary Béres emphasized the importance of the declaring this right unconditionally in the text of the law. Author interview, ibid.

[137] "Proiectul legii pentru modificarea legii învățământului," Article 31 and Article 32, paragraph 1.

[138] András Béres, author interview, Bucharest, Romania, June 11, 1997.

[139] "Proiectul legii pentru modificarea legii învățământului," Article 33.

[140] Senators and deputies of the other coalition partners also dissented from their leaders' agreement on the issue during the parliamentary debate. The RMDSZ, however, reported the most divisive differences in opinion with PNȚCD. See *RMDSZ Tájékoztató*, September 24, 25, 1997;

government remained committed to a consensual resolution of the education battle.[141] The final text of the amendments adopted on July 1, 1999, although it retained the 1995 law's restriction on the teaching of Romanian history and geography, preserved the initial liberalizing amendments largely unchanged, reflecting the moderate majority parties' acceptance of the Hungarian preference for language maintenance over language shift. To provide access to native language education for minority students, the new legislation permitted the formation of native-language classes in communities where the number of minority students fell under formerly established limits. The recognition of the right of minorities to maintain their language was evident in this text. The government went so far as to promote the values of two-way bilingualism, encouraging Romanian professionals to learn minority languages voluntarily in order to increase their ability to interact in multiethnic regions.[142]

The expectation that Hungarian schools would provide their students with a high competence in the majority language remained strong among these majority elites. The law preserved the obligation of minority students to acquire native-level proficiency in the majority language if they wanted to pass the baccalaureate after secondary school. The teaching of Romanian as a second language was allowed in elementary and middle school. At the end of high school, however, minority students were examined in Romanian language and literature from materials developed for their peers in Romanian classes.[143] At the same time, the coalition agreed to the RMDSZ request to lift the obligation under the 1995 law of "mastering" the majority language and instead to require students to "study" it.[144]

In the debate about minority education in Slovakia, the majority's demand that Hungarian students acquire high-level competence in Slovak was

excerpts from Pruteanu's speech on the Senate floor in "Commission Head Addresses Senate on Minority Education," FBIS-EEU–97–329, November 25, 1997.

[141] The PNȚCD expelled Senator Pruteanu from the party's ranks for his defiance of party discipline. See "PNTCD Expels Senator Pruteanu 'From Party Structures,'" FBIS-EEU–98–077, March 18, 1998. For reports on efforts to find a consensual solution, see for example, "PNTCD, UDMR Leaders Agree on Commission to Solve Dispute," FBIS-EEU–97–269, September 26, 1997; "Miniszterelnöki látogatás az RMDSZ-frakciónál: Radu Vasile támogatja jogainkat," *Szabadság,* April 10, 1998.

[142] "Proiectul legii pentru modificarea legii învățământului," Article 33. Education Minister Petrescu emphasized that ethnic Romanians were in no way obliged to learn minority languages and this option was only made available for them, so that they might "maintain positions" in mixed regions, see Petrescu interview with Ghimpu, "Învățământul 'susține' interesul național pentru integrarea Europeană," 5.

[143] "Proiectul legii pentru modificarea legii învățământului," Article 30.

[144] Education Minister Virgil Petrescu explained in a television talk show that in the ministry's definition, the term *study* already contained the requirement that students master the Romanian language at each respective grade level, otherwise they could not pass the necessary examination. *Televiziunea Antena 1* (Bucharest, Romania), June 25, 1997, voice recording by author.

even more forceful. Many Slovak moderates perceived the preservation of a separate language as both a tool for preserving national identity and a source of division between language communities.[145] To illustrate the legitimacy of requiring Hungarian schools to provide both Hungarian language mainte-nance and a mastery of the Slovak language, the Education Ministry under the Moravčik government issued a report on the preferences of Hungarian parents. This report indicated that the overwhelming majority of Hungarian parents regarded the maintenance of Hungarian public schools to be a dem-onstration of the Slovak government's respect for their rights and that most of these parents also considered the mastery of Slovak an important asset in Slovakia.[146] Unlike the nationalists, the Slovak moderate elites were willing to accept methods that Hungarian linguists recommended for improving the learning of Slovak as a second language, rather than introducing "lan-guage immersion" in Hungarian schools.[147]

As architects of a new national state, majority moderates in Slovakia were less inclined to create new institutional spaces for Hungarian edu-cation than their Romanian counterparts. The preelection agreements be-tween the Slovak Democratic Convention and the Hungarian Coalition in December 1997 did not address Hungarian aspirations for higher educa-tion in the native language and promised instead a public education system that would allow for education in Hungarian only up to the end of second-ary school.[148] The Slovak governing parties also rejected their Hungarian coalition partner's request to include educational rights in the minority language law adopted in 1999.[149] By contrast, the dominant view among majority moderate leaders in Romania throughout the decade was that the Hungarians had legitimate claims to native language education from preschool through university. Consequently, these leaders sought ways of expanding higher education in Hungarian after the formation of the new government in 1996.

A Consistent National Canon

Moderate majority political parties in Romania and Slovakia considered the teaching of the majority national canon to minority students instrumental to

---

[145] Slavo Ondrejovič, "Contact Languages and Minorities in The Slovak Republic," *Human Affairs* 3, no. 2 (1993): 187; Ondrejovič, author interview, Bratislava, Slovakia, April 26, 1996.

[146] Rosa, "Education and Science," 182–83.

[147] Deputy Prime Minister Pál Csáky listed this as an important achievement of the first year of power-sharing government in Slovakia. See *Új Szó,* April 9, 1999.

[148] For full text of the agreement, see *Új Szó,* December 3, 1997.

[149] "SMK's Bugar Hopeful Language Law Agreement Can Be Reached," FBIS-EEU–1999–0623, June 23, 1999.

achieving minority socialization in the spirit of loyal citizenship. Nonetheless, these moderates favored different methods for achieving this goal. Instead of requiring the teaching of canon subjects exclusively in the majority language, Slovak moderates relied on ministerial control over the content of instruction in all schools. They pointed out that only the state could guarantee a nationally acceptable quality of education in all schools and prevent potential tensions among Slovak and Hungarian parents and educators in southern Slovakia.[150] In Romania, moderate parliamentarians manifested a strong consensus on the necessity to preserve the policy of teaching the subjects most directly related to ideas about the national space (Romanian literature, history, and geography) exclusively in the Romanian language. In the parliamentary debate, the overwhelming majority of moderate Romanian deputies voted in favor of the nationalizing position on this issue.[151] The issue gained such significance that prominent PNȚCD leaders in late 1997 claimed that the idea of an independent Hungarian university was more acceptable than the instruction of history and geography in Hungarian.[152]

Meanwhile, the possibility of schools choosing among alternative textbooks rendered the task of maintaining a traditional Romanian national canon difficult. A heated parliamentary controversy over newly available alternative history textbooks in the fall of 1999 illustrated the ongoing political salience of centrally designed interpretations of the past.[153] Eventually, the language liberalization that the moderates adopted put an end to the practice of teaching Romanian history and geography in higher grades exclusively in Romanian. The condition remained, however, that Hungarian-language instruction of these subjects be based on exact translations of the curricula and teaching materials developed for Romanian-language schools.[154]

---

[150] This view was expressed especially by KDH Chairman Čarnogurský, author interview, Bratislava, Slovakia, April 24, 1996.

[151] *RMDSZ Tájékoztató,* July 1, 5, 1999; "Diaconescu: History, Geography To Be Taught in Romanian," FBIS-EEU–97–316, November 12, 1997; and "PNȚCD Agrees to Compromise on Education Law," FBIS-EEU–97–316, November 12, 1997.

[152] Radu Vasile, later prime minister of Romania, expressed this opinion in December 1997. See *Szabadság,* December 16, 1997.

[153] "O nouă dispută încinge Parlamentul României: Scandalul cu manualul," *Evenimentul zilei,* October 6, 1999, www.expres.ro/arhive/1999/octombrie/06/politica/3–2.html; "Cine îl lucrează pe Vlad Țepeș?" *Evenimentul zilei,* October 10, 1999, www.expres.ro/arhive/1999/octombrie/10/editorial/9oct.html; "Autorii manualului de istorie de clasa a XII-a sînt gata să se supună oricărei anchete, inclusiv penale," *Evenimentul zilei,* October 7, 1999, www.expres.ro/arhive/1999/octombrie/07/politica/3–5.html; "Manualele de istorie," *Revista 22,* www.dntb.ro/22/1999/50/3niculescu.html; and Christian Preda, "Acuz!" *Revista 22,* www.dntb.ro/22/1999/42/1cp-edi.html.

[154] "Proiectul legii pentru modificarea legii învățământului," Article 30, paragraph 2.

Higher Education: Integration under Majority Oversight

Although Romanian moderates were less willing than their Slovak counterparts to allow minority schools to teach the majority national canon in minority languages, they were considerably more generous than the Slovak moderates in creating minority-language educational opportunities within state universities. The 1990s in Slovakia were the first decade of independent state formation, and in this context majority moderate elites demonstrated no desire to facilitate the reproduction of a Hungarian minority elite. Slovak had to remain the exclusive language of higher education, except for the training of Hungarian teachers. The new Slovak leadership agreed to expand instruction in the Hungarian language only in this area, and only within existing institutional structures. The Education Ministry supported the improvement of Hungarian-language teacher training at the Pedagogical College in Nitra but denied Hungarian aspirations for the establishment of a separate Hungarian department within the college. (A newly elected rector and university governing body in Nitra endorsed the expansion of Hungarian training, increased Hungarian representation in the university management, and expressed support for an independent Hungarian-language department in the long run.)[155] Efforts to obtain Hungarian-language university education in other professions, however, remained outside the debate for majority moderates. In January 2004, the government allowed the establishment of a private Hungarian-language institution, the Selye János University, which offers higher education in teacher training, economics, and theology.

In Romania, the leaders of the coalition government formed after November 1996 agreed that Hungarians had a right to higher education in Hungarian. A communiqué issued by Romanian President Emil Constantinescu argued that since Hungarian aspirations for comprehensive native language education were legitimate and in agreement with European norms, the practical uses of such education in Romanian society were irrelevant from the perspective of democratic rights.[156] The question Romanian coalition leaders had to answer was whether they could agree to establish a separate Hungarian public university and to reopen the Hungarian public university in Cluj. In answering this question, the leadership of the Romanian governing

---

[155] *Új Szó*, March 11, 1999, July 6, 1999, September 28, 29, 1999, October 16, 25, 30, 1999, November 9, 1999, December 6, 1999.
[156] "President Approves of Hungarian Language Education," FBIS-EEU–97–072, March 13, 1997. The right to education in Hungarian at all levels of the education system was also guaranteed in governmental decree No. 36/1997; see Article 32, paragraph 1.

parties moved from hesitant approval in the spring of 1997 to firm rejection in the summer of 1998.

On a visit to Budapest in March 1997, Prime Minister Victor Ciorbea stated that the coalition had agreed to restore the independent Hungarian university in Cluj in a two-step process, first creating a separate Hungarian section within the existing structure, then establishing a fully independent Hungarian university.[157] The Romanian president also declared public support for developing a Hungarian section "alongside" the Romanian section within Babeş-Bolyai University.[158] These high-level public contemplations of a highly controversial solution, however, triggered strong reactions within the Romanian coalition parties and the Romanian academic community. In Cluj, the rector of BBU, Andrei Marga, called a "crisis meeting" to discuss the government's proposal.[159] The president retreated and issued a "clarification"—no less controversial than his initial communiqué—to the effect that he did not support the idea of splitting the BBU into two parts. Instead, he proposed, the Hungarian section would remain part of an integrated university and the leadership of BBU would be consulted before any reorganization.[160] Thus, in a highly charged political debate, what the Hungarians had framed as the reopening of the historical Hungarian university in Cluj the Romanian side redefined as the "splitting up of the BBU along ethnic lines."[161] Clearly, the university was considered an important arena for the formation of socioeconomic and political authority.[162] As discussed earlier, the university in Cluj had particular significance as one of the primary arenas in which the reversal of power between Romanians and Hungarians took place after the incorporation of Transylvania in Greater Romania in 1919. In a passionate address to RMDSZ leaders on the parliament floor, Education Committee Chairman Pruteanu (of PNŢCD) articulated the view that reopening the Bolyai University through a process of dividing the BBU would

---

[157] *Magyar Nemzet,* March 13, 1997; Claudiu Săftoiu, "Riscul de imagine şi chestiunea maghiară," *Sfera Politicii* 47 (1997): 38.

[158] "President Approves of Hungarian Language Education," FBIS-EEU–97–072, March 13, 1997; see also Săftoiu, "Riscul de imagine şi chestiunea maghiară," 39.

[159] For a discussion of the internal process triggered by Ciorbea's comments, see Magyari-Vincze, *Analiza antropologică a naţionalismelor Est-Europene.*

[160] "Presidency Denies Intending to Split Up Cluj University," FBIS-EEU–97–073, March 14, 1997.

[161] Education State Secretary Béres discussed Hungarian views in author interview, Bucharest, Romania, June 11, 1997.

[162] For a discussion of the university as a "field of power" in the post-Communist elite transformations in Romania, see Adrian Neculau, "Construirea câmpului de putere şi transmiterea moştenirii în instituţiile de învăţământ superior," *Revista de cercetări sociale* 1 (1994): 62–69. For the change of power relations in the educational system after the creation of Greater Romania, see Livezeanu, *Cultural Politics in Greater Romania.*

have signified Hungarian separatism and ultimately a defiance of Romanian cultural dominance in Romania.[163]

Thus, by October 1997 a consensus had formed within the coalition leadership that the Bolyai University could not be reopened and that Cluj could not become the site of any independent Hungarian public university. In December 1997, the Senate voted overwhelmingly against reopening the Hungarian university in Cluj.[164] Yet the coalition leaders continued to express willingness to discuss the establishment of a Hungarian university.[165] In June 1998, they accepted the RMDSZ initiative to form a committee that would assess the possibility of such a university and to create new Hungarian departments within BBU as well as in the Gheorghe Dima Music Academy in Cluj.[166] Under pressure from parliamentarians and the Romanian academic community, however, the government adopted the "multicultural" solution advocated by Education Minister (and former BBU rector) Andrei Marga.[167] "Multiculturalism" was the idea that Romanian would remain one of the languages of instruction in any public university that offered instruction in other languages. Its advocates believed that "multiculturalism" would prevent Hungarian "separatism" by including minority languages in higher education without endangering social and political integration. Besides increasing the

[163] "Commission Head Addresses Senate on Minority Education," FBIS-EEU–97–329, November 25, 1997. The view that the division of BBU would have served Hungarian separatism was advanced forcefully by Andrei Marga, rector of BBU and education minister in 1998. For his statement, see *România liberă*, August 1, 1998. PNT ̦ CD leader Nicolae Cerveni expressed the same view; see "All Sides Reach 'Full Agreement' on Cluj University," FBIS-EEU–97–094, April 4, 1997.

[164] *Szabadság*, December 19, 1997.

[165] "PNTCD Agrees to Hungarian University, But Not in Cluj," FBIS-EEU–98–173, June 22, 1998.

[166] The Hungarian press reported Prime Minister Ciorbea stating at meeting with Hungarian Prime Minister Gyula Horn that a Hungarian university would be acceptable, but not in Cluj. See *Szabadság*, October 23, 1997. On President Constantinescu's stance in December 1997, see *Szabadság*, December 11, 1997. On the agreement to form a commission, see *RMDSZ Tájékoztató*, June 10, 1998. See also "Coalition Leaders Agree on Hungarian-Language Instruction," FBIS-EEU–98–161; "Ciorbea Confers with Cluj University, Fourth Army Leaders," FBIS-EEU–997–281.

[167] For Marga's statement, see *România liberă*, August 1, 1998. For a joint protest against a separate Hungarian university by prominent Romanian university professors from several universities in Romania, see *Curentul*, May 19, 1998. For the government's turn to multiculturalism, see "Radu Vasile Says Multicultural University 'Only Solution,'" FBIS-EEU–98–261, September 18, 1998. The BBU Senate adopted a joint committee decision about the "multicultural" character of the institution in April 1997, See "All Sides Reach 'Full Agreement' on Cluj University," FBIS-EEU–97–094. Education Minister Virgil Petrescu also expressed his choice for a multicultural university in Cluj; see "Minister Backs Multicultural University in Cluj-Napoca," FBIS-EEU–97–248, September 5, 1997. The government's decree No. 36/1997 also encouraged the establishment of "multicultural structures and activities" in higher educational institutions; see Article 33, "Proiectul legii pentru modificarea legii învăţământului."

"multicultural" character of BBU, Marga also made a less popular proposal in the fall of 1998 to establish a Danubian University that would have Hungarian departments in Arad and Satu-Mare and Romanian departments in similar cities in Hungary.[168]

Although "multiculturalism" became the popular solution among Romanian moderates, coalition leaders in Bucharest continued to search for a consensual response to the Hungarian demand for a separate university. In September 1998, they issued a decree to allow the establishment of a Hungarian-German bilingual university called Petőfi-Schiller.[169] This option also guaranteed that the Hungarians were not "on their own" in a separate public university. Although the government had not consulted the representatives of the German minority, the Democratic Forum of Germans in Romania accepted the offer and joined an ad hoc leadership of the Hungarian-German language university in October 1998.[170] The idea of a bilingual Hungarian-German university, however, found weak support within the moderate political parties.[171] As the education law amendments adopted in July1999 indicated, the farthest that these parties were willing to go was to allow the establishment of loosely defined "multicultural" institutions for minority education.[172]

Decentralization with Majority Oversight

The position of Romanian and Slovak moderates concerning community authority over schools reflected the same search for balance between majority interests and minority demands for institutional autonomy. In both cases, majority political parties called for decentralization in public education while emphasizing the need to integrate Hungarian schools into a national educational system. Romanian Education Minister Andrei Marga, the most vocal supporter of multiculturalism, also indicated a consistent interest in decentralizing Romanian education and connecting educational

---

[168] Romanian coalition leaders argued that the Romanian community in Hungary and the Hungarians in Romania were not comparable in size and therefore provided no basis for such reciprocity. "Education Minister Suggests Funding 'Danube University,'" FBIS-EEU–98–252, September 9, 1998.

[169] The government issued a decree (No. 687/1998) to allow for the establishment of the Petőfi-Schiller University, see "Government Offers to Set Up 'Petőfi-Schiller' University," FBIS-EEU–98–273, September 30, 1998; and *Szabadság,* October 21, 1998.

[170] *Szabadság,* October 10, 1998

[171] Among others, PNȚCD President Ion Diaconescu; PNȚCD Vice President Remus Opriş; the leaders of the National Liberal Party; and the National Council of University and College Presidents expressed strong opposition to the Petőfi-Schiller university. *RMDSZ Sajtófigyelő,* December 15, 1998; and *Szabadság,* October 21, 1998.

[172] *RMDSZ Tájékoztató,* July 1, 5, 1999.

institutions both to their local communities and to a broader international network.[173] The government also amended the 1995 education law to provide teachers, parents, community leaders, and civic organizations a greater role in operating local schools.

RMDSZ leaders failed to convince their coalition partners of the legitimacy of a separate Hungarian educational system. Under the new government, the administrative supervision of schools remained under the authority of school inspectorates accountable to the Ministry of Education. The RMDSZ's coalition partners agreed to increase the presence of Hungarians in these ministerial decision-making structures. After the formation of the governing coalition, the RMDSZ was able to appoint state secretaries of education and culture. As Education Minister Virgil Petrescu (Marga's predecessor) had explained, from the perspective of majority moderates, greater Hungarian authority meant "a guarantee for minority-majority integration [through] internally autonomous structures, but not separation."[174]

In Slovakia, the issue of local community authority over schools gained particular salience after the Mečiar government used the dismissal of Hungarian school principals as a method for controlling Hungarian educational institutions. After they had attained power in late 1998, the Slovak moderates agreed to restore the right of school boards to appoint and recall principals. The Hungarian preference for giving local self-governments authority over schools, however, remained controversial among majority moderates.[175]

As occurred in Romania after 1996, the majority coalition partners allowed the Hungarian party to appoint an education state secretary.[176] Unlike the Romanian moderates, however, the Slovak coalition partners were reluctant to create a separate Hungarian office within the ministry. Instead, the new Slovak government established a minority department with officials representing the Ukrainian, Roma, and German communities as well as the Hungarian minority.[177]

A Pluralist Majority Position

As an alternative to the moderate majority position, politically active liberal intellectuals in Romania and Slovakia articulated a pluralist perspective that accepted the Hungarian aspiration for language parity in minority education

---

[173] Marga's ideas on decentralization appeared in *România liberă*, April 3, 1998.
[174] Ghimpu, "Învăţământul 'susţine' interesul naţional pentru integrarea Europeană."
[175] Čarnogurský, author interview, Bratislava, Slovakia, April 24, 1996.
[176] "SMK's Szigeti To Be Education Ministry State Secretary," FBIS-EEU-98-307, November 3, 1998.
[177] *Új Szó*, April 9, 1999.

allowing minorities equal rights to participate in public education in their language at all levels and to reproduce a national elite in all professions. In Romania, this approach was articulated primarily by the liberal circle at the Romanian Helsinki Committee in Bucharest.[178] Without endorsing the RMDSZ concept of educational autonomy, this group called for a genuinely public (rather than state-controlled) educational system in which local communities would have considerable autonomy over schools. This group proposed "distinct" school units for minority education, challenged the majority's efforts to impose a Romanian national canon in the teaching of history and geography, and advocated the Hungarian community's right to reestablish their historical educational institutions, including the university in Cluj.[179] Slovak liberals did not develop a similar pluralist legislative proposal, but the Slovak Helsinki Committee strongly criticized the nationalist government's policy of language shift, and a prominent Slovak intellectual, political scientist and former VPN deputy Miroslav Kusý, articulated a pluralist approach to Hungarian institutional demands.[180] Although not influential in the legislative debate of either parliament, the pluralist majority approach was nevertheless significant for presenting an alternative to the moderate perspective and questioning the legitimacy of majority predominance in all segments of the public school system.

The decade-long debates over language use in education demonstrated the extraordinary significance of the public educational system to both majority and minority political elites in reproducing national cultures. As all of the important political actors in both states conceived of democratic government as popular sovereignty over "national spaces," the public school became a strongly contested domain. The key issue of the debate was the relationship between the territorial state and the public school. Should the school primarily serve the interests of the state or the interests of the local community? To what extent could the minority school become a minority

---

[178] Gabriel Andreescu, president of the Helsinki Committee's Bucharest office, articulated the pluralist democratic foundation of his position, author interview, Bucharest, Romania, May 29, 1996.

[179] Andreescu, Stan, and Weber, "Un proiect de lege privind minoritățile naționale elaborat de Centrul pentru drepturile omului." See also Weber, "Legea învățământului," 16. Some individual Romanian parliamentarians, such as Laurențiu Ulici, Romanian Alternative Party senator and president of the Romanian Writers' Union, argued during the parliamentary debate over the amendments to the 1995 education law that the Hungarians, as a historical national community as opposed to an immigrant group, had aspirations for national reproduction that the majority was obliged to respect. See *RMDSZ Tájékoztató*, September 21, 1997.

[180] "Helsinki Committee: Education Measures 'Discriminatory,'" FBIS-EEU–97–127, May 7, 1997. Miroslav Kusý explained his pluralist perspective on the Hungarian demands in author interview, Bratislava, Romania, April 23, 1996.

"national space"? Was the purpose of the minority school to prepare students for life under majority language dominance or predominance in all settings, or should the school help create language parity in bilingual communities that included the minority language in all domains of public life?

The similarities and differences in the answers that nationalist and moderate majority and Hungarian minority parties gave to these questions mirrored these parties' positions in the broader debate about the new social contract. Majorities that sought to establish or consolidate a unitary national state represented the interests of such a state in public education. They designed educational policies that would simultaneously strengthen state sovereignty and achieve majority cultural dominance. From this perspective, the public school served minority students best by facilitating language shift rather than language maintenance in the minority community. Majority nationalists also demanded that minority schools teach a centrally sanctioned canon in literature, history, and geography. The story of past and present links to the territory, national heroes, and literary figures had to reinforce ideas of loyalty to the state. Because this task was especially salient in minority language schools, these schools had to remain fully consolidated in a centralized system of education. Separate minority institutions at any level were undesirable. The unitary national state that majority nationalists envisioned also required loyal and undivided political, cultural, and economic elites. Strong minority national elites educated in the minority language endangered the unitary character of the state. Individual members of the minority could gain access to higher education in a majority environment and in the majority language.

The conditions under which Slovak and Romanian nationalizing political elites designed their educational policies provided different possibilities and constraints. Building a new national state, Slovak nationalists articulated a more explicit connection between the language of education and loyalty toward the state than their Romanian counterparts, who sought to complete the "nationalization" of a relatively older state. The Slovak nationalist government developed a much more ambitious plan for language shift in Hungarian schools than the Romanian nationalizing government. Because it represented a drastic change from the previous structure of minority education, however, the Slovak "alternative education" plan was ultimately unsuccessful. The Romanian policies of language shift continued and legally formalized Communist-era practices. Consequently, by the end of the period of nationalist majority governments, limitations on the language of minority education in the two states remained by and large unchanged from the Communist era. Hungarians in Slovakia faced fewer language limitations than Hungarians in Romania throughout pre-university education but more in the sphere of higher education. In this sense, the strategy of gradual shift away from minority language usage by the end of secondary education was more consistently applied in Slovakia.

Hungarian minority political elites, for their part, expected the post-Communist social contract to establish a fundamentally different relationship between the state and the minority education system. They envisioned education policies that would strengthen their community rather than the state, and they called on majority political elites to lift all previous restrictions on language use in education. In both states, Hungarians reacted particularly strongly against the new limitations that the post-Communist governments attempted to impose. For Hungarians in Romania, the Iliescu regime's formalization of previously informal restrictive practice in the 1995 education law was seen as a betrayal of trust. The Hungarians in Slovakia received news of the introduction of "alternative education," the dismissals of Hungarian school principals, and prohibition of bilingual certificates with similar disillusionment.

The purpose of minority schools, from the perspective of the Hungarian minority elites, was to help create parity among national groups and national languages in ethnically mixed regions—a bilingualism of equal cultures. They envisioned minority schools as sites of socialization that would help students maintain Hungarian as their primary language while learning the majority language as a second language used for communication in the broader society. These elites expected the minority school to create a link between students and their own national space, the story of which they believed should be told in their language and also from their perspective. To preserve the minority language and culture in their complexity, Hungarian elites claimed the right to separate institutional spaces in education that would allow a large decree of independence from majority language dominance. They envisioned a separate network of schools placed under the authority of community self-governments and overseen by a Hungarian "peak" organization.

The legacies of the Communist period created dramatically different conditions for Hungarian higher education, and it was in this domain that the choices of Hungarian political elites in Romania and Slovakia differed significantly. Although Hungarians in both states sought to expand Hungarian higher education and achieve more autonomy in this sphere, the Hungarian parties in Slovakia limited the scope of their demands primarily to teacher training. The Hungarian political elites in Romania, on the other hand, articulated a strong call for the reopening of an independent Hungarian public university.

It was precisely these calls for separate institutional spaces that created a fault line between the minority Hungarian and the moderate Romanian and Slovak positions on educational policy. On the one hand, moderates in both states wanted to make public schools more "public" and less state-centered and recognized the legitimacy of minority public demands for language maintenance. On the other, they maintained a "titular" preference for language predominance (asymmetric bilingualism) in all settings and institutions within the territorial boundaries of the state. Consequently, these elites expected minority schools to compel students to achieve *native-level* competence in the majority language even as they were taught mainly in the minority language. They wanted schools to prepare minority students for a broader society in which the majority language would be predominant. They also feared that if minority schools became separate "national spaces," they would not adequately create the necessary link between minority citizens and the state. As their policy choices indicated, majority elites regarded this link as an important guarantee for territorial integrity. In both states, moderate majority parties opted for continued control over the content of education in minority schools, especially in history and geography—although Romanian moderates were significantly more forceful in this respect than their Slovak counterparts. The Slovak moderates did not join nationalist efforts to introduce new legislation to teach history and geography in Slovak; rather, they favored ministerial control over the content of instruction in minority schools.

Bound by their coalition agreement with the Hungarian party to reopen the legislative debate about minority education, Romanian moderate elites lifted most of the restrictions that the nationalizing government had instituted on minority language use in education (leaving in place the requirement to teach history and geography in Romanian in higher grades). After the change in power, the Slovak consensual government also adopted liberalizing amendments to alter the previous government's restrictive legislation. At the same time, the Slovak moderates were less willing to create new institutional spaces for minority education than their Romanian counterparts, who made considerable efforts to increase higher educational opportunities for Hungarian and German minorities. Moderate political elites in Romania and Slovakia shared concerns about independent Hungarian higher educational institutions. These concerns were much more pronounced in Slovakia, however, where even the creation of a separate Hungarian teacher training department in a Slovak-language institution was controversial. In Romania, the leadership of the moderate coalition parties could conceive of a bilingual Hungarian-German public university—even though this solution found little support among moderate parliamentarians and in the end did not materialize. As an alternative solution, Hungarians established private colleges with the support of the Hungarian state.

The education policy choices that emerged from more than a decade's worth of debates in these countries were anchored in divergent positions that majority and minority political actors maintained about the relationship between national communities outside the public school, in the broader institutional structure of the reconstituted state. Although Hungarian demands for community autonomy over minority education remained unacceptable to a spectrum of majority parties, in both states an increasingly pluralist relationship emerged by the end of the first decade after Communism, as moderate majority and minority political parties renegotiated their positions and cooperated in the democratic process.

Chapter 6

Language and Democratic Competition

The question of language use is a fundamental component of the social contract in multilingual democracies, no matter how recently the territorial boundaries of a state were drawn or how eagerly governments pursue transnational integration. The territorial nation-state model that emerged in Europe in the process that we associate with modernity has become influential around the world, ascribing special status to the place and importance of national languages in the political process. This study has demonstrated that, despite European integration, nationalism remains a powerful principle of social organization, as national majorities and minorities alike aspire to reproduce their cultures on territories defined as "national homelands" and expect their languages to mark cultural ownership over those territories. The broadly shared notion of linguistic territoriality also includes an expectation that the national language be inextricably linked to institutional spaces associated with sovereignty and those that guarantee cultural reproduction.

Ultimately, the language debates explored in this study revolved around the question of who has to right to the institutions that guarantee cultural reproduction on nationally defined territories. As the study has also revealed, when more than one "nation" claims rights to cultural reproduction on the same "national homeland," competing concepts of sovereignty and inclusion emerge, and the issue of language use can become deeply divisive. When both language majorities and politically well-organized language minorities see themselves as national entities and define popular sovereignty in linguistic terms, they are likely to push for divergent institutional agendas, such as the national majority for linguistic assimilation and the minority for institutionally guaranteed language pluralism.

Indeed, the strategies that democratic territorial states around the world are likely to continue to pursue are either various forms of linguistic assimilation or various degrees of institutionalized language pluralism. As the language debate in Romania and Slovakia demonstrates, the question of whether such strategies will bring more cohesion than conflict and more legitimacy than challenge to democratic states hinges on a combination of key domestic and international factors, among which majority and minority political elites and parties hold a prominent place.

Democratically elected for the first time after decades of Communist Party rule, the political elites in charge of the transformation process drafted new constitutions and restructured the fundamental institutions of government. Taking turns in government and opposition, they laid down the contract that would serve as a new foundation for popular sovereignty. As part of this process, the question of how to establish the relationship between majority and minority national communities in the new or reconstituted state was fiercely debated, as majority and minority political elites opted for different institutional structures: majorities for a unitary nation-state and minorities for a pluralist state allowing various forms of minority institutional autonomy. In the former Yugoslavia, similarly conflicting visions about the post-Communist state derailed the process of democratization and European integration, and led to massive violence.[1] In Romania and Slovakia, however, competitive nation-building did not turn violent—not even under the conditions of new state formation or dramatic regime change in a region of mutually claimed national homelands.

One of the most important lessons that post-Communist democratization provides to other parts of the world, where societies are emerging, or hoping to emerge, from long periods of undemocratic rule, is that democratic competition can lead to the resolution of deeply divisive issues. Outside influence can encourage and reinforce commitments to democracy, but it is the internal process (domestic electoral alliances and at times vicious debates in parliaments that force majority and minority parties to articulate, fight, and negotiate their positions peacefully) that leads to a broadly acceptable social contract.

This study also demonstrates that both the continuing power of linguistic territoriality and the potential for majority-minority consensus are greatly influenced by the challenges of institutional transformation and the way that majority and minority elites respond to those challenges—the way

---

[1] Chip Gagnon, *The Myth of Ethnic War* (Ithaca: Cornell University Press, 2004).

they define the "national interest," and the leadership they demonstrate. The leadership that mattered in these cases was not the power of one charismatic leader—indeed, most charismatic leaders in the region in this period were highly divisive—but the perseverance of majority and minority political elites who forged interethnic alliances despite deep disagreements and mutual distrust. Ethnic majorities feared the fragmentation of their state, and minorities feared the loss of their culture. Yet they managed to reach consensus on deeply divisive issues.

This study confirms the notion that state formation and regime change can increase the salience of the language issue and raise the potential for conflict over multilingualism.[2] In both Romania and Slovakia, language contestations that were heightened in the first decade of post-Communist transformation have become more moderate in recent years. In Slovakia, where political elites were engaged in creating a new nation-state after the breakup of Czechoslovakia in 1992, language became directly linked to the debate about independence. The nationalist majority demand for a specific language law to establish Slovak as the exclusive official language compelled all political parties to take a stand on multilingualism. Throughout the first decade of the independent state, the ongoing battles over the language law helped define majority and minority positions on the relationship between the state and the Hungarian minority. The language laws adopted in 1990, 1995, and 1999 were the major landmarks of this process. In the absence of a similar debate about independent statehood in post-Ceaușescu Romania, majority nationalizing elites did not call for a specific language law. Instead, they incorporated policies of language dominance into laws concerning local public administration and public education.

Although the key domains of contestation were the same in both cases, Slovak majority nationalists expressed the link between language rights and territorial sovereignty more boldly than their Romanian counterparts. Slovak nationalists articulated stronger interest in the exclusion of minority languages from the official domain and in achieving language shift in minority schools. Slovak moderates were also less generous to their Hungarian coalition partners than their Romanian counterparts.

Although the Romanian and Slovak governments faced different challenges after the collapse of Communism (state formation in one case, state consolidation in another), they chose similar strategies to contend with these challenges, and their strategies contributed to similar dynamics. The framers of the debate about the new social contract (the dominant political elites

---

[2] Laitin, *Language Repertoires and State Construction in Africa*; Snyder, *From Voting to Violence*.

during the first years of post-Communism) were majority nationalists who opted for a traditional unitary nation-state and approached the question of linguistic diversity as a threat to state stability. They sought to establish complete majority control over the institutions of government and cultural reproduction at all levels and in all regions of the country. These elites also chose to exclude from the process of institutional design not only minority elites but also those majority elites and parties that represented different approaches to regime change. Therefore, the institutional and legislative strategies of the first period of democratization created divisions both between and within national groups.

In both cases, the nation-state design caused Hungarian minority parties and organizations to form a united front and demand substate institutional autonomy, while majority parties remained united on the salience of state stability and on the rejection of minority claims for institutional autonomy, but they were deeply divided over the question of whether the state should maintain centralized control over all institutions. On the latter point, the Romanian and Slovak democratic opposition found itself in agreement with Hungarian minority parties, and this commonality of interest in decentralization and governmental accountability led to strategic alliances between them.

These alliances established minority parties as integral parts of a political community even as they continued to define themselves as a separate national community. Later, the presence of the minority party in government also created the conditions for a broader acceptance in society of the propositions that multiple nation-building processes could peacefully coexist within the state and that minority parties could represent shared interests with the majority. Majority-minority divisions over multilingualism became increasingly possible to bridge—not because the importance of language as a national marker decreased but because pluralist solutions emerged in the debate.

There were three competing positions on the ordering of languages. They were the same in the two countries, and they matched conceptions of sovereignty: (1) Those majority elites who pursued a unitary and centralized nation-state designed policies of language dominance aimed at establishing the language of the state's "titular" nation as the exclusive official language in the domains of government and education; (2) Hungarian minority parties, pressing for a pluralist state, sought language parity, coequal status for the minority language in local and regional government as well as the educational system in the regions where they claimed homeland community status; (3) Romanian and Slovak moderates, seeking to accommodate minority demands within the framework of a majority nation-state, preferred language predominance for the majority, a situation where majority speakers could not be forced to learn the minority language in any part of the state, but minority speakers would be allowed one-sided bilingualism in certain settings.

The majority elites who formed the moderate cluster during the early days of transformation in Romania and Slovakia preferred silence to vocal participation in the debate over linguistic territoriality, yet they represented a relatively consistent position through their institutional and legislative choices. They opted against regions of language parity and in favor of limited language inclusion and majority language predominance in all institutions of public authority. The influence of territoriality in the preferences of these elites was particularly evident in contestations over the official domain, and this influence became especially conspicuous in the battles over bilingual place markers. Linguistic territoriality was also expressed in the debate over language use in education. The question that created the main fault line among moderate majority and minority positions in this debate was whether minority schools could become autonomous spaces for national reproduction. Another key point of contestation was whether history and geography—the stories of past and present links to the territory—could be taught in Hungarian and in accordance with a Hungarian national canon.

Perhaps most telling about the potential that the democratic process created for certain changes were the points of fissure over which consensus seemed most difficult to reach, even under the conditions of majority-minority "power-sharing" in coalition governments. Minorities could not conceive of a fully legitimate democratic government without autonomous institutional spaces for the minority, and majorities could not accept such separate spaces or the idea of language parity even in limited regions of the state. For majority moderates, the predominance of their language in all public institutions within the state's territorial boundaries was a guarantee of continued territorial sovereignty. Over time, however, the specific points of the language conflict became increasingly less divisive among the majority moderates and the Hungarian elites, as they began articulating the institutional debate in mutually acceptable terms. Although they disagreed on a pluralist state structure and language parity, they agreed on the need to devolve power from the centralized state to local communities.

By the end of the decade, majority moderate positions were persistently different from those of majority nationalists. Hungarian minority and majority moderate positions grew increasingly compatible, and, in the Romanian case at least, some of the majority elites who had adamantly pursued nationalist positions moved to the moderate camp and shifted to policies of language pluralism. This dynamic demonstrated that political elites had significant freedom to shape the "mental map" provided by the Westphalian state model in ways that could accommodate both majority and minority interests, and cooperation created possibilities for a change in preferences. Today, the key legislative issues concerning language use are resolved in Romania, although problems remain in the implementation of new laws. In Slovakia, the 2002 elections reinforced a governing alliance between Slovak moderates and Hungarians, and this coalition also made substantive progress in resolving the issues of the language debate. The solutions that emerged necessarily involved some form of institutional pluralism, at least in the form of limited inclusion of minority languages in contested domains.

Thus, a broadly acceptable language policy in contested domains can only emerge if minority demands become an integral part of the democratic process rather than "problems to solve."[3] In Romania and Slovakia, the majority elites who took an adversarial approach to minority language rights triggered questions by minority elites about the legitimacy of the state (as a territorial entity) and regime (as a form of government). By contrast, majority elites who followed a consensual approach were able to build minority support for both state and regime. In these cases, minority parties joined the government and demonstrated a high degree of loyalty even during periods of political crisis, or when they disagreed intensely with their majority allies on certain aspects of minority policy and other issues. Minority parties presented continuous opposition to the government during periods of conflict (when the governing parties refused to address their demands for language rights) and developed a relatively solid partnership with the ruling majority elites during periods of consensus (when the governing parties made efforts to accommodate language rights). This logic was particularly evident in Romania, where the Hungarian minority party signed cooperation agreements with the reconstituted government of President Ion Iliescu, whom the Hungarian party had helped oust from power in the 1996 elections. The first Iliescu regime (1990–1996) had antagonized the Hungarian minority through policies that excluded the Hungarian language from local government and territory markings and significantly restricted its use in public education. After another reversal of fortune returned him to power in 2000, Iliescu chose a consensual relation with the Hungarian party, and their cooperation resulted in the passage of a number of bills that created a minority-friendly institutional framework in Romania.

---

[3] The concept of ongoing political debate in contemporary democracies about fundamental democratic values is particularly well developed in the literature on deliberative democracy. See, for example, James Fishkin, *Democracy and Deliberation* (New Haven: Yale University Press, 1971); Bernard Manin, "On Democracy and Political Deliberation," *Political Theory* 15 (August 1987), 338–68; and Amy Gutmann and Dennis Thompson, *Democracy and Disagreement* (Cambridge, MA: Belknap Press of Harvard University Press, 1996).

Another significant lesson emerging from this study is that international influences reinforce both nationalist competition and commitments to democracy. The most significant international factors influencing the power of linguistic territoriality and the potentials for consensus were the legacies of past state- and nation-building in the region (including memories of past relationships among "national groups" during the Hungarian kingdom through Soviet-dominated Communism) and the opportunities of European integration.[4]

The ethnically mixed territories in which these Hungarians live had been part of a Hungarian state for centuries and became incorporated into Romania and Slovakia through twentieth-century border changes, and Hungarian elites (both in Hungary and in neighboring states) use the traditions rooted in past statehood to reproduce shared Hungarian nationhood.[5] National minority elites in both Romania and Slovakia defined Hungarians as autochthonous groups whose strong sense of separate nationhood was precipitated by their formerly dominant status and by the proximity of the Hungarian state. Indeed, the governments of Hungary were active participants in the language debate, expressing this support in their bilateral relations with the governments of Romania and Slovakia and lobbying for international support for minority autonomy claims. From the beginning of the 1990s, Hungarian elites also pursued a trans-sovereign nation-building project aimed at strengthening the links between Hungarians across state borders and at helping ethnic kin maintain and perpetuate Hungarian culture in their historic "homelands." While the engagement of the Hungarian kin-state encouraged continuing Hungarian minority interest in nation-building, it also strengthened Romanian and Slovak majority wariness of this Hungarian interest, especially against the backdrop of secessionist demands elsewhere in the post-Communist region—for instance, Romanian and Slovak majority elites followed the Kosovo crisis with particular apprehension. At the same time, the absence of irredentism in the strategies of the post-Communist Hungarian governments strengthened the resolve of Hungarian minority elites to seek substate institutional solutions rather than secessionist alternatives. The European integrative framework also provided incentives for the governments of Hungary to work toward the consensual resolution of issues rooted in competitive nation-building.

[4] Scholars of post-Communist developments have made a particularly compelling case for the importance of legacies. See Herbert Kitschelt et al., *Post-Communist Party Systems* (Cambridge: Cambridge University Press, 1999), chapter 1, "Historical Legacies and Strategies of Democratization"; Bunce, *Subversive Institutions*; and Sharon Wolchik, "The Politics of Transition and the Break-Up of Czechoslovakia" in *The End of Czechoslovakia*, ed. Musil.
[5] Roger Brubaker and Margit Fleischmidt, "1848 in 1998," in *Ethnicity without Groups*, ed. Brubaker, 161–204.

Common institutional legacies in the two cases as well as the revival of cross-border relations among Hungarians in the region after the collapse of Communism raise the question (also known as "Galton's problem") of whether the similarities observed in majority-minority relations in Romania and Slovakia today are the consequences of independent processes or of the diffusion of the same phenomenon from one culture to the other. Although the institutional processes analyzed in this study are clearly interlinked in many ways, institutional traditions in the two countries differ significantly. While all of Slovakia had been part of the Austro-Hungarian monarchy before the end of World War I, Romania (except for Transylvania) did not experience Hungarian domination, and even multiethnic Transylvania had an autonomous "Transylvanist" history within the monarchy. The momentous shifts in authority patterns after the two great wars in this region during the twentieth century created different conditions for majority-minority relations. The era of totalitarian social engineering after 1945, when—adopting Ildikó Szabó's insightful phrase—"human beings were taken into state ownership," had a similarly dramatic impact on the structure of these societies.[6] Both Czechoslovakia and Romania found themselves in the common Soviet sphere of influence. This influence, however, took different forms in the evolution of majority-minority relations, as domestic political elites played a decisive role in shaping the relationship between the reconstituted states and their minority citizens.

International actors influenced the post-Communist institutional debate under dramatically changed conditions at the end of the twentieth century. Luckily for Hungarians, the interest of Romanian and Slovak governments in "returning to Europe" provided Western institutions opportunities for involvement in their respective domestic political processes, and this involvement encouraged the accommodation of cultural diversity. The opportunities for EU integration provided incentives for democratic parties to join forces and create cross-ethnic political alliances. At the same time, however, the international norm of states' territorial sovereignty reinforced the asymmetrical power of national majorities over policies of cultural reproduction.

European institutions were presented with a historic opportunity to establish substantive standards for language rights, but the potential for the emergence of "European norms" in this domain was also constrained by these institutions' continued emphasis on state sovereignty over cultural policies. The duality in the European approach that promotes minority protection while upholding state rights remained evident. Across Europe,

---

[6] Ildikó Szabó, *Az ember államosítása* (Budapest: Tekintet könyvek, 1991).

states maintain control over the institutions of national cultural reproduction even as they give up other important areas of authority. Some scholars argue that, despite the absence of unified European standards, EU membership conditionality has achieved significant change toward minority-friendly policies in post-Communist states, but only when the EU has taken its own conditionality seriously by increasing the credibility of enforcement and moving to more active use of leverage in the EU accession process.[7] Yet this study questions whether improvement in the likelihood of Romania's EU accession or in the methods of enforcing EU conditionality would have substantively altered the dynamics of the language debate in Romania under the first Iliescu regime or in Slovakia under the Mečiar government. Although the general norm of minority protection that European officials took to the Romanian and Slovak capitals remained relatively consistent, the results that external influence achieved varied substantively, depending on the way domestic political elites defined their own "national" goals. Ruling elites who defined this interest with an overwhelming emphasis on state sovereignty showed little willingness to respond to European pressure. Those stressing the necessity of decentralization demonstrated substantial flexibility. There were obvious limits to EU influence on minority accommodation even when governing elites were strongly committed to satisfying the conditions of membership. In Slovakia, the moderate majority elites in power after the 1998 elections were especially eager to satisfy EU requirements, yet they made fewer concessions to their Hungarian governing partners on language inclusion than their counterparts in Romania had after 1996, when the probability of EU membership in the near future was significantly lower. When it came to questions of cultural reproduction, the impact of international expectations was always sifted through the filter of how domestic elites defined the "national interest."

Thus, although the participation of international actors was highly important in providing incentives for change, the goals of international actors had to match those of domestic political elites in order to lead to meaningful change. The story of EU influence on the language debate in Romania and Slovakia also demonstrates that majority-minority conflicts unfolding in domestic arenas influence the evolution of European norms. Majority and minority political elites referred repeatedly to "European" norms of language rights, but European norms themselves had not yet evolved into a set of standards applicable across the EU. The debates concerning minority language use in post-Communist countries—especially those involving kin-states seeking an active role in the fate of "external minorities,"

---

[7] Kelley, *Ethnic Politics in Europe*; and Vachudova, *Europe Undivided*.

such as the Hungarian minorities or the Russian minorities in the Baltic states—highlighted the significance of the issue and compelled European institutions to begin formulating a more coherent approach.

An important hindrance to the emergence of a unified European approach to language rights is that language minorities are of different kinds. The patterns that emerged in Romania and Slovakia indicate that linguistic territoriality drives language minorities that define themselves as homeland communities to use democratic contestation to claim institutionalized language rights. The particular language claims that minority elites formulate reflect the influence of their political resourcefulness (especially the size of their constituency and the degree of unity among minority elites about the scope of language claims). During the first years after Communism, Hungarian minorities in both Romania and Slovakia constituted the only sufficiently large and politically resourceful minority to articulate claims for language inclusion in the domains of government and public education. Today, these minorities are the two largest Hungarian minority communities in Central Europe and among the best politically organized historic minorities in Europe that can rely on significant electoral support as well as on the support of a kin-state. These minorities have been able to use the opportunities of democratic competition and those of the EU accession process to press for institutionalized language rights.

Not all sizeable language minorities, however, are politically resourceful national minorities. The case of Hungarian minorities raises the question of what the potentials for minority language rights are in a different setting, where language minorities do not make historic "national homeland" claims in their state. The conflicts over language use in the reestablished Baltic states offer particularly intriguing points of comparison, especially as these cases share many domestic and international influences that shaped the language debate in Romania and Slovakia.

During the gradual dissolution of the Soviet Union at the end of the 1980s, the "titular" political elites of Latvia, Estonia, and Lithuania began pursuing classic "nation-state" strategies: with the end of Soviet control, they proclaimed the majority languages in their respective republics to be official and, after regaining political independence from Moscow, designed policies to establish a dominant position for these languages. Language minorities promptly contested these policies throughout the Baltics. The situation of Russian speakers who made up a significant portion of these states' populations was especially complicated. Most Russian speakers in these states were ethnic Russians who had settled in the Baltic republics during the Soviet era, while others were non-Russians who had shifted to the Russian language during the period of Soviet dominance. The political leaders of Russian speakers in these countries contested nationalist language policies and turned to the Russian government for support.[8] The Russian government, in turn, called on European institutions to pressure the Baltic governments to observe European norms for minority protection. (The relatively large Polish minority in Lithuania, a historical minority, also strongly opposed nationalist language policies.)

The legacy of Soviet-era language and demographic policies created similar language hierarchies in the three Baltic states.[9] The relationship between Russian and "titular" national languages during the Soviet era has been described as one-sided bilingualism: according to Soviet language policy, non-Russians had to be fluent in Russian in order to function fully and advance socioeconomically, but Russian speakers were not expected to learn the languages of the republics in which they resided.[10] This language policy and the massive influx of Russians into the Baltic republics after Soviet occupation in the aftermath of World War II considerably weakened the relative status of all three Baltic languages.[11] At the end of the 1980s, Russian was the predominant language in the public domain, especially in urban centers, despite language legislation adopted in the final years of Soviet political reform in an attempt to "emancipate" the "titular national" languages. In 1989, Estonian, Latvian, and Lithuanian were each proclaimed official languages in the respective Soviet republics. The purpose of the 1989 laws was to achieve language parity with Russian. After the collapse of the Soviet Union in 1991, national majorities in these states opted for language dominance over language pluralism.[12]

In Latvia and Estonia the debates over language use were strikingly similar to each other. Both states established citizenship laws that required residents to pass a language proficiency test in order to become citizens of the reestablished states. By contrast, in Lithuania all residents who had lived in the republic before independence obtained citizenship simply by applying. The new governing elites in Estonia and Latvia made significant

---

[8] "Estonia: Ethnic Russian Voters May Play Key Role," *RFE/RL Special Report,* www.rferl.org/nca/features/1999/F.RU.990305140105.html. See also *RFE/RL Newsline,* February 12, 1998.

[9] On Soviet language policy, see Karklins, *Ethnopolitics and Transition,* 151–52.

[10] Karklins notes, for example, that in Latvia parallel courses were taught at universities in Russian and Latvian, but Russians were not required to learn Latvian, while it was impossible for Latvian students to obtain higher education without fluency in Russian. She also observes that after 1987, some Russian reformers began criticizing the policy of one-sided bilingualism. Ibid., 152–53.

[11] Only Latvian and Lithuanian are "Baltic" languages in the linguistic sense of the word. Estonian belongs to the Finno-Ugric language family, together with Finnish and Hungarian.

[12] Mathiassen suggests that the three states cooperated in formulating their language policies after 1991. Terje Mathiassen, "Regulations and Language Planning in Latvia and Lithuania" in *Language Contact and Language Conflict,* ed. Unn Royneland (Volda, Norway: Volda College, 1997), 200–201.

legislative efforts to mandate the use of the state language in the domain of government. They also shared a desire to establish the majority language gradually as the only language of instruction in public schools.[13] In 1990, the Lithuanian government also indicated an interest in majority language dominance. After a forceful reaction from the Polish minority in the Vilnius area, including a demand for regional autonomy, the Lithuanian government abandoned this pursuit in favor of a more moderate policy that guaranteed Lithuanian predominance but allowed for language pluralism in local administration. At the same time, the Lithuanian elite shared the commitment of Estonian and Latvian political elites to compelling minorities in government positions to learn the state language.[14]

A plausible explanation for differences between language policies in Lithuania and its Baltic neighbors is the variation in the relative size of minority populations in the three states. Because the national majority constitutes a comfortable 80 percent of the population in Lithuania, the Lithuanian majority had less reason to fear that language inclusion would threaten territorial sovereignty. By contrast, the majority makes up only 55 percent of the population in Latvia; Estonians account for 64 percent in Estonia.[15] Based on this comparison, some analysts have contended that demographic conditions prompted Latvian and Estonian political elites to choose more aggressive policies than their Lithuanian counterparts in order to protect the status of their language in the state.[16]

It is equally important, however, to consider the role of another component of Lithuanian demography. The Polish minority articulated a stronger challenge to the Lithuanian "nation-state" than the Russian minority had, although the two groups were approximately the same size.[17] The 20 percent minority population in Lithuania is composed of 10 percent Poles and 10 percent Russians. The Polish challenge to the "nation-state" contributed significantly to the Lithuanian government's shift from a strategy of language dominance to a greater acceptance of minority languages in the official sphere. Clearly, the demands of the minority with the stronger historic connection to the land it inhabited (the Polish minority) were considered

---

[13] Aija Priedite, "The Relationship between Minority and Majority Languages in Latvia," in *Language Contact and Language Conflict*, ed. Royneland, 118–19. See also *OMRI Daily Digest*, February 22, 1995, May 17, 1996; *RFE/RL Newsline*, September 11, 1997, November 6, 1997, September 1, 1998; and Karklins, "Ethnic Integration and School Policies in Latvia," *Nationalities Papers* 26, no. 2 (1998), 292.

[14] Ellen J. Gordon, "Legislating Identity," Ph.D. dissertation, University of Michigan, 1993, 6; and Mathiassen, "Regulations and Language Planning," 195.

[15] These estimates are commonly used in studies on the Baltic states.

[16] Mathiassen, "Regulations and Language Planning," 204.

[17] Ibid., 195.

more legitimate than the claims of recent settlers representing a recently dominant power (the Russians). In both Latvia and Estonia, Russian speakers composed the largest minority group. Analysts of the language debate in these states argue that nationalizing language policies were aimed at reversing the dominance of the settlers' language over the languages of historic majorities.[18] Karklins noted that for Latvian elites "an equitable policy meant differentiating among subgroups of the non-Latvian population" and that such policies needed to take into account the remarkably weak position of Latvian in relation to Russian at the beginning of independence and "to redress the neglect experienced by the smaller historical minorities of Latvia such as Poles, Jews, and Gypsies."[19]

Policies of language dominance, no matter how justified, encountered significant obstacles when embedded in the larger process of democratization. The parallel goals of building a "nation-state" in a multilingual society and of creating an inclusive political community without forcible assimilation have been impossible to reconcile.[20] Like Romania and Slovakia, the Baltic governments applied for European integration, and European institutions, especially the OSCE and the Council of Europe, repeatedly called on them to design language policies that complied with "European norms." These pressures compelled an increasing number of political actors in Estonia and Latvia to argue for more moderate language policies, so in 1998, both governments passed amendments to the citizenship laws that made it easier (if not automatic, as the OSCE had recommended) for children of non-Latvian citizens born in Latvia after 1991 to acquire citizenship.[21]

Although language legislation in Latvia and Estonia continued to reflect a nationalist state-building strategy, in most cases these laws were only slowly and moderately implemented. Karklins argued that by 1993 the Latvian government was moving toward a policy of language pluralism, allowing the continued presence of Russian in governmental offices and the existence of two sets of educational institutions, a system of Latvian schools and a parallel system of Russian schools. In 1998, she found that Latvian educational policy was unsuccessful in achieving bilingual education for Russian students. Instead of integration into the Latvian language environment, Russians managed to maintain their autonomous educational institutions.[22] Still,

---

[18] Priedite, "The Relationship between Minority and Majority Languages"; and Mathiassen, "Regulations and Language Planning," 111.
[19] Karklins, *Ethnopolitics and Transition,* 141–42.
[20] The two processes, nationalism and democratization, are not necessarily opposite—indeed, they went hand in hand in Europe during the nineteenth century.
[21] *RFE/RL Newsline,* October 31, 1997, May 21, 1998, July 15, 1999.
[22] Karklins, "Ethnic Integration," 284.

language policies in Latvia remain divisive, as bilingual curricula were introduced in the 2002–2003 school year, requiring minority language schools to
provide education in Latvian as well instead of teaching Latvian as a second
language.[23] This policy continues to foment vehement opposition from the
Russian-speaking minority.

Similarities between the Baltic states and Romania and Slovakia reinforce
the main arguments of this study. The process of state formation in Baltic
states, just as in Slovakia, heightened the desire of majority nationalist elites
to design strategies of language dominance and language minorities to challenge these strategies. Like Romania and Slovakia, these states moved away
from policies of language dominance (albeit to varying degrees) under the
conditions of democratization and the expectation of future European integration. The Russian government played a similar role to the government
of Hungary in the language debate, lobbying for European pressure for minority language inclusion, although it did not pursue a similarly consistent
kin-state policy.[24]

The differences among these cases are equally intriguing. The Russian
minority in the Baltic states is composed overwhelmingly of relatively recent
settlers, while Hungarians in Transylvania and southern Slovakia and the
Polish minority in Lithuania have lived in the same territory for centuries.
The Russians were a politically and culturally dominant group in the Baltic
republics until the collapse of the Soviet Union, and the power shift was an
ongoing process during their first decade of independence. In Romania and
Slovakia, by contrast, the power shift took place during the Communist
period. The Russian minority in the Baltic states was largely monolingual,
while the Hungarians in Romania and Slovakia were overwhelmingly bilingual. Clearly, the majorities in these states faced different challenges from
language minorities.

Comparisons between Lithuania and the two cases analyzed in this study
confirm the argument that historical national minorities tend to be more
successful in their pursuit of inclusive language policies. The problems related to Russian language claims, on the other hand, illustrate the difficulties experienced by language minorities that are considered non-historical.
This hierarchy of historical and nonhistorical language groups reflects the
expectation that a language will provide a link between a community and a
territory through a national literary canon, history, and geography in order
to make its speakers "eligible" for institutional spaces within a state. The

---

[23] Ojarrs Kalnins, "Latvia: The Language of Coexistence," www.tol.cz/look/TOL/home, accessed
September 1, 2004.
[24] Csergo and Goldgeier, "Virtual Nationalism in Comparative Context."

same expectation is the basis of established language hierarchies within the European Union, where—as Esman notes—immigrant communities "have no claims at all to official status for their languages."[25]

This comparative account suggests that linguistic territoriality will continue to trigger important questions about the European norms of democratic inclusion and equality. One question that Hungarian minority demands brought back into the broader European debate is whether cultural "groups" should be considered legitimate actors in the democratic process and be granted institutional rights. For a brief period at the end of World War I, major international actors like Woodrow Wilson promoted collectivist ideas of both majority national self-determination and minority protection in a system of democratic nation-states. But the failure of the League of Nations and the horrors of World War II (committed in the name of strong collective identities) expelled the concept of collective rights from the vocabulary of legitimate international terms. The founding documents of the United Nations provided international support for states to impose cultural policies that served their territorial stability.[26]

Recent decades have seen a renewed acceptance in international organizations not only of the notion of minority rights but also of the existence of multiple collective identities in democratic states. It is becoming more widely recognized that the modern state system, which many expected to foster citizenship with individualistic and universalistic values, in reality has created and perpetuated strong collective identities.[27]

The concepts of national majority, ethnic minority, and all related political concepts (such as majority-minority relations, rights, and identities) capture the notion that people share collective cultural allegiances. But should this notion—or the evidence emerging from the study of political elites and their political strategies—convince us that coherent "majority" and "minority" positions exist about language rights and visions about the social contract? Do "national groups" exist just because minority political elites *claim* to represent such groups and demand group rights? If the debate over language rights in Romania and Slovakia was also about popular sovereignty, then where were "the people" in the debate?

Clearly, in the framework of democratic government, language disputes concern not only the way political elites "play the language game" but also the way people in society evaluate languages and the way these language

---

[25] Milton J. Esman, "The State and Language Policy," *International Political Science Review* 13, no. 4 (1992): 392.

[26] Stephen D. Krasner, *Sovereignty* (Princeton, NJ: Princeton University Press, 1999), 90–97.

[27] Kymlicka, *Multicultural Citizenship*.

choices and loyalties affect the democratic process. Rogers Brubaker warns us that intense elite-level nationalist mobilization should not lead us to expect similar popular mobilization or even interest in contested issues. He argues that consistently high electoral performance by Hungarian minority parties is no evidence that these parties' demands match those of their constituencies.[28] The analysis in this book confirms that there is no "ethnic" unity on questions of nation-building. It is a major paradox of nationalism that its fundamental unifying logic becomes a source of division not only between but also within the "nations" its advocates aim to unite. Majorities in both states have been deeply divided over "national" questions, and the Hungarian minority elites also maintained recognizable disagreements despite the strategic unity they formed in response to the nation-state design.

Political elites have a higher stake in shaping cultural reproduction into particular "national" forms, as it is more likely that they would assume control of the institutions of cultural reproduction for which they fight—and therefore more incentives to fight for them. Still, language contestations are not merely elite-level power games. In Romania and Slovakia, the enduring political salience of the issue assured the continuous presence of the language debate in multiple arenas of the public space, and it was against this backdrop that majority and minority voters in both states gave their support primarily to leaders and parties that opted for collectivist approaches to language rights. It was due to these electoral dynamics that parties representing liberal individualist approaches to language rights became marginalized and national community-based approaches to cultural reproduction became dominant.[29]

This study reveals that collective identities are just as firmly rooted in the European state model as the ideology of liberal individualism. The majority-minority contestations explored are manifestations of a decidedly "nationalist" process of cultural reproduction. By placing the concept of cultural reproduction at the center of analysis, the study lends support to theories of nationalism that question the utility of the classic dichotomy of "civic vs. ethnic" (or "political vs. cultural") nations—a dichotomy that has been widely used in the literature on nationalism to describe differences between the supposedly more "ethnically" nationalist eastern Europeans and their more "civic" western counterparts.[30] The language debates in post-Communist Europe

---

[28] Brubaker, *Ethnicity without Groups*, 2, 22–23.

[29] For a comparative analysis, see Zsuzsa Csergo and Kevin Deegan-Krause, "Why Liberalism Failed," paper presented at the annual meeting of the American Political Science Association, Philadelphia, PA, August 28–31, 2003.

[30] About the "civic vs. ethnic" dichotomy, see Bernard Yack, "The Myth of the Civic Nation," in *Theorizing Nationalism,* ed. Ronald Beiner (Albany: State University of New York Press, 1999), 103–18; Rogers Brubaker, "'Civic' and 'Ethnic' Nationalism," in Brubaker, *Ethnicity Without Groups*; Zsuzsa Csergo, "National Strategies and the Uses of Dichotomy," *Regio: A Review of Studies on Minorities, Politics, and Society* (2003), 95–101.

demonstrate that processes of nation-building always are both cultural and political and that nation-building in culturally diverse societies always challenges the democratic potentials of the territorial state. Still, that broadly accepted language rules emerged in these countries through democratic competition should give us reasons for optimism that democracy might "work" even under conditions of nationalist competition.

Beyond their obvious significance for the future evolution of state and democracy in Europe, the lessons that Romania and Slovakia offer are relevant for other societies that are struggling to use or have yet to begin using democratic competition in an effective way to find their own balance in a polity that accommodates multiple processes of cultural reproduction.

References

Abdelal, Rawi. *National Purpose in the World Economy: Post-Soviet States in Comparative Perspective.* Ithaca: Cornell University Press, 2001.

Agárdy, Gábor. "A megalakulás időszaka." In *Közösségünk Szolgálatában: A Magyar Keresztényemokrata Mozgalom öt éve: 1990–1995.* Pozsony: Microgramma; MKDM, 1995.

Agenda 2000. "Commission Opinion on Slovakia's Application for Membership of the European Union; DOC/97/20," Brussels, Belgium, July 15, 1997. Available at europa. eu.int/comm/enlargement/dwn/opinions/slovakia/sk-op-en.pdf, accessed July 7, 2004.

Agnew, Hugh. *The Czechs and the Lands of the Bohemian Crown.* Stanford: Hoover Institution Press, 2004.

Agnew, John. "The Territorial Trap: The Geographical Assumptions of International Relations Theory." *Review of International Political Economy* 1 (Spring 1994): 53–80.

Anderson, Benedict. *Imagined Communities: Reflections on the Origins and Spread of Nationalism.* London: Verso, 1991.

Andreescu, Gabriel. "Iugoslavia: secesiunea Kosovo și 'încremenirea în proiect'" *Revista 22* 17 (March 27–May 3, 1999). Available at www.dntb.ro.

———. "Un comunicat al MAE sau cum face Adevărul politica externă a României." *Revista 22* 11 (1999). Available at www.dntb.ro.

———. "Universal Thought, Eastern Facts: Scrutinizing National Minority Rights in Romania." In *Can Liberal Pluralism Be Exported? Western Political Theory and Ethnic Relations in Eastern Europe,* ed. Will Kymlicka and Magda Opalski. London: Oxford University Press, 2001.

Andreescu, Gabriel, and Renate Weber. *Evolutions in the D.A.H.R. Conception on Hungarian Minority Rights.* Bucharest: APADOR-CH, 1994.

Andreescu, Gabriel, Valentin Stan, and Renate Weber. "Două proiecte de lege privind drepturile minorităților naționale." *Legislația în tranziție* (January 1995): 75–93.

———. "Un proiect de lege privind minoritățile naționale elaborat de Centrul pentru drepturile omului." *Legislația în tranziție* (January 1995): 102–12.

Barany, Zoltan. "Ethnic Mobilization without Prerequisites: The East European Gypsies." *World Politics* 54, no. 3 (2002): 277–307.

Bárdi, Nándor. ed. *Autonóm magyarok? Székelyföld változása az "ötvenes" években.* Csíkszereda: Pro-Print, 2005.

Barkin, Samuel J., and Bruce Cronin. "The State and the Nation: Changing Norms and the Rules of Sovereignty in International Relations." *International Organization* 48, no. 1 (Winter 1994): 107–30.

Barrington, Lowell W. "'Nation' and 'Nationalism': The Misuse of Key Concepts in Political Science." *PS: Political Science and Politics* 30, no. 4 (December 1997): 712–14.

Barry, Brian. *Culture and Equality.* Cambridge, MA: Harvard University Press, 2001.

Beissinger, Mark. "How Nationalisms Spread: Eastern Europe Adrift the Tides and Cycles of Nationalist Contention." *Social Research* 63, no. 1 (Spring 1996): 97–146.

——. *Nationalist Mobilization and the Collapse of the Soviet Union.* New York: Cambridge University Press, 2002.

Ben-Rafael, Eliezer. *Language, Identity, and Social Division.* Oxford: Clarendon Press, 1994.

Berényi, József. *Nyelvországlás: A szlovákiai nyelvtörvény történelmi és társadalmi okai.* Bratislava: Fórum, 1994.

Billig, Michael. *Banal Nationalism.* London: Sage Publications, 1995.

Biró, Zoltán. "A restaurációs kísérletektől a pragmatikus modellekig. Intézményesedési folyamatok a romániai magyar társadalomban 1989–1995 között." Manuscript, 1996.

Blocker, Joel. "Romania/Hungary: Historic Basic Treaty Signed Today." *RFE/RL Newsline,* September 16, 1996.

Borneman, John. "Towards a Theory of Ethnic Cleansing: Territorial Sovereignty, Heterosexuality, and Europe." In John Borneman, *Subversions of International Order: Studies in the Political Anthropology of Culture.* Albany, NY: State University of New York Press, 1997.

Bottoni, Stefano. "The Creation of the Hungarian Autonomous Region in Romania (1952): Premises and Consequences," *Regio* (2003): 71–93.

Bourdieu, Pierre. *Language and Symbolic Power.* Cambridge, MA: Harvard University Press, 1991.

——. "The Economy of Linguistic Exchanges." In *Language and Symbolic Power,* ed. Pierre Bourdieu. Cambridge: Harvard University Press, 1991.

Breuilly, John. *Nationalism and the State.* Manchester, UK: Manchester University Press, 1982.

Brubaker, Rogers. *Nationalism Reframed: Nationhood and the National Question in the New Europe.* Cambridge: Cambridge University Press, 1996.

——. "'Civic' and 'Ethnic' Nationalsim." In Rogers Brubaker, *Ethnicity Without Groups.* Cambridge: Harvard University Press, 2004.

——. *Ethnicity without Groups.* Cambridge: Harvard University Press, 2004.

Brubaker, Rogers, and Margit Fleischmidt. "1848 in 1998." In *Ethnicity without Groups.* Cambridge: Harvard University Press, 2004.

Brusis, Martin. "The European Union and Interethnic Power-Sharing Arrangements in Accession Countries." *JEMIE: Journal of Ethnopolitics and Minority Issues in Europe* 1 (2003). Available at www.ecmi.de/jemie, accessed August 25, 2003.

Bucken-Knapp, Gregg. *Elites, Language, and the Politics of Identity: The Norwegian Case in Comparative Perspective.* Albany: State University of New York Press, 2003.

Bunce, Valerie. *Subversive Institutions: The Design and the Destruction of Socialism and the State.* Cambridge: Cambridge University Press, 1999.

Butora, Daniel. "Meciar and the Velvet Divorce: Journalist Sheds New Light on Czechoslovakia's Peaceful Split." *Transitions* 5, no. 8 (August 1998): 72–75.

Bútora, Martin, and Zora Bútorová. "Political Parties, Value Orientations, and Slovakia's Road to Independence." In *Party Formation in Central Eastern Europe,* ed. G. Whitman and M. Waller. Cheltenham, UK: Edward Elgar Publishing, 1994.

——. "Slovakia: The Identity Challenges of the Newly Born State." *Social Research* 60, no. 4 (Winter 1993): 705–36.

Bútora, Martin, and Thomas Skladony, eds. *Slovakia 1996/1997: A Global Report on the State of Society.* Bratislava: Institute for Public Affairs, 1998.

Bútorová, Zora, Olga Gyárfášová, and Marián Velšic. "Public Opinion." In *Slovakia 1998–1999: A Global Report on the State of Society,* ed. Grigorij Mesežnikov et al. Bratislava: Institute for Public Affairs, 1999.

Carens, Joseph H. "Justice and Linguistic Minorities." Paper delivered at the 2002 meeting of the American Political Science Association, Boston, MA, August 29–September 1, 2002.

Castle, Stephen, and Paul Waugh. "'New Europe' Strikes Back after Vitriolic Chirac Attack." *The Independent* (London), 11. Accessed via Lexis-Nexis, July 7, 2004.

Checkel, Jeffrey. "Why Comply? Social Learning and European Identity Change." *International Organization* 55, no. 3 (2001): 553–88.

Chirot, Daniel. "What Provokes Violent Ethnic Conflict?" In *Ethnic Politics after Communism,* ed. Zoltan Barany and Robert G. Moser. Ithaca: Cornell University Press, 2005.

Coltea, Tibor. "Mire alapozhat egy kisebbség, ha önálló intézményrendszert kíván kiépíteni." *Magyar Kisebbség* 4, no. 18 (1994).

Cooper, Robert L. *Language Planning and Social Change.* Cambridge: Cambridge University Press, 1989.

Cornea, Andrei. "Ce va fi?" *Revista 22* 34 (1998). Available at www.dntb.ro.

Crăiuțu, Aurelian. "A Dilemma of Dual Identity: The Democratic Alliance of Hungarians in Romania." *East European Constitutional Review* 4, no. 2 (1995): 43–49.

Creppell, Ingrid. *Toleration and Identity: Foundations in Early Modern Thought.* New York: Routledge, 2003.

Csáky, Pál. "Introduction," *A Magyar Kereszténydemokrata Mozgalom az Autonómiáért. Dokumentumok I.* Bratislava: MKDM, 1995.

Csapó, József. "Székelyföld autonómia-statútuma (Tervezet)." *Magyar Kisebbség* 2 (1995): 174–200.

Csergo, Zsuzsa. "Beyond Ethnic Division: Majority-Minority Debate about the Postcommunist State in Romania and Slovakia." *East European Politics and Societies* 16, no. 1 (Winter 2002): 1–29.

——. "National Strategies and the Uses of Dichotomy." *Regio* (2003): 95–101.

Csergo, Zsuzsa, and James M. Goldgeier. "Virtual Nationalism." *Foreign Policy* 125 (July/August 2001): 76–77.

——. "Nationalist Strategies and European Integration." *Perspectives on Politics* 2, no. 1 (March 2004): 21–37.

——. "Virtual Nationalism in Comparative Context: How Unique is the Hungarian Approach?" Paper prepared for the international conference on "The Status Law Syndrome: A Post-communist Nation Building or Post-modern Citizenship?" at the Institute of Legal Studies, Budapest, Hungary, October 14–16, 2004.

Csergo, Zsuzsa, and Kevin Deegan-Krause. "Why Liberalism Failed: Majorities and Minorities in European Enlargement." Paper presented at the annual meeting of the American Political Science Association, Philadelphia, PA, August 28–31, 2003.

Datculescu, Petre. "Cum a votat România: O analiză a alegerilor generale și prezidențiale de la 27 septembrie 1992." *Revista de cercetări sociale* 1 (1994), 43–61.

Deets, Stephen. "The Hungarian Status Law and the Specter of Neo-Medievalism in Europe." Paper presented at the annual meeting of the International Studies Association, Montreal, Canada, March 17–20, 2004.

De Swaan, Abram. *The Language Constellation of the European Union: A Perspective from the Political Sociology of Language.* Amsterdam, the Netherlands: Amsterdam School for Social science Research, 1995.

De Witte, Bruno. "Politics versus Law in the EU's Approach to Ethnic Minorities." In *Europe Unbound: Enlarging and Reshaping the Boundaries of the European Union,* ed. Jan Zielonka. New York: Routledge, 2002.

Deutsch, Karl. *Nationalism and Social Communication.* Cambridge: MIT Press, 1953.

Dolník, Erzsébet. "A szlovákiai magyar oktatásügy helyzete." *Regio* 5, no. 3 (1994): 28–45.

——. "Az egyes tantárgyak alternatív oktatásának koncepció–javaslata a nemzetiségileg vegyes területek iskoláiban (Elemzés)." Undated document.

Dostál, Ondrej. "Minorities." In *Global Report on Slovakia: Comprehensive Analyses from 1995 and Trends from 1996,* ed. Martin Bútora and Péter Hunčík. Bratislava: Sándor Márai Foundation, 1997.

Doyle, John. "Challenges to the Hegemonic Image of Westphalia: New Models of Sovereignty in Practical Cases from Northern Ireland and Kosovo." Paper presented at the 45th Annual ISA convention, Montreal, Canada, March 17–20, 2004.

Duka Zólyomi, Árpád. "A szlovák-magyar kiegyezés felé?" In *Önkormányzat az önrendelkezés alapja: A szlovákiai magyar választott képviselők és polgármesterek országos nagygyűlésének hiteles jegyzőkönyve. Komárom, 1994. január 8.* Komárom, Hungary: Komáromi Lapok—Szinnyei Kiadó, 1995.

Duray, Miklós. "A komáromi nagygyűlésen elfogadott állásfoglalás rövid elemzése." In *Önkormányzat az önrendelkezés alapja.*

——. "Önrendelkezés a Szlovákiában élő magyarság torekvéseiben." In *Az Önkormányzat az önrendelkezés alapja: A szlovákiai magyar választott képviselők és polgármesterek országos nagygyűlésének hiteles jegyzőkönyve. Komárom, 1994. január 8.* Komárom, Hungary: Komáromi Lapok—Szinnyei Kiadó, 1995.

Eckstein, Harry. *Division and Cohesion in Democracy: A Study of Norway.* Princeton, NJ: Princeton University Press, 1966.

Egletis-Stukuls, Daina. "Imagining the Nation: Campaign Posters of the First Postcommunist Elections in Latvia." *East European Politics and Societies* 11, no. 1 (Winter 1997): 131–54.

Ertman, Thomas. *Birth of the Leviathan: Building States and Regimes in Medieval and Early Modern Europe.* Cambridge: Cambridge University Press, 1997.

Esman, Milton J. *Ethnic Politics.* Ithaca: Cornell University Press, 1994.

——. "The State and Language Policy." *International Political Science Review* 13, no. 4 (1992).

European Commission for Democracy through Law [Venice Commission]. "Report on the Preferential Treatment of National Minorities by their Kin-State." Adopted by the Venice Commission at its 48th Plenary Meeting, Venice, Italy, October 19–20, 2001.

Ferko, Milan. "Zásady zákona Národnej Rady Slovenskej Republiky o štátnom jazyku Slovenskej Republiky." *Slovenská Republika,* August 26, 1995: 10–11.

Fisher, Sharon. "Meeting of Slovakia's Hungarians Causes Stir." *RFE/RL Research Report* 3, no. 4 (January 28, 1994).

——. "Making Slovakia More 'Slovak.'" *Transition* 2, no. 24 (November 29, 1996): 14–17.

Fishkin, James. *Democracy and Deliberation: New Directions for Democratic Reform.* New Haven: Yale University Press, 1991.

Fishman, Joshua. *Handbook of Language and Ethnic Identity.* Oxford: Oxford University Press, 1999.

Fukuyama, Francis. "The End of History?" *National Interest* 16 (Summer 1989): 3–35.

Gábos, András. "Adatok a romaniai tanugyi torvenyhez." *Regio* 5, no. 3 (1994): 46–68.

Gabdilová, Soňa. "Schools in the Slovak Republik with instruction in the Hungarian language—Present Status." In *Minorities in Politics: Cultural and Language Rights,* ed. Jana Plichtová. Bratislava, 1992.

Gabdilová, Soňa, and Mária Homosinová. "Az iskolaügy a szlovákiai magyar politikai pártok és mozgalmak tevékénységében." *Regio* 5, no. 3 (1994): 19–27.

Gagnon, V. P. *The Myth of Ethnic War: Serbia and Croatia in the 1990s.* Ithaca: Cornell University Press, 2004.

Gal, Susan. *Language Shift: Social Determinants of Linguistic Change in Bilingual Austria.* New York: Academic Press, 1979.

Gallagher, Tom. "Nationalism and the Romanian Opposition." *Transitions* 2, no. 1 (January 1996): 30–32.

Gellner, Ernest. *Nations and Nationalism.* Ithaca: Cornell University Press, 1983.

———. *Thought and Change.* London: Weidenfeld and Nicolson, 1964.

Gezalis, Nida M. "The European Union and the Statelessness Problem in the Baltic States." *European Journal of Migration and Law* 6 (2004): 225–42.

Ghimpu, Aurel. "Învăţământul 'susţine' interesul naţional pentru integrarea Europeană." *Opinia naţiona* (June 2, 1997): 5.

Gordon, Ellen J. "Legislating Identity: Language, Citizenship, and Education in Lithuania." Ph.D. dissertation, University of Michigan, 1993.

Gramstad, Sigve. "The European Charter for Regional or Minority Languages." In *Language Contact and Language Conflict: Proceedings of The International Ivar Aasen Conference 14–16 November 1996, University of Oslo,* ed. Unn Royneland. Volda, Norway: Ivar Aasen Institute, Volda College, 1997.

Greenberg, David. *Language and Identity in the Balkans: Serbo-Croatian and its Disintegration.* New York: Oxford University Press, 2004.

Greenfeld, Liah. *Nationalism: Five Roads to Modernity.* Cambridge, MA: Harvard University Press, 1992.

Grillo, Ralph D. *Dominant Languages: Language and Hierarchy in Britain and France.* Cambridge: Cambridge University Press, 1989.

Gumperz, John. *Language in Social Groups.* Stanford, CA: Stanford University Press, 1971.

Gutmann, Amy, ed. *Multiculturalism and "The Politics of Recognition": An Essay by Charles Taylor.* Princeton, NJ: Princeton University Press, 1992.

Gutmann, Amy, and Dennis Thompson. *Democracy and Disagreement.* Cambridge, MA: Belknap Press of Harvard University Press, 1996.

Gyimesi, Éva Cs. "Kolozsvár-központû erdélyi magyar felsőoktatási hálózat." *Romániai magyar szó* (February 11, 1998).

Gyivicsán, Anna. "Szempontok a lakosságcsere magyarországi szlovák értékeléséhez." Conference on the Hungarian-Czechoslovak population exchange, Central Europe Institute, Budapest, Hungary, March 27, 1996.

Gyurcsik, Iván. "About the Passing of the Constitution of the Slovak Republic." Undated manuscript.

Gyurgyík, László. *A szlovákiai magyarság a népszámlálási és a népmozgalmi adatok tükrében.* Bratislava: Kalligram, 1994.

Haas, Ernst B. *Beyond the Nation-State: Functionalism and International Organization.* Stanford, CA: Stanford University Press, 1964.

Henrard, Kristin. "Devising an Adequate System of Minority Protection in the Area of Language Rights." In *Minority Languages in Europe: Frameworks, Status, Prospects,* ed. Gabrielle Hogan-Brun and Stefan Wolff. New York: Palgrave Macmillan, 2003.

Hobsbawm, E. J. *Nations and Nationalism since 1780: Programme, Myth, Reality.* Cambridge: Cambridge University Press, 1990.

Hoffmann, Stanley. "Nationalism and World Order." *World Disorders: Troubled Peace in the Post–Cold War Era.* Lanham, MD: Rowman and Littlefield, 1998.

Hogan-Brun, Gabrielle, and Stefan Wolff. "Minority Languages in Europe: An Introduction to the Current Debate." In *Minority Languages in Europe: Frameworks, Status, Prospects,* ed. Gabrielle Hogan-Brun and Stefan Wolff. New York: Palgrave Macmillan, 2003.

Hogan-Brun, Gabrielle, and Stefan Wolff, eds. *Minority Languages in Europe: Frameworks, Status, Prospects.* New York: Palgrave Macmillan, 2003.

Horowitz, Donald L. "Ethnic Conflict Management for Policymakers." In *Conflict and Peacemaking in Multiethnic Societies,* ed. Joseph V. Montville. Lexington, MA: Lexington Books, 1990.

Horváth, Gabriella. "Blowing with the Nationalist Wind," *Balkan War Report* 29 (October/November 1994): 37.

Hroch, Miroslav. "From National Movement to the Full-Formed Nation: The Nation-Building Process in Europe." *New Left Review* no. 198 (1993): 3–20.

Hughes, James, and Gwendolyn Sasse. "Monitoring the Monitors: EU Enlargement Conditionality and Minority Protection in the CEECs." *JEMIE: Journal on Ethnopolitics and Minority Issues in Europe* 1 (2003). Available at www.ecmi.de/jemie, accessed 17 June, 2005.

Hunčík, Péter, and Fedor Gál. "The Historical Background to the Formation of Slovak-Hungarian Relations." In Pavol Frič et al., *The Hungarian Minority in Slovakia*. Prague, Czech Republic: Institute of Social and Political Science, Charles University, 1993.

Hungarian Christian Democratic Movement—Coexistence, "Draft of Fundamental Principles of a Constitutional Law of the National Council (Parliament) of the Slovak Republic about the Legal Status of National and Ethnic Minority Communities in the Slovak Republic." Undated document.

Hunya, Gábor, Tamás Réti, Andrea R. Süle, and László Tóth. *Románia 1944–1990: Gazdaság-és politikatörténet*. Budapest: Atlantisz, 1990.

Igric, Gordana. "Education is the Key in Serb-Kosovar Negotiations." *Transition* 3, no. 4 (March 7, 1997): 19–23.

Iliescu, Ion. *Integration and Globalization: A Romanian View*. Bucharest: Romanian Cultural Foundation Publishing House, 2003.

———. "Keep Russia Away From the Danube; So Says Romania, With Reason to be Wary of the Federation's Involvement." *Washington Post*, May 23, 1999, B05. Accessed via Lexis-Nexis on May 26, 2004.

———. "Romania's Example." *Washington Post*, March 17, 2003, A19. Accessed via Lexis-Nexis on May 26, 2004.

Innes, Abby. "The Breakup of Czechoslovakia: The Impact of Party Development on the Separation of the State." *East European Politics and Societies* 11, no. 3 (Fall 1997): 393–435.

Ionescu, Dan. "More Controversy in Romania over Treaty with Hungary." *RFE/RL Newsline*, September 16, 1996.

———. "Romania Complains about Treaty Talks with Hungary." *OMRI*, September 1, 1994.

Janics, Kálmán. *A hontalanság évei: A szlovákiai magyar kisebbség a második világháború után 1945–1948*. Budapest: Hunnia, 1989.

Jürgens, Eric. "Preferential Treatment of National Minorities by Their Kin-States: The Case of the Hungarian Status Law of 19 June 2001." Council of Europe, Parliamentary Assembly. Doc. 9744 rev., May 13, 2003. Available at assembly.coe.int, accessed July 7, 2004.

Kačala, Ján. "Naša jazyková suverenita." *Slovenský národ*, June 14, 1990.

———. "Čo je to jazyková suverenita." In *Slovenčina—vec politická?* ed. Ján Kačala. Martin, Slovakia: Matica slovenská, 1994.

Kalnins, Ojarrs. "Latvia: The Language of Coexistence," Accessible at www.tol.cz/look/TOL/home, accessed September 1, 2004.

Kántor, Zoltán. "Status Law and 'Nation Policy': Theoretical Aspects." In *The Hungarian Status Law: Nation Building and/or Minority Protection*, ed. Zoltán Kántor et al. Sapporo, Japan: Slavic Research Center, Hokkaido University, 2004.

Kántor, Zoltán, and Nándor Bárdi, The DAHR (Democratic Alliance of Hungarians in Romania) in the Government of Romania from 1996 to 2000, *Regio* 13 (2002): 188–226.

Kántor, Zoltán, and Balázs Majtényi, "Autonómiamodellek Erdélyben: Jövőkép és stratégia," available at kantor.adatbank.transindex.ro. Accessed November 20, 2006.

Kantorowicz, Ernst Hartwig. *The King's Two Bodies: A Study in Medieval Political Theology*. Princeton, NJ: Princeton University Press, 1957.

Kaplan, Robert B., and Richard B. Baldauf Jr. *Language Planning from Practice to Theory*. Clevedon, UK: Multilingual Matters, 1997.

Karklins, Rasma. "Ethnic Integration and School Policies in Latvia." *Nationalities Papers* 26, no. 2 (1998): 283–302.

———. *Ethnopolitics and Transition to Democracy: The Collapse of the USSR and Latvia.* Washington, D.C., and Baltimore: The Woodrow Wilson Center Press and the Johns Hopkins University Press, 1994.

Keating, Michael, and John McGarry, eds. *Minority Nationalism and the Changing International Order.* Oxford: Oxford University Press, 2001.

Kelley, Judith G. *Ethnic Politics in Europe: The Power of Norms and Incentives.* Princeton, NJ: Princeton University Press, 2004.

Kincses-Ajtay, Mária. "A kolozsvári magyar egyetem ügye." *Szabadság,* March 19, 1998.

King, Charles. *The Moldovans: Romania, Russia, and the Politics of Culture.* Stanford, CA: Hoover Institution Press, 2000.

———. "The Myth of Ethnic Warfare." *Foreign Affairs* 80, no. 1 (November/December 2001): 165–70.

King, Robert R. *Minorities under Communism: Nationalities as a Source of Tension among Balkan Communist States.* Cambridge, MA: Harvard University Press, 1973.

Kingston, Klara. "The Hungarian Status Law." *East European Perspectives* 3, no. 17 (October 2001). Available at www.rferl.org/reports/eepreport/2001/10/17–031001.asp, accessed August 30, 2006.

Kiss, János. "Ultikultúra." *Szabadság,* August 4, 1998.

Kitschelt, Herbert et al. *Post-Communist Party Systems: Competition, Representation, and Inter-Party Cooperation.* Cambridge: Cambridge University Press, 1999.

Kolumbán, Gábor. "Autonómia törekvések és konszociáció, a szövetségi demokrácia esélyei Romániában." *Hitel—Erdélyi Szemle* (March–April 1994): 3–9.

Kötő, József. "Kiművelt fők közössége." Undated manuscript.

———. "Önrendelkezés—az identitás megőrzésének garanciája." *Magyar Közélet* 1, no. 8 (January 1998).

Kovrig, Bennett. "Peacemaking after World War II: The End of the Myth of National Self-Determination." In *The Hungarians: A Divided Nation,* ed. Stephen Borsody. New Haven: Yale Center for International and Area Studies, 1988.

Krasner, Stephen, ed. *Problematic Sovereignty: Contested Rules and Political Possibilities.* New York: Columbia University Press, 2001.

———. *Sovereignty: Organized Hypocrisy.* Princeton, NJ: Princeton University Press, 1999.

Krause, Kevin. "Slovak-Hungarian Issues in the Political Party System of Slovakia." Paper presented at the Association for the Study of Nationalities, Columbia University, New York, 1996.

Krivý, Vladimír. "The Parliamentary Elections 1994: The Profile of Supporters of the Political Parties, the Profile of Regions." In *Slovakia: Parliamentary Elections 1994,* ed. Soňa Szomolányi and Grigorij Mesežnikov. Bratislava: Interlingua Publishing House, 1995.

———. "Slovakia and its Regions." In *Slovakia 1996–1997: A Global Report on the State of Society,* ed. Martin Bútora and Thomas Skladony. Bratislava: Institute for Public Affairs, 1998.

Krupa, András. "A magyarországi szlovákok az önvallomások tükrében." Conference on the Hungarian-Czechoslovak population exchange, Central Europe Institute, Budapest, Hungary, March 27, 1996.

Kus, Miroslav. "Dvojitá identita národnostnej menšiny." *Národná obroda,* February 22, 1996.

———. "Národný štát a etnická autonómia." *Národná obroda,* March 20, 1996.

———. "Slovak Exceptionalism." In *The End of Czechoslovakia,* ed. Jiří Musil. Budapest: Central European University Press, 1995.

Kymlicka, Will. "Introduction." In *Can Liberal Pluralism Be Exported? Western Political Theory and Ethnic Relations in Eastern Europe,* ed. Will Kymlicka and Magda Opalski. London: Oxford University Press, 2001.

Kymlicka, Will, *Multicultural Citizenship: A Liberal Theory of Minority Rights.* Oxford: Clarendon Press, 1995.

Kymlicka, Will, and Alan Patten, eds. *Language Rights and Political Theory.* Oxford: Oxford University Press, 2003.

Laitin, David. "The Cultural Identities of a European State." *Politics and Society* 25, no. 3 (September 1997): 277–302.

———. *Identity in Formation: The Russian-Speaking Populations in the Near Abroad.* Ithaca: Cornell University Press, 1998.

———. *Language Repertoires and State Construction in Africa.* New York: Cambridge University Press, 1992.

Laitin, David, and Rob Reich. "A Liberal Democratic Approach to Language Justice." In *Language Rights and Political Theory,* ed. Will Kymlicka and Alan Patten. Oxford, UK: Oxford University Press, 2003.

Lanstyák, István. "Az anyanyelv és a többségi nyelv oktatása a kisebbségi kétnyelvűség körülményei között." *Regio* 5, no. 4 (1994): 90–116.

Lanstyák, István, and Gizella Szabómihály. *Magyar Nyelvhasználat—iskola—kétnyelvűség: Nyelvi változók a szlovákiai és magyarországi középiskolások néhány csoportjának magyar nyelvhasználatában.* Bratislava: Kalligram Könyvkiadó, 1997.

Lanstyák, István, and László Szigeti. *Identitásunk alapja az anyanyelvű oktatás: Érveinkaz ún. alternatív—kétnyelvű oktatással szemben.* Bratislava: Mécs László Alapítvány, May 1995.

Leška, Dušan, and Viera Koganová. "The Elections 1994 and Crystallization of the Political Parties and Movements in Slovakia." In *Slovakia: Parliamentary Elections 1994,* ed. Soňa Szomolányi and Grigorij Mesežnikov. Bratislava: Interlingua Publishing House, 1995.

Liebich, André. "Ethnic Minorities and Long-term Implications of EU Enlargement." In *Europe Unbound: Enlarging and Reshaping the Boundaries of the European Union,* ed. Jan Zielonka. New York: Routledge, 2002.

Linden, Ronald, ed. *Norms and Nannies: The Impact of International Organizations on the Central and East European States.* Lanham, MD: Rowman and Littlefield, 2002.

Livezeanu, Irina. *Cultural Politics in Greater Romania: Regionalism, Nation Building, and Ethnic Struggle, 1918–1930.* Ithaca: Cornell University Press, 1995.

Magocsi, Paul Robert. "Magyars and Carpatho-Rusyns." In *Czechoslovakia 1918–88: Seventy Years from Independence,* ed. Gordon H. Skilling. Oxford: Macmillan, 1991.

Magyari-Vincze, Enikő. "Analiza antropologică a naționalismelor Est-Europene." Ph.D. dissertation, Babeş-Bolyai University, June 1997.

Malová, Darina. "The Development of Hungarian Political Parties during the Three Election Cycles (1990–1994) in Slovakia." In *Slovakia: Parliamentary Elections 1994,* ed. Soňa Szomolányi and Grigorij Mesežnikov. Bratislava: Interlingua Publishing House, 1995.

Manin, Bernard. "On Democracy and Political Deliberation." *Political Theory* 15 (August 1987): 338–68.

Marga, Andrei. "Cultural and Political Trends in Romania before and after 1989." *East European Politics and Societies* 7, no. 1 (Winter 1993): 14–32.

Marin, Ruth-Mario. "Language Rights: Exploring the Competing Rationales." In *Language Rights and Political Theory,* ed. Will Kymlicka and Alan Patten. Oxford: Oxford University Press, 2003.

Markó, Béla. "Közakarat és érdekképviselet." *Romániai magyar szó,* October 11, 1994.

———. "Romania's Hungarians Face a Catch-22 Situation." *Transitions* 5, no. 12 (December 1998): 76–77.

Mathiassen, Terje. "Regulations and Language Planning in Latvia and Lithuania." In *Language Contact and Language Conflict: Proceedings of the International Ivar Aasen Conference 14–16 November 1996, University of Oslo,* ed. Unn Royneland. Volda, Norway: Ivar Aasen Institute, Volda College, 1997.

Mato, Zsolt. "Romanian Parliament Ratifies Treaties with Budapest, Belgrade." *RFE/RL Newsline,* October 4, 1996.
McMahon, Patrice. "Managing Ethnicity in Eastern Europe: The Effects of Globalization and Transnational Networks." Paper presented at the annual meeting of the International Studies Association, Montreal, Canada, March 17–20, 2004.
Mesežnikov, Grigorij. "Domestic Political Developments and the Political Scene in the Slovak Republic." In *Global Report on Slovakia: Comprehensive Analyses from 1995 and Trends from 1996,* ed. Martin Bútora and Péter Hunčík. Bratislava: Sándor Márai Foundation, 1997.
———. "The Parliamentary Elections 1994: A Confirmation of the Split of the Party System in Slovakia." In *Slovakia: Parliamentary Elections 1994,* ed. Soňa Szomolányi and Grigorij Mesežnikov. Bratislava: Interlingua Publishing House, 1995.
Mikó, Imre. *Huszonkét év: Az erdélyi magyarság politikai története 1918. december1–től 1940 augusztusz 30–ig.* Budapest: Studium, 1941.
Moravčik, Andrew. "The Myth of a European Leadership Crisis in an Era of Diminishing Returns." *Challenge Europe* (March–April 2004). Available at www.theepc.net, accessed March 26, 2004.
Morris, Helen M. "EU Enlargement and Latvian Citizenship Policy." *JEMIE: Journal of Ethnopolitics and Minority Issues in Europe* 1 (2003). Available at www.ecmi.de/jemie, accessed June 17, 2005.
Mostny, Vojtech. "The Beneš Thesis: A Design for the Liquidation of National Minorities: Introduction." In *The Hungarians: A Divided Nation,* ed. Stephen Borsody. New Haven: Yale Center for International and Area Studies, 1988.
Mungiu-Pippidi, Alina. "Intellectuals as Political Actors in Eastern Europe: The Romanian Case." *East European Politics and Societies* 10, no. 2 (Spring 1996): 333–64.
Murvai, László. *Fekete fehér könyv.* Cluj: Studium, 1996.
Neculau, Adrian. "Construirea câmpului de putere şi transmiterea moştenirii în instituţiile de învăţământ superior." *Revista de cercetări sociale* 1 (1994): 62–69.
Neményi, Ágnes. "Az önálló magyar egyetem időszerűségéről." *Szabadság,* August 5, 1998.
Németh, Júlia. "Multimaszlag." *Szabadság,* September 4, 1998.
Okey, Robin. *The Habsburg Monarchy: From Enlightenment to Eclipse.* New York: St. Martin's Press, 2001.
Ondrejovič, Slavo. "Contact Languages and Minorities in The Slovak Republic: An Encyclopedic Overview." *Human Affairs* 3, no. 2 (1993).
Paler, Octavian. "Problema noastră." *România liberă,* May 14, 1999. Available at www.romanialibera.com/1POL/14c2pedi.htm.
Pasti, Vladimir. *România în tranziţie: Căderea în viitor.* Bucharest: Editura Nemira, 1995.
Patapievici, H.-R. "Minorităţile imperiale." *Revista 22* 38 (1998). Available at www.dntb.ro/22/1998/38/1edit-hr.html.
———. "Regimul Iliescu: Un Portret." In *Politice,* ed. H.-R. Patapievici. Bucharest: Humanitas, 1997.
———, ed. *Politice.* Bucharest: Humanitas, 1997.
Patten, Alan. "Liberal Neutrality and Language Policy." Paper presented at the American Political Science Association Annual Conference, Boston, MA, August 29–September 1, 2002.
Patten, Alan. "What Kind of Bilingualism?" In *Language Rights and Political Theory,* ed. Will Kymlicka and Alan Patten. Oxford: Oxford University Press, 2003.
Paulston, Christina Bratt. "Introduction." In *International Handbook of Bilingual Education,* ed. Christina Bratt Paulston. New York: Greenwood Press, 1988.
———. "Linguistic Minorities and Language Policies." In *Sociolinguistics: The Essential Readings,* ed. Christina Bratt Paulston and G. Richard Tucker. Malden, MA: Blackwell, 2003.
———. *Linguistic Minorities in Multilingual Settings: Implications for Language Policies.* Amsterdam: John Benjamins, 1993.
Péntek, János. "Factori de asimetrie in bilingvismul social." National Conference on Bilingualism, University of Bucharest, June 16–17, 1997.

Petőcz, Kálmán. "The Slovak Law on the State Language." Manuscript, November 1995.
Phillipson, Robert. "Political Science." In *Handbook of Language and Ethnic Identity,* ed. Joshua Fishman. Oxford: Oxford University Press, 1999.
——, ed. *Rights to Language: Equity, Power, and Education: Celebrating the 60th Birthday of Tove Skutnabb-Kangas.* Mahwah, NJ: Lawrence Erlbaum Associates, 2000.
Pillich, László. "Pótcselekvéseink kora lejárt." *Hitel—Erdélyi Szemle* (March–April 1994): 10–13.
Pilon, Juliana Geran. *The Bloody Flag: Post-Communist Nationalism in Eastern Europe: Spotlight on Romania.* New Brunswick, NJ: Transaction Publishers, 1992.
Pippidi, Alina Mungiu. "Problema democraţiei transetnice." *Sfera politicii* 37 (April 1996): 36–41.
——. *Românii după '89: Istoria unei neînţelegeri.* Bucharest: Humanitas, 1995.
Pleşu, Andrei. *Chipuri şi măşti ale tranziţiei.* Bucharest: Humanitas, 1996.
Pogány, Erzsébet et al. "A komáromi nagygyűlés sajtóvisszhangja." *Önkormányzat az önrendelkezés alapja: A szlovákiai magyar választott képviselők és polgármesterek országos nagygyűlésének hiteles jegyzőkönyve. Komárom, 1994. január 8.* Komárom, Hungary: Komáromi Lapok—Szinnyei Kiadó, 1995.
"Political Transformation and the Electoral Process in Post-Communist Europe." Available at www2.essex.ac.uk/elect/database/aboutProject.asp, accessed November 30, 2006.
Preda, Marian. "Partidele politice in România: clasificare şi relaţii parlamentare." *Revista de cercetări sociale* 3 (1994): 7–10.
Priedite, Aija. "The Relationship between Minority and Majority Languages in Latvia." In *Language Contact and Language Conflict: Proceedings of the International Ivar Aasen Conference 14–16 November 1996, University of Oslo,* ed. Unn Royneland. Volda, Norway: Ivar Aasen Institute, Volda College, 1997.
"Private Education in Central Europe: Less of the State, Please." *The Economist,* January 3, 2002. Available at www.economist.com/displayStory.cfm?story_id=922868, accessed July 18, 2004.
Ram, Melanie. "Transformation through European Integration: A Comparative Study of the Czech Republic and Romania." Ph.D. dissertation, George Washington University, 1999.
Rawls, John. *A Theory of Justice.* Cambridge, MA: Harvard University Press, 1971.
Reisch, Alfred A. "Slovakia's Minority Policy under International Scrutiny." *RFE/RL Research Report* 2, no. 49 (December 10, 1993).
Reiter, Dan. "Why NATO Enlargement Does Not Spread Democracy." *International Security* 25, no. 2 (2001): 41–67.
Riagain, Donall O. "Unity in Diversity: Language Policies in the New Europe." In *Language Contact and Language Conflict: Proceedings of the International Ivar Aasen Conference 14–16 November 1996, University of Oslo,* ed. Unn Royneland, Volda, Norway: Ivar Aasen Institute, Volda College, 1997.
Romaine, Suzanne. "Language Contact in Relation to Multilingualism, Norms, Status and Standardization." In *Language Contact and Language Conflict: Proceedings of the International Ivar Aasen Conference 14–16 November 1996, University of Oslo,* ed. Unn Royneland, Volda, Norway: Ivar Aasen Institute, Volda College, 1997.
Rosa, Vladislav. "Education and Science." *Slovakia 1996–1997: A Global Report on the State of Society.* Bratislava: Institute for Public Affairs, 1998.
Rothschild, Joseph. *East Central Europe between the Two World Wars.* Seattle and London: University of Washington Press, 1974.
Ruggie, John Gerard. "Continuity and Transformation in the World Polity: Toward a Neorealist Synthesis." In *Neorealism and Its Critics,* ed. Robert O. Keohane. New York: Columbia University Press, 1986.
Săftoiu, Claudiu. "Riscul de imagine şi chestiunea maghiară." *Sfera Politicii* 47 (1997): 38.

Salat, Levente. "A bénultság természetrajza: polemikus esszé az RMDSZ-ről." *Korunk* 3 (1994): 23–27.

Sándor, Elenóra. "The Slovak-Hungarian Basic Treaty." In *Global Report on Slovakia: Comprehensive Analyses from 1995 and Trends from 1996,* ed. Martin Bútora and Péter Hunčík. Bratislava: Sándor Márai Foundation, 1997.

Schlett, István. *Kisebbségnézőben: Beszélgetések és dokumentumok.* Kossuth Könyvkiadó, 1993.

Schöpflin, George. "Transylvania: Hungarians under Romanian Rule." In *The Hungarians: A Divided Nation,* ed. Stephen Borsody. New Haven: Yale Center for International and Area Studies, 1988.

Shafir, Michael. "Agony and Death of an Opposition Alliance." *Transition,* May 26, 1995, 23–28.

———. "Controversy Over the Romanian Education Law." *Transition* 2, no. 1, January 12, 1996, 34–37.

———. "Government Encourages Vigilante Violence in Bucharest." *Report on Eastern Europe* 1, no. 27 (1990): 32–39.

———. "A Possible Light at the End of the Tunnel." *Transition* 2, no. 19 (September 20, 1996): 30.

———. "Ruling Party Formalizes Relations with Extremists." *Transition* 1, no. 5 (1995): 42–46.

———. "Three Legacies." *Transition* (December 27, 1996): 5.

Sidó, Zoltán. *A magyar anyanyelvért folytatott küzdelem Szlovákiában.* Bratislava: Szent László Akadémia, 1999.

———. "Magyar nyelvű oktatás Szlovákiában." Manuscript, April 1999.

Smith, Anthony D. "Culture, Community and Territory: The Politics of Ethnicity and Nationalism." *International Affairs* 72, no. 3 (1996).

———. *Nationalism and Modernism: A Critical Survey of Recent Theories of Nations and Nationalism.* London: Routledge, 2001.

———. *Nationalism: Theory, Ideology, History.* Malden, MA: Blackwell, 2001.

Smith, David. "Minority Rights, Multiculturalism, and EU Enlargement: The Case of Estonia." *JEMIE: Journal on Ethnopolitics and Minority Issues in Europe* 1 (2003). Available at www.ecmi.de/jemie, accessed June 17, 2005.

Snopko, Ladislav. "Culture." In *Slovakia 1996/1997: A Global Report on the State of Society,* ed. Martin Bútora and Thomas Skladony. Bratislava: Institute for Public Affairs, 1998.

Somai, József. "A 69–es Közigazgatási Törvény és a Helyi Önkormányzatok Európai Chartája." *Valóság és lehetőség: Tanulmányok az önkormányzatokról.* Csíkszereda: Pro Print, 1995.

Snyder, Jack. *From Voting to Violence: Democratization and Nationalist Conflict.* New York: Norton, 2000.

Sorbán, Attila. "Kis lépések, kis remények, kis csalódottság." *Erdélyi napló* 4, no. 162 (October 19, 1994).

Stewart, Michael. "The Hungarian Status Law: A New European Form of Transnational Politics." Available at www.transcomm.ox.ac.uk/working%20papers/WPTC-02–09%20Stewart.pdf, accessed May 27, 2004.

Strmiska, Maxmilián. Article in *Středoevropské politické studie* 3, no. 2 (Spring 2001). Available at www.iips.cz/cisla/texty/clanky/romanian201.html.

Šutaj, Štefan. "A Beneš-dekrétumok a magyar kisebbségek történeti tudatában." *Régió* 1–2 (1995): 185–91.

Szabó, Ferenc A. "A második világháború utáni magyar-szlovák lakosságcsere demográfiai szempontból." *Régió* 4 (1991): 49–71.

Szabó, Ildikó. *Az ember államosítása: Politikai szocializáció Magyarországon.* Budapest: Tekintet könyvek, 1991.

Szarka, László. "Közigazgatási reform és kisebbségi kérdés," *Kisebbségkutatás* 2 (2001): 208–22.

——. "A szlovákiai Magyar Koalíció Pártjának kormányzati szerepvállalásáról. *Régió* 4 (2000): 122—49.

Szigeti, László. *Oktatásügyünk helyzete.* Pozsony: Magyar Kereszténydemokrata Mozgalom, 1995, 11.

Szilágyi, Sándor N. "Tervezet. Törvény a nemzeti identitással kapcsolatos jogokról és a nemzeti közösségek méltányos és harmonikus együttéléséről." *Korunk* 5, no. 3 (March 1994): 131–50.

Szilagyi, Zsofia. "Hungarian Minority Summit Causes Uproar in Slovakia and Romania." *Transition* 2, no. 18 (September 6, 1996): 45–48.

Szomolányi, Soňa. "Does Slovakia Deviate from the Central European Variant of Transition?" In *Slovakia: Parliamentary Elections 1994,* ed. Soňa Szomolányi and Grigorij Mesežnikov. Bratislava: Interlingua Publishing House, 1995.

Tabajdi, Csaba. Keynote speech at the Conference on Minority Interest Representation, Self-Government, and Autonomy Forms, manuscript, Budapest, Hungary, November 9–10, 1995.

Tamás, Miklós Gáspár. "A Bolyai Egyetem ügyéről." *Élet és Irodalom,* December 12, 1997, 3–4.

Tilly, Charles. *The Formation of National States in Western Europe.* Princeton, NJ: Princeton University Press, 1975.

Tismăneanu, Vladimir. *Fantasies of Salvation: Democracy, Nationalism, and Myth in Post-Communist Europe.* Princeton, NJ: Princeton University Press, 1998.

——. "Romania: Democracy, What Democracy?" *East European Reporter* 4, no. 2 (1990).

——. "Tenuous Pluralism in the Post-Ceausescu Era." *Transition,* December 27, 1996.

Tismăneanu, Vladimir, and Pavel Ondrejovič. "Romania's Mystical Revolutionaries: The Generation of Angst and Adventure Revisited." *East European Politics and Societies* 8, no. 3 (Fall 1994): 402–38.

Tőkés, László. "Az RMDSZ pere." *Erdélyi napló.* 3, no. 111 (October 14, 1993): 10.

Törzsök, Erika. "The National Minorities and Stability." Manuscript, translation of article published in *Magyar Hirlap,* July 4, 1996. English-language manuscript.

Turcone, Diana. "Pumnul opoziţiei." *Revista 22* 45 (November 6–12, 1996).

Vachudova, Milada Anna. *Europe Undivided: Democracy, Leverage, and Integration after Communism.* Oxford: Oxford University Press, 2005.

Vadkerty, Katalin. *A reszlovakizáció.* Bratislava: Kalligram, 1993.

Van Oudenaren, John. *Uniting Europe: An Introduction to the European Union,* 2d ed. Lanham, MD: Rowman and Littlefield, 2005.

Vatchkov, Vesselin. "Divided by a Mutual Tongue: Do Bulgarians and Macedonians Speak One Language or Two? Their Search for Understanding Raises Issues of Territory, History, and Ethnic Identity." *Transition* 4, no. 4 (September 1997): 76–81.

Vekov, Károly. "A romániai magyarság tömbszerveződésének okairól." *Regio* 2, no. 1 (1991): 101–2.

Verdery, Katherine. *National Ideology under Socialism: Identity and Cultural Politics in Ceauşescu's Romania.* Los Angeles: University of California Press, 1991.

Verdery, Katherine, and Gail Kligman. "Romania after Ceausescu: Post-Communist Communism?" In *Eastern Europe in Revolution,* ed. Ivo Banac. Ithaca: Cornell University Press, 1992.

Vermeersch, Peter. "EU Enlargement and Minority Rights Policies in Central Europe: Explaining Policy Shifts in the Czech Republic, Hungary and Poland." *JEMIE: Journal on Ethnopolitics and Minority Issues in Europe* 1 (2003). Available at www.ecmi.de/jemie, accessed June 17, 2005.

Vincze, Gábor. *Illúziók és csalódások: fejezetek a romániai magyarság második világháború utáni történetéből.* Csíkszereda: Státus, 1999.

Vincze, Gábor, and János Lázok, *Erdély magyar egyeteme 1944–49.* Marosvásárhely: Custos, 1995 (vol. I) and Marosvásárhely: Mentor, 1998 (vol. II).

Vogel, Sándor. "Kisebbségi dokumentumok Romániában." *Regio* 5, no. 1 (1994).

Wagner, István. "Nesze neked autonómia!" *Erdélyi napló* 4, no. 162 (October 19, 1994): 4.

Walker, J. B. *Inside/Outside International Relations.* Cambridge: Cambridge University Press, 1993.

Waterbury, Myra A. "Beyond Irredentism: Domestic Politics and Diaspora Policies in Post-Communist Hungary." Paper presented at Western Political Science Association, 2004.

Waterman, Harvey, and Dessie Zagorcheva. "Correspondence: NATO and Democracy." *International Security* 26, no. 3 (2002): 221–35.

Weber, Eugen. *Peasants into Frenchmen: The Modernization of Rural France.* Stanford, CA: Stanford University Press, 1976.

Weber, Renate. "Legea învăţământului: între contestare şi supra-apreciere." *Revista română de drepturile omului* (May–June 1995): 16–27.

Weinstein, Brian, ed. *Language Policy and Political Development.* Norwood, NJ: Ablex, 1990.

Williams, Margit Bessenyei. "European Integration and Minority Rights: The Case of Hungary and Its Neighbors." In *Norms and Nannies: The Impact of International Organizations on the Central and East European States,* ed. Ronald Linden. Lanham, MD: Rowman and Littlefield, 2002.

Wolchik, Sharon L. *Czechoslovakia in Transition: Politics, Economy, and Society.* New York: Pinter, 1991.

——. "The Politics of Transition and the Break-Up of Czechoslovakia," In *The End of Czechoslovakia,* ed. Jiří Musil. Budapest: Central European University Press, 1995.

Woolard, Kathryn A. *Double Talk: Bilingualism and the Politics of Ethnicity in Catalonia.* Stanford, CA: Stanford University Press, 1989.

Young, Crawford, ed. *The Accommodation of Cultural Diversity: Case-Studies.* New York: St. Martin's Press, 1999.

——, ed. *Ethnic Diversity and Public Policy: A Comparative Inquiry.* New York: MacMillan, 1998.

——, ed. *The Rising Tide of Cultural Pluralism: The Nation-State at Bay?* Madison: University of Wisconsin Press, 1993.

Zalabai, Zsigmond. *Mit ér a nyelvünk, ha magyar? A "táblaháború" és a "névháború" szlovákiai magyar sajtódokumentumaiból 1990–1994.* Bratislava: Kalligram Könyvkiadó, 1995.

Zolberg, A. "The Formation of New States as a Refugee-Generating Process." *Annals of the American Academy of Political and Social Sciences* 467 (1983): 24–38.

Index

Page numbers with an *f* indicate figures; those with *t* indicate tables.